CH01455497

YOU KNOW THE DRILL

THE PRIVATE MUSINGS OF A DENTIST

DR BILL

You Know The Drill Kindle Edition
© 2024 Dr Bill

ISBN: 9798309810970

The names of any individuals, patients, doctors, dentists, nurses, in-
patients, deranged members of the public, escaped convicts or
otherwise are all fictional and figments of the author's vivid
imagination. No breaches of GDPR or patient confidentiality are
within these pages. We don't want a case being dragged before the
General Dental Council, now do we?! After all, we don't want to upset
anyone – and there are many laws that must not be broken. This book
is a complete work of fiction, although some of the tales within may
be influenced by the author's personal trip down Memory Lane…

For all the dentists who fake-smile and fake-laugh each time a new patient snarls, 'I hate you.'

Special thanks to my wonderful partner. Alex has endured me whinging, whining, crying, and despairing, as well as supporting me throughout obsessive daily research on how to get out of this profession.

Oh, and a mention to Google. Thanks for the random name generator. It stopped everyone within these pages being called Mr Twit... Mrs Twit... Miss Twit... Master Twit... Professor Twit... Sir Twitty Twit...
You get the idea...

Prologue

'What made you choose to be a dentist?'

I get asked this a lot. Like a *lot...*

My university application answer was:

I want to do something where every day is different. Where I use my hands. Where I interact with the public. I want to have a career that is both rewarding and helps people. A job that I'm respected for. That challenges. Where I strive to always do my best while learning and progressing.

But that's the university answer. The real answer is:

Not a Scooby.

When you're sixteen and have to make certain choices from '*What to study in Sixth Form*' and, later, '*What to do at University*', you really have no clue.

I remember asking my mum what she thought. I was the first person in my family to even consider going to university. It was, therefore, quite a big deal. Even more so on what choice of career to aim for. I can remember her response clearly. She looked at me and said, 'What about dentistry?'

'What about dentistry?' I said – possibly with a bit of an eyeroll.

'Well, Dr Peter Vaneman, who works at the local practice, drives a Porsche, and seems to go on holiday every other week. You never see a poor dentist! You're a smart kid. You should look into it.'

'Okay.'

And so I did. I investigated. To get into dental school, a student required a Level Seven in chemistry and a Level Six in biology. At this point I should add that I didn't do *A Levels*. My school was one of those weird academies that ditched such 'old-fashioned' examinations for a crazy-ass test called the *International Baccalaureate* (IB). This was basically A levels on steroids. A student had to study English, maths, a language, a science, a humanity, an extra subject of choice, plus *Theory of Knowledge* which was meant to be a version of philosophy - I guess?

On top of having to smash your exams, you had to do a beefed-up 11+ examination called the *UKCAT*. This was done on a computer, usually at the same centre as people taking driving theory tests. You'd be shown a bunch of irrelevant maths and shape-related questions designed to bewilder any reasonable person. You'd muddle (or guess) your way through and, if you hit a certain score, then you could apply to dentistry (or medicine).

The test was ridiculous. It didn't demonstrate any real ability or critical thinking and it had no relevance to university, dentistry, or the big wide world. But hey, I passed! I got the *lowest* mark possible in order to apply. To give you a clue how ridiculous the UKCAT test is - despite getting the minimum pass score, I later graduated with Honours and an additional award for the best all-round student. The UKCAT should be scrapped. It discourages so many amazing and capable individuals from applying.

Anyway, I did it. Passed.

I applied to five dental schools: Barts (Queen Mary's), Kings, Bristol, Manchester, and Liverpool. I was interviewed by them all. Special shout-out to the complete asshole interviewers at Bristol. They were possibly the rudest, most over-privileged toffs I've ever had the misfortune to meet!

My university advisor had warned me that Bristol only took private school students. As a state schoolboy I was lucky to even be granted an interview.

I got asked questions about *primary care trust acronyms* and *the intricacies of the NHS dental band system*. Even now, as a seasoned veteran dentist, I would not be able to explain that.

I looked on as the interviewer picked up a black sharpie and wrote NO on a piece of paper. He was sitting right in front of me. He then gave me a supercilious look and smiled.

'Any questions?' he asked,

'No,' I said, hoping he caught the irony.

And that was that. I left disheartened, disillusioned, but also defiant.

Having since been on the other side as an interviewer for prospective students, I can honestly say I have never treated any sixteen/seventeen-year-old the way I was treated by that fella. Anyway, this isn't about axe-grinding (or is it?!). In the end, I achieved what I'd set out to do. I secured a place at a dental school. I went to Barts & The London School for Medicine and Dentistry.

I did my extracurriculars, passed my exams, and was as proud as anything. I convinced myself that I was going to make a difference. I honestly thought that this profession was for me. To be fair - dear reader - I *do* enjoy the act of dentistry. It's just everything else that goes with it that makes it so horrible.

But back to the age of eighteen. There I was, bright-eyed, bushy-tailed and brimming with enthusiasm.

University here I come.

1

Dental School

It always surprises me when a patient asks if I learnt to do dentistry 'on the job', or if the nurse is training to be a dentist.

Dentistry is a five-year university course. The same as medicine. I have a few doctor friends who will likely give me a stick and call me a *failed doctor*. However, at the risk of upsetting all the medics, dentistry - as a course - is far more intense and hands-on than medicine. A student is basically studying all of medicine whilst, at the same time, specialising in dental surgery.

Indeed, I studied every body system – endocrine to excretory. Every condition – autoimmune to idiopathic (without cause). Every piece of anatomy – head and neck to feet and toes. You name it, I did it. And by God, did I get grilled on it.

That isn't to say that I didn't enjoy it. I loved it. I felt like I was spending my time in the most useful of ways. I was gaining knowledge of the human body along with how to 'fix' it.

I would test the student doctors and tie them in knots with what I was learning. I don't write this to gloat or boast, I write it to emphasise that dentists are **not** carpenters of the mouth.

We are highly trained *medical* professionals. We are in the unique position of spotting diseases or conditions before a GP does. This is because we see our patients every six months.

Many, many times, I have seen patients who have been

on inappropriate medications. And many, many times I've had to call their irked GP to get medications removed or changed.

I've spotted dementia years before an official diagnosis and been rebuffed by the patient's GP. Usually, the doctor tells me that if the patient has a problem, they can contact the surgery themselves (with me, at this point, doing an eyeroll).

I've picked up on deficiencies, stresses, cancers, and nerve-compressing cysts. I've reported and rescued children from abuse and neglect. I've identified and counselled mental health conditions, commonly bulimia.

Dentistry is so much more than just the mouth... because, well, *everything* presents in the mouth first.

Syphilis? The lip - a sore that doesn't heal.

Anaemia? Pale, grey-like gums without colour.

Bulimia? A unique erosive-wear pattern on the upper incisors and canines.

Immune suppression? A sudden unexplained onset of thrush with a build up like cottage cheese on the throat and tongue.

Dementia? Loss of dentures multiple times or a sudden worsening in dental health accompanied by verbal repetition and confusion.

This is why I love dentistry. You *do* make a difference. This is why I studied it. As I write this, I'm reminded how I loved university. How much I learnt. How motivated I was to stay in the library until almost midnight, trawling through dusty medical tomes.

But hey, that's boring right? You, my dear reader, want to know the gory details... the toe-curling, cringeworthy stories... the darkly sadistic world of dentistry... not the all-hallowed good.

So let me tell you about the best (or worst?) parts of my dental studies at Barts & The London School of Medicine and Dentistry!

❖

Local Anaesthetic. This tiny needle draws fear into the hearts of the mightiest of men – and trust me, men are the worst. When it comes to the dental chair, they are the biggest babies.

As well as learning the theory of local anaesthetics and what different esters and amides (chemical formulae) do to nerve endings, we also had to learn how to *give* an injection.

My practical session on administering local anaesthetic (which I shall refer to as *LA*) is forever etched in my brain. It was so memorable that, years later, when teaching my own students, I delivered it exactly how my tutor instructed me.

This is how it went:

'Gather round, gather round!' said Dr Bowman. 'I need a volunteer.'

Silence.

Cue a nervous exchange of glances between students.

'Oh, for goodness' sake,' he huffed. 'You'll do!'

Dr Bowman pointed to Ananya, a meek Indian student. She squeaked fearfully and shuffled forward.

'Come on, come on! Hop on to the dental chair.'

Ananya reluctantly obeyed. She looked at Dr Bowman fearfully. Everyone was deathly silent. We were like a bunch of ghouls, unable to look away, grimly delighting at Ananya's plight, while privately thankful to have escaped a stabbing.

Dr Bowman pulled on his latex gloves, ensuring they made a satisfying snap as he released them around his wrists. Just like a movie, he was going for drama. He then assembled the syringe. Upon unsheathing it, a twenty-seven-gauge needle was revealed. This is the longer of the two standard needles used for dental anaesthetic. He waved it around in the air, then squirted out some LA in front of Ananya. Not surprisingly, she was starting to look a little faint.

'Right, open wide. This is going to hurt – a lot!'

Dr Bowman faced Ananya, holding the needle like a fencing sword poised to strike. Anaya's eyes widened but she obeyed the instruction and opened her mouth. The cruel tip of the hypodermic lunged toward her.

He suddenly and dramatically stopped, turned to his captivated audience, and gave a half smile.

'And that is... how *not* to do it.'

There was a palpable sigh of relief as everyone exhaled at the same time, not least Ananya who'd come perilously close to fainting.

What followed next was Dr Bowman educating us on how you *should* do it:

Hide the syringe – nobody wants to see that.

Always apply numbing gel, even if it has only a placebo effect – it's kinder to give something than nothing.

Don't lie. Say, 'A little scratch is coming up.' Never say *pain coming now* or *sharp scratch*, and forget all about *little prick* (although there are some patients I wouldn't mind saying that to!).

Remind the patient to breathe. I've had many a patient tense up, forget to inhale and then faint.

To this day, I follow the principles that Dr Bowman taught. However, if a patient is a real piece of work, I might accidentally forget to apply the numbing gel (wink).

❖

Do you know how hard it is to drill upside down? That was the realisation I came to when working on the phantom heads in our dental-simulation clinic. At this point I suggest you google *phantom head*. It's literally a half head with some pink latex and jaws with plastic teeth that unscrew.

When you drill a tooth on the upper arch, you must use a mirror to see what you're doing. You basically have to teach your brain to drill the opposite way to what you're looking at, as it's all... well... mirrored!

God, I used to get so frustrated when I'd botched it up and smacked through to the tooth next door. Thankfully, it wasn't a real patient. Sometimes, when the tutor wasn't looking, I'd unscrew the jaws, quickly finish the drilling, then put it back inside the phantom's gaping mouth.

These sessions were run by a most patronising tutor by the name of Dr Hemeres (referred to by students as Dr Haemorrhoids due to his constant pacing and inability to sit down). He would march around the sim-lab, then peer over your shoulder and blast you with his awful coffee breath. If you thought you'd done a good job, guess what? You hadn't.

'OHHH, you think you did a good job, eh?' he'd roar.

He would then take the tooth you'd be working on and put it on the projector for the entire class to see. It would be blown up at times five magnification so everyone could see *exactly* how you'd fucked up.

'Yes, right here. See this scratch? You've destroyed the tooth next door. And this box that you've drilled – look at the line positions. They're all rough and at acute angles!'

What made drilling upside down even more difficult was working on *plastic* teeth. If you skim enamel with a slow drill, it will do nothing. If you skim a plastic tooth with a slow drill, it will look like you've mullered it.

Luckily, I wasn't alone in my apparent inability to use a drill. My boyfriend, at the time, had a complete emotional breakdown over it.

'I CANNOT DO IT,' he sobbed, totally distraught. 'I'm never going to be able to do this. I'm not cut out for dentistry.'

'I promise you, it's the same for me,' I assured. 'I think at some point, and with enough practice, it will just click and we will both be okay.'

Of course, I was right (I'm always right!). Suddenly, there came the day when we could both just *do* it. But at the time, the struggle had been real. My boyfriend had been in *doomsday* mode, and I'd similarly often resigned myself to that feeling too. BOGOF Domino's pizza (buy-one-get-one-free for those who aren't familiar) and a large glass of wine helped put the world to rights many a time.

Throughout my time at uni, many students experienced *the wobbles* – over trying to learn all the head and neck anatomy (after all these years I'm still crap at this) to finding all the canal openings in a root canal treatment (a needle in a haystack comes to mind) to the truly mundane – like pulling an all-night rager then turning up for clinic hungover (you'd do it once, but never again). It was normal. The tears would dry, and that day's worry would be replaced by an excitement for tomorrow.

❖

My first patient experience was at the end of my second year at university. It was terrifying and traumatic for both the patient and me alike. It took place at the now 'old' dental hospital in Whitechapel, fourth floor.

The dental hospital was old when it was new. The only upgrade it ever received was key card locks on the doors to the clinics - and this was to stop the local homeless population from entering the building and drinking the hand sanitiser!

Each floor had a designated clinic for a different speciality. The fourth floor was *general restorative*, where 'normal' dentistry went on –fillings, root canal treatments, crowns etc. Each clinic was then set out with a number of low-lying partition walls that surrounded a bay where a patient dental chair was set. The walls were low enough to see directly over into adjoining bays and witness what was going on. To make matters worse, the patient chairs in opposite bays faced each other. This meant a patient could observe another patient's treatment – a rather awkward and uncomfortable situation. This design feature was later rectified in the new hospital that eventually came about the following year, but during this particular episode of my training, I could look into any bay and see the hopelessness etched on a patient's face as he or she reclined in their chair.

Patients were randomly assigned by a central office. Often you did not know anything about the patient apart from what their general dental practitioner (GDP) had referred them in for. It might be read as *routine fillings* or *root canal treatment* or *complex wear and tear*.

Anyway, my first patient was a middle-aged lady by the name of Denise. She worked in the Barts NHS trust as an administrator. Denise sat down on the patient chair, and I took a clinical history while we both waited for the tutor to arrive. I asked the usual questions – why she was here, if there were any issues or pain, the duration of the pain, etc. If Denise hadn't had any problems before this moment, she soon would have!

Dr Sanford bounced into the room. She was a short lady with a girth that rivalled her height. Her lips were always pursed. Her eyes – which alternately glared at students or performed somersaulting eye rolls – were crowned by a pair of manicured eyebrows. One eyebrow was always raised, just like Dwayne *The Rock* Johnson's. It would elevate even higher if you did something wrong. If you thought you knew something, you didn't. Every question Dr Sanford asked was designed to trip the student up and get those eyes rolling. She was affectionately known to her students as *The Bulldog*, but her bite was definitely worse than her bark.

'RIGHT!' barked The Bulldog as she stood by Denise. 'What's wrong with this one?'

Quaking, I read from my notes.

'Uhhh, pain in the lower left first molar. It's a sharp shooting pain made worse by—'

She snatched the notes from my hands. Scowling, she skim-read the words I'd written. Her frown deepened to the point where I wondered if it might become a ravine on her forehead.

'You eat too many sweets Denise. That's the problem. Let me look in your mouth!'

Dr Sanford abruptly put the patient chair into reverse sending the meek Denise catapulting backwards. Denise was gripping the arm rests with such force her knuckles had turned white. The Bulldog advanced with mirror and probe. She dug about, as if seeking oil.

'Ah ha! Lower left six. Large cavity!'

Oil strike.

'OUCH!' Denise shrieked, as The Bulldog poked and prodded.

'Yep, you need a filling. Let's put in a temporary today. Hey, you – whatever your name is.' She pointed at me. 'I'll numb up the patient, and you can remove the decay and temporise.'

There was no question there, just a statement. Dr Sanford assembled the LA syringe, then cackled evilly. (Okay, maybe I made up the cackle, but she might as well have.)

'Open up, Denise!'

'AHHHHHHH!' Denise screamed, as Dr Sanford injected the LA. Her Bulldog hackles went up when Denise's arms and legs flailed about. For a moment, Denise looked a bit like Olive Oyl calling for Popeye. (If you can't picture the reference, then Google search it. God, that makes me feel old). Denise then went limp, with a defeated look upon her frozen face. Dr Sanford snapped off her gloves, then dumped them in front of me.

'Tut tut, Denise. Was such fuss *really* necessary?' The Bulldog delivered so many eye rolls, I thought her eyeballs might fall from her head. 'Hey, YOU!' she growled at me. 'Crack on with the temporary filling. I'll be back in five. I need a coffee.'

And with that, The Bulldog took her hackles and huge girth off for a mid-clinic refreshment break.

❖

Extractions. Not as bad as a root canal treatment, right? Across the country, every day, thousands of patients opt for an extraction over a root canal treatment (RCT) because of how bad a rap RCTs have. Anyway, let's talk about taking out teeth. Oral Surgery sounds so... primal? Exotic? *Dangereux*?

By the end of my third year at dental school, I'd taken out a few teeth. My stint in oral surgery (extraction clinic) was hampered by a pair of bumbling tutors – Dr Patronise-The-Shit-Out-Of-You and Dr Give-Me-Another-Gin. The latter had a
bright red conk that could have rivalled Rudolph's hooter.

I remember my first extraction as if yesterday. Dr

Patronise took my hand, placed it on the forceps, then held both the forceps and my hand within his. He then ripped the tooth from the patient's mouth before congratulating me on doing an extraction. I immediately impersonated Dr Sanford and did a number of eye rolls.

Anyway, one lucky clinic day, neither Dr Patronise nor Dr Gin turned up, which meant we had a substitute. What a great day that was – we actually got to *do* the extractions and learn some skills.

Oral surgery clinics are where I started to develop my interest in surgical dentistry (implants, wisdom teeth extractions, sinus lifts etc). Throughout my career, there have been specific cases vividly remembered. They are usually either the really good, or the truly terrible.

As a student, one particular extraction has stayed with me, not because it was difficult, more because it was different to anything I've experienced before or since.

An elderly Bengali lady arrived at the emergency clinic in pain. In her upper jaw, there remained one single tooth – an upper left canine. It was giving severe pain. It was also very decayed. After taking x-rays and confirming a plan of action with the patient via her translator (Whitechapel has a high Bengali population so we had translators to assist with the consent process), I numbed up the patient.

I know that you, my reader, will likely have never taken out a tooth! So let me explain what it *should* feel like. Extractions are all about *pushing* (no pulling is involved). You push upwards and apply pressure down the root to help 'dilate' the space between the bone and the root that holds the tooth in place. It should feel firm. The tooth is hard, so there should be resistance. Well, there *should*. Except this tooth did *not*.

I put the luxator (a flat, semi-screwdriver-cum-mini-spoon shaped instrument designed to loosen teeth) against the tooth and wiggled it about. There was some mild resistance, and the tooth began to loosen. I then took a narrow pair of forceps, held the tooth, then started to apply some pressure. The tooth started to move, but it felt odd. It *squelched*. And with this peculiar sensation came a stench so terrible that the entire clinic paused to look on in disbelief. Despite wearing a mask, the reek was putrid enough to send me reeling backwards.

'ROOTS!' I shouted to my equally aghast colleague.

She quickly grabbed the root forceps and hurled them at me. Thus armed, I staggered forward, weapon raised, grabbed the offending tooth and, with a final tug, released it from its gummy prison.

We quadruple-wrapped the brown canine, desperate to quell the smell, and then quickly disposed of it. Windows were thrown open and a nurse discreetly sprayed some Oust toilet spray around the clinic.

The patient gave me a gleaming gummy smile.

'Thank you, thank you!' she cried.

'You're welcome,' I said, before running through the post-operative instructions – albeit at a distance...

After it was all over and done with, one of the experienced dental nurses (the one who had been spraying Oust) sought me out.

'Alvogyl,' she said.

'Alvogyl?' I repeated.

This is a medicine that contains cloves and iodine-based ingredients. It is used to treat dry sockets (infections that can occur after a tooth is extracted). However, I wasn't sure of its relevance on this occasion.

'Yeah, Alvogyl,' the nurse confirmed. 'Got a smelly patient? Rub a small amount into your mask. It'll stop the worst of the whiffs,' she said with a knowing smile.

What excellent advice. I can't tell you the number of times in my career that me and my nurse have rubbed Alvogyl into our masks before the smellier clientele have walked through the door. It is a godsend in our profession.

That reminds me. How many times have patients asked me, 'Why do you want to look in smelly dirty mouths?'

I often ask myself the same question!

❖

Pain is a big part of dentistry. Not inflicting it, mind you, but treating it. Dear reader, if you've ever had a toothache, you know you will go to the ends of the Earth to stop the pain. A large part of my dental training was diagnosing dental pain and then treating dental emergencies.

When I later worked in the NHS, the personally favoured emergencies were swollen faces and abscesses. You'd never run late because you could prescribe antibiotics and quickly get the patient in and out. The emergencies you hated were the hot pulps (when the nerve of a tooth was dying) because you either had to take the tooth out there and then or start a root canal treatment. Let me assure you that *neither* could ever be done in the fifteen-minute emergency appointment that the NHS system allowed for. Even worse was the payment for such complex treatment in that limited time – just ten pounds!

Anyway, I digress. Let me tell you about an interesting perspective on how to deal with emergencies from a dinosaur's point of view. Sorry reader, that was a typo. That should be read as *from a dinosaur dentist's point of view.*

My fourth year involved several placements in the dental hospital's emergency clinic. We would triage and treat patients as appropriate. Normally this would be run by Dr Li. She was a no-nonsense, efficient tutor. She knew her shit and, by God, expected you to know yours or else you'd be off her clinic and instead have your nose in a book.

However, on this particular day she was off sick. We waited for the substitute to arrive. By 8:45am – when the clinic should have been well underway – no had had arrived. We waited. Then waited some more. After a while, we called the office and asked what was happening. The staff assured that someone would be along shortly.

At half past nine, Dr Blackwood-Reid shuffled into clinic. He was wearing ancient trousers that sagged at both knee and backside, a scruffy scrub top and an extraordinary pair of carpet slippers. The bags under his eyes could rival a shopping bag and I swear the lines on his forehead could have been counted – much like a tree – to determine his age. He looked like a man who'd been hauled out of a deep sleep. Possibly hibernation. As he regarded us all with befuddlement.

'What are you all doing standing around?' he asked.

We all gave each other sideways glances and raised eyebrows.

'What clinic is this?' asked Dr Blackwood-Reid.

'Dental emergency clinic, Sir,' said one of my braver compatriots.

'Ah, yes. Very good. Okay, get your patients in then children.'

Okay, maybe he didn't really say *children,* but you get the vibe.

In came the patients, neatly filtering into the dental bays. My patient, a middle-aged lady by the name of Carla, was complaining of soreness around the gums in the upper right quadrant. It had been going on for two to three weeks and was now getting steadily worse. It was a seven out of ten on the pain scale (where ten is the worst).

I took an x-ray but couldn't see anything untoward. After collecting all the information – like a fact-finding mission – I approached Dr ~~Bumble~~-Blackwood-Reid to discuss Carla's case and her best course of action. As I explained my findings and showed him the x-ray, he nodded and frowned, then pursed his lips.

'Pah! Nothing wrong with this one. I reckon it's probably just her gums.'

'Her gums?' I repeated.

'Yeah, I can't see anything wrong. She's probably imagining it. Just give the gums a really *deep* clean. You know, make them bleed a bit, so she thinks you've done a good job. That's half of dentistry, lad – making the patient think you've done something amazing for them.' I stared at him, agog. 'And close your mouth, sonny. You don't want a bug flying in.' I shut my mouth.

I went back to my patient, explained that my tutor believed the issue was her gums, that I would give them a scale and polish, and then we'd see how things went.

15

I did the treatment, talked about how to improve oral hygiene – that food might be getting trapped and making things sore – then discussed flossing. Finally, I bid adieu to the patient (and no I didn't forcibly make her gums bleed). She also thought I'd done an okay job, despite not leaving with a red river pouring out of her mouth.

So, what did I learn that day? That dentistry has come a long way since the Middle Ages.

❖

Dental materials were an exciting and engaging part of my dental training. Said no-one ever. Dental materials were the dullest, driest, most draining subject that we ever covered. Unfortunately, it was not limited to one year of study, but covered the entire five years. If you are ever struggling to sleep, read some lecture notes on the spherical properties of the metal globules in amalgam fillings and you'll immediately drift off.

Regardless, we had to learn it. The lecturer was a dental materials scientist by the name of Mrs Pattison. She was as exhilarating as her course content. Her grey hair was worn in a bob which she accessorised with large milk-bottle spectacles. On her feet were the smallest kitten heels you can ever imagine, and her Victorian skirts were cut in such a way as to teasingly reveal the occasional flash of ankle.

In one double lecture (yes, two hours of dental materials with a five-minute coffee break – and by God strong caffeine was required) Mrs Pattison was droning away, monotone in full swing. As she burbled on about the fascinating properties of Bis-GMA polymers in composite, multiple students began to doze off. Mrs Pattison appeared unfazed by her lecturing's soporific effect until one student began loudly snoring.

Suddenly, there was a loud bang. Everyone jolted upright.

'Excuse me!' Mrs Pattison quavered indignantly. 'If you

want to sleep, you can leave!'

All eyes swivelled to the student who'd been impersonating a farrowing pig. Hamza was a large oaf of a man. He'd somehow managed to achieve a place at dental school despite lacking in capability (and personal hygiene).

'Nah, nah, Miss,' he said, hastily rubbing the sleep from his eyes. 'I'm staying, like, yeah.'

'This is very important,' snapped Mrs Pattison. 'This will impact upon your patients' clinical care.'

'Nah, Miss. I don't fink so. That's, like, rubbish. When am I ever gonna talk to patients about this, eh? Yer just put the filling in the hole and then yer done, right?'

Mrs Pattison's face changed to a disturbing shade of maroon. We could almost see the steam pouring forth from her ears. This normally meek and mild-mannered woman was about to blow.

'If *you* think this is irrelevant to your studies,' she said ominously, 'then leave NOW!'

'Nah, Miss. It's fine. I'll, like, stay for now.'

'NO!' she roared. 'I insist you GET OUT NOW!'

A silent stand-off then ensued with both lecturer and student embroiled in a horribly lengthy staring contest.

After about half a century, Mrs Pattison left the room in a whirl of skirts. Hamza remained sitting there, looking vacant. Whispered chuntering broke out. *Where had Mrs Pattison gone?*

A minute or two later, The Bulldog (aka Dr Sanford) erupted into the room, closely trailed by Mrs Pattison.

'YOU!' she barked at Hamza, 'OUT!'

His face paled.

'Nah, Dr San–'

'NOW!' she growled.

Hamza grabbed his things and exited the room with Dr Sanford snapping at his heels.

Mrs Pattison then cleared her throat, and continued to deliver the rest of the lecture on spherical molecules and tensile strengths in her best monotone.

The incident certainly served to make us pay more attention (or not get caught nodding off!).

Worryingly, Hamza went on to become a fully-fledged dentist despite failing every single exam at least once. He also had a fitness-to-practice case brought against him due to homophobia against a staff member. Finally, he got caught cheating in exams. Eventually he managed to scrape a pass by the skin of his teeth (forgive the pun).

I think the above is a sad reflection on how bleak the dental world really is. There is a vast shortage of dentists and a huge need to prop up the NHS system.

Happily, this was limited to *one* student in the entire year, but it's always bothered me to know that this *gentleman* is out there, somewhere, somehow, and possibly working on *your* teeth!

❖

Failure. That was the topic of The Bulldog's lecture. 'Everything you do will fail,' announced Dr Sanford, her muzzle compressing. 'No matter what you do, what treatment you complete, what care you take, what courses you do, what skills you *think* you have, every single restoration or piece of work you put in a patient's mouth will, eventually, fail.'

Her words were met with a gloomy silence.

She did the Dwayne Johnson thing with one eyebrow before continuing.

'We can only imitate what God gave us. Nothing you put in a patient's mouth will be the same as Nature's intended enamel and dentine.'

'That's depressing,' someone dared to mutter.

'Yes, it is,' she agreed, showing a sudden and surprising soft side. 'I'm not telling you this to put you down, but to be realistic. Dentistry is about kicking the can down the road as far as you can. When the filling fails, the tooth will need a crown. At some point the nerve will die, and then the tooth will need a root canal treatment. Eventually that too will fail and the tooth will need to be extracted. Every time we take a drill to a tooth, we are setting a timer on how long we can keep that tooth ticking over.'

This was a pivotal moment in my training. Don't ask me

why. Maybe it was simple naivety. But up until now it hadn't registered in my head that the work *I* was doing wouldn't last the test of time. This realisation was massive. Almost enlightening. Like having a weight lifted from my shoulders.

At the time I'd been a young man of twenty-one and feeling the pressure. My work *must* be perfect. My work *must* last. At times I'd felt like a machine. But Dr Sanford went on to say that it was okay to remember our 'human-ness'. Indeed, it was important to accept that failure would one day happen. It was necessary – for one's own mental health and peace of mind – to remember that, eventually, everything fell apart. Phew!

'In the end, you must remember, no matter what happens, no matter what breaks or fails, it is *just* teeth,' she concluded. Her words echoed into the abyss of my thoughts. 'Right,' she barked. 'Everyone out. Lecture over. Get back to your clinics!'

And with that, a somewhat spellbinding moment was broken.

Off we went. Back to work. Nonetheless, I couldn't help but feel a little changed from the experience. She was right, of course. Dentistry is a litigious career – as you'll read later, dear reader. But in the end, why do people sue? It's *just* teeth!

❖

Sunny Milford-on-Sea is where our next episode takes place. Hampshire was my home for eight weeks of my fourth year of dental school. This eight-week placement was what we called *Outreach*.

Basically, there weren't enough NHS dental services in the Hampshire region, so the NHS set up a student clinic. The university would house us, and we'd do nothing but patient clinics, nine to five, for eight weeks of the year.

This was a fantastic experience from an educational point of view. You could really hone your skills, increase the amount of patient contact you had, and get a true taste of being a general dentist.

Also, the tutors were local dentists to the area. Dr Popa was one of them. She was a fifty-something Ukrainian intent on channelling a twenty-something hipster and always dressed in *charity-shop-chic* outfits.

Dr Popa loved 'alternative' patients – like my middle-aged female patient who told me fluoride was poison, we were being brainwashed by the government into believing fluoride was a preventive, whereas the reality was that all toothpastes had been personally manufactured by David Cameron to cull the population.

This particular patient puffed twenty ciggies a day but steered clear of toothpaste.

I tentatively suggested that her cigarettes might be more likely to contribute to her demise, but she wasn't receptive to this and dismissed my words with a wave of the hand.

Dr Popa *loved* this patient. Overhearing, she zoomed over and told my patient to try Miswak sticks. This is a type of bark that contains chemicals that may help disinfect the mouth. No doubt Dr Popa had come across this particular find while backpacking across Asia – probably in the early 1900s.

Another tutor, Dr Doyle, was memorable because of her flaming red hair and dry sense of humour. I was never sure if she was laughing with me, or at me. Nonetheless, she was an excellent dentist and gave me enough freedom to really learn while working.

Finally, there was Dr Andrews. He was a plump sweaty little man. Despite being married to a woman he came across as camper than a row of pink tents. He strutted around the bays, flirting with patients, nurses, and staff alike – both female and male. Gender wasn't an issue!

So, now that you've been introduced to the cast of Milford Outreach Clinic, let me tell you about a dramatic tale. Well, to be honest, it wasn't dramatic at all, the patient was simply a drama Queen (yes, capital Q).

Mrs Larsen was a forty-five-year-old homemaker from Milford-on-Sea. When I say *homemaker*, what I actually mean – and no disrespect to the *real* homemakers out there – is that she was unemployed. She ate enough sugar to give Willy Wonka a toothache and drank so much cola that it was a wonder she didn't bounce off the walls from the caffeine high. Unsurprisingly, she had several cavities that required a number of fillings.

I greeted Mrs Larsen, and she parked her bottom in the chair. I ran through the plan of action for the appointment – a filling in the lower left first molar. She nodded, then looked at her watch, as if she soon had somewhere else to be (or perhaps just seeing when she could have her next cola hit).

I popped her back in the chair, applied numbing gel, then administered a dental block to numb the lower jaw. I then sat her upright again so she could rinse away any bitter aftertaste.

'I feel weird,' she said, suddenly pawing at her throat. 'My throat... my THROAT!' she gasped. 'I can't swallow,' she squealed, eyes widening, pupils dilating.

'You've swallowed some of the numbing gel,' I soothed. 'It can make the throat feel a little numb. It's nothing to worry about. Have a sip of water and the sensation will soon pass,' I reassured.

But Mrs Larsen was having none of it.

'You've poisoned me,' she shrieked. 'What was in that injection? ARGHHHH!'

What the...?

Mrs Larsen's reaction momentarily rendered me speechless. Hastily, I mentally ran through past communication skills training, all textbooks and lectures on anaesthetic and anxiety management, then finally a subsection of notes on batshit crazy individuals. Every single one drew a blank on what to do.

Mrs Larsen was now thrashing around in the chair.

'You're trying to kill me,' she screamed. 'I need help.' Her caterwauling went up an octave. 'HELP!'

By this point, Mrs Larsen's behaviour had attracted the attention of all three tutors. Dr Popa, Dr Doyle, and Dr Andrews dropped everything and dashed into my bay.

'What on earth ith going on?' lisped Dr Andrews.

'Your student has poisoned me,' screeched Mrs Larsen. 'I've gone all itchy. My throat is closing up. I'm slowly being murdered!!'

'Now, now, dear lady,' soothed Dr Andrews. 'It's a combination of numbing gel and anxiety. Take some deep breaths. I'll get you some glucose to raise your blood sugar.'

'NO MORE POISON!' she howled. Dr Andrews stepped back in alarm. 'GET ME AN AMBULANCE,' Mrs Larsen roared.

Meanwhile, the no-nonsense Dr Doyle had had enough.

'Calm down, Mrs Larsen. You don't need an ambulance. You're being quite ridiculous.'

Mrs Larsen gave Dr Doyle a look of contempt, then reached into her back pocket and pulled out an ancient phone. I think it may have been an original Nokia 3310. She called 999 and requested both the police and an ambulance.

'I've been poisoned at the student dental clinic in Milford and am now being held against my will,' she informed.

I looked helplessly at my three tutors who, in turn, were staring incredulously at the crazy Mrs Larsen. Was it my imagination, or was she starting to foam at the mouth like a rabid dog? I jest. She wasn't really frothing at the mouth. Rather, dribbling everywhere and acting like a Grade A asshole.

The ambulance duly arrived (no police though, which was a shame as we all could've used their protection from this nutter).

The paramedic strode into clinic. Checked her out. Blood pressure. Temperature. Oxygen saturation. Glucose levels. Conclusion: ~~I had poisoned her~~ she was absolutely fine.

'No, I'm not!' Mrs Larsen protested shrilly. 'Take me to A&E. Now! I need someone competent to check me out.'

She continued to behave belligerently, now arguing with the paramedic.

I stood outside my bay. The entire clinic had come to a halt. Students and patients alike were watching this bit of drama. Everyone was agog at what might happen next.

'Ma'am,' said the paramedic. 'You are fine. You do not

need to go to A&E, and we are certainly not taking you there in our ambulance. This is a waste of NHS resources.'

'How *dare* you,' hissed Mrs Larsen. 'If I die because of being poisoned, I will sue you. Do you hear me? I WILL SUE YOU and PERSONALLY HOLD YOU ACCOUNTABLE FOR MY DEATH!'

I didn't dare point out that if she died, she wouldn't be able to hold the paramedic accountable, let alone sue him, because she would be – well – dead.

The paramedic shook his head before taking himself off. Meanwhile, Mrs Larsen gave everyone a look of disgust. She scrambled to her feet and snatched up her coat. A can of cola fell from one pocket. As it hit the floor, it burst open, fizzing everywhere.

'Now look what you've done,' she screamed at me. 'I'm going to drive myself to A&E all because of YOU!'

And with that she turned on her heel and flounced off. No doubt, she was absolutely fine by this point but didn't want to lose face.

Thankfully I never saw Mrs Larsen again, and the Milford Echo never ran a scoop headlined *Dastardly Dental Student Spikes Nutty Nora with Narcotics*.

❖

Sedation is the art of calming a patient down through the use of drugs. Dental phobia is very common and, in some cases, cannot be managed through the usual behavioural routes such as small, repeated exposures to the dental environment (what we call *acclimatisation*). In such cases, sedation is employed.

Sedation is usually given intravenously and creates a twilight state for the patient. They'll feel tired, relaxed and more carefree. Midazolam – the preferred choice of drug – also has an amnesic effect, meaning the patient will likely not remember anything of the treatment.

One unfortunate side-effect of Midazolam can be inappropriate behaviour, and by that I mean sexual in nature. This is because Midazolam, as well as being a sedative, is also a mild hypnotic. It depresses the central nervous system so that inhibitions ebb away and (as Freud might say) the true id of the psyche can be revealed.

Despite never performing sedation (and I have no plans to!), it is still important to have a rounded education. As a result, sedation clinics were part of our dental training. We didn't administer the sedative, but we did cannulate and then do the dental work on sedated patients. Throughout, a sedation dentist or anaesthetist would be monitoring.

I had an uncomfortable experience with one such sedated patient.

Gene Appleby was an eighty-five-year-old woman who wore upper and lower partial dentures. She had very few of her own teeth left. She was a cantankerous old lady at the best of times. In hindsight, the crankiness was likely a defence mechanism due to her fear of dentists and dental work.

On this particular day, she walked into the clinic smartly dressed in a long gingham skirt, with coordinated blouse and cardigan. Her shoes were so highly polished I could see the surgery lights reflecting in them. Around her neck was a thick chain from which hung an enormous gold crucifix.

'I don't want to be here long,' was her opening gambit. 'My daughter is waiting to take me home and she's a very busy lady.'

'Of course, Mrs Appleby,' I said. 'Now then, I understand you have a loose upper tooth and today we're going to take it out.'

'Yes, yes,' she said irritably. 'Can we get on with it?'

'Absolutely. However, I need to go through your medical history first,' I said.

She sighed with annoyance and gave me an eyeroll.

'Young man. Are you quite sure you're fully competent to do this treatment, because I've already given my medical history.'

I reassured her that checking the medical history was part of the protocol, also that I wouldn't be the one giving her the sedative but would be the person performing the tooth extraction.

Reluctantly, Mrs Appleby went through her medical history with me. She then removed her dentures and set them to one side.

I cannulated the patient. The tutor delivered the sedation and double-checked everything. I noticed that Gene's knuckles were very white as she gripped the arms of the dental chair and decided that she was more nervous than she cared to admit.

The Midazolam was duly administered. Gene's hands gently relaxed and returned to their normal colour. She gave a deep contented sigh, as if getting into a deliciously fragrant bubble bath at the end of a tiring day.

'Okay, Mrs Appleby,' I soothed. 'You're doing really well. I'm now going to get you nice and numb.'

'Oh boy,' she breathed. 'You're going to give me the prick, are you?' She winked lasciviously.

'Just a small scratch, then everything will go numb.'

'Ha!' she giggled naughtily. 'I bet you'd like that, eh? A gorgeous damsel like me.'

Gene stuck a finger in her mouth and licked it suggestively. Dribble waterfalled down her chin.

I administered the LA and Gene's drooling intensified.

'Okay, Gene,' I said. 'I'm now going to take the tooth out.'

'Ooh, you naughty *naughty* boy! Here we are, all alone, and you want to have your wicked way with me, don't you?' She thrust her chest out, then stroked her crucifix. 'Let's start with a little kiss, young man.'

Not only did Gene pucker up, but she also abruptly sat up and lunged at me. I leapt backwards, crashed into the instruments trolley, sent the whole lot flying, and fell painfully arse over tit.

The patient greeted this scenario with delight. Her wish to be snogged gave way to childish giggles. The tutor helped me up and, to my relief, said he would take over. I limped towards the exit, grateful to escape. As I pushed through the swing doors, Gene's voice floated over, loud, and clear.

'Where's the young man gone?' she slurred. 'He's done

a runner. Well, fuck me.'

'Not today,' said my tutor wryly.

❖

Exam season came round all too quickly. My fifth-year finals came round in April. A series of grueling papers, face-to-face viva exams (where you're questioned one-on-one with an examiner) and ultimately the presentation of your *finals case*. We'll talk about the finals case a little later. First, I want to tell you about my Oral Pathology examination – the driest and hardest of all the exams.

Oral Pathology is where one assesses microscope slides to identify different types of conditions, such as cancers or cysts. In addition to being able to identify different types of cells and their appearances, you had to be able to describe the mechanism that caused the condition, then suggest the treatment, prognosis, and drug actions. Finally, this all had to be written in fluent Mandarin. Okay, that last bit is a joke, but I can't emphasise enough how tough, how taxing, this three-hour exam was.

Together, my friend Joelle and I, had spent months with flash cards while frequenting a local restaurant by the name of *Marrakech*. Once a week, regular as clockwork, we'd test each other extensively while consuming a lamb tagine, until we identified every condition perfectly (or so we thought).

On the day of the test, Joelle and I quietly reassured each other, then shuffled nervously into the exam hall.

Here, within this ancient building that had stood since the late 1800s, I sat silently at my desk, paper in front of me.

The hall was dark and musty with lacquered wooden walls and a floor covered in a faded green carpet. At the front were three exam invigilators.

Dr Sanford aka The Bulldog entered the hall.

'Right,' she barked. 'Good luck to you all today. I'm sure you'll all do fine because you've all worked your socks off.

You have three hours for this paper. If you finish early, please go back and re-read the questions. I will now leave you in the care of the invigilators and will return at the end of the exam. The time is a quarter past ten. Your exam starts... now!'

There was the whispering sound of papers being turned and ballpoint pens clicking, ready to fill blank pages with knowledge. We were off!

I turned to the first question and mentally punched the air in delight. I knew the answer! Eagerly, I jotted it down, taking care to make my writing a legible as possible.

Fifteen minutes into the exam, I was distracted by one of the invigilators. He was a tall slim man wearing square geek-style spectacles. He was holding a brown paper bag. From this, he extracted a bottle of wine. I glanced about to see if anyone else was observing this invigilator. Just me apparently.

Fascinated, I watched as he proceeded to open the bottle, put it to his lips and then neck the entire bottle.

My mouth dropped open. Hastily shutting it, I quickly looked back at my paper, desperately trying to forget what I'd just witnessed.

I continued to work my way through the questions. Twenty minutes later, another bottle appeared! The other two invigilators exchanged a look while their colleague downed a bottle of pinot noir.

My concentration fragmented. This particular invigilator was visibly inebriated. He got to his feet, then staggered up and down the aisles between our desks. When someone asked for a spare pen, he lurched over and nearly upon their desk. All the students were now aware of what was going on.

After ninety minutes – the midway point – the man opened a third bottle and greedily gulped the contents down. He was now completely smashed. He looked squiffily at the clock on the wall and opened his mouth to speak.

'You have ten minutes left,' he announced.

A palpable frisson of shock rippled around the hall. Everyone glanced at each other in confusion.

'N-No, Tim,' stammered one of the invigilators. 'They have another hour and a half.'

'Oh,' he said, his eyes briefly crossing. 'Ah, shorry 'bout that,' he slurred. 'Carry on,' he said, before convulsing.

Things quickly descended into chaos as he repeatedly tripped and fell over in various aisles, giggling hysterically every time he uprighted himself. Eventually, I put up my hand. The female invigilator approached.

'Look, this is ridiculous,' I hissed. 'He's drunk three bottles of wine. Can't you get him out of here? It's impossible to concentrate.'

The woman was most apologetic and did her best to usher him from the hall. However, he was having *none* of it!

'Who do you think you are?' he roared. 'You're not the boss, you silly tart!'

By now, he had everyone's attention. Literally no one was writing a word. One invigilator left the room. I could see him, outside, making a phone call. Less than a minute later, Dr Sanford stormed in accompanied by a security guard from the hospital.

The drunken invigilator gulped. The Bulldog hooked a finger and beckoned him to her side. Meekly, he obeyed – albeit tripping over his own foot as he staggered from the hall.

'Continue with your exam,' Dr Sanford growled.

And we did.

Needless to say – and most peculiarly – not one single student failed that exam. Indeed, everyone achieved excellent scores. I mean, for me it was clearly all down to the copious revision Joelle and I had done. But I couldn't help but wonder if a certain alcoholic's outrageous performance might have contributed to bumping up our grades. Just a teeny bit...

❖

Final's case presentation: This is the exam that reduced students to terrified babbling idiots. Half the class – including me – visited their GPs begging for propranolol (a blood pressure medication). This drug helped to slow down heart rate and provide a sense of relaxation around examination time.

So, why did the final's case presentation cause such fear? Let me explain. It involved your most complex patient. This patient – one who'd been party to your shed-load of work throughout your fifth and final year – also had to attend the clinic. This patient would be inspected by two different tutors, along with your notes and a review of all x-rays. You would then be grilled in front of the patient. This also included justifying why you performed such treatment, and quoting a hundred different evidence-based articles that would confirm you'd done everything correctly. At the same time, nurses would jab you with hot sticks and molten liquid would rain down from the clinic's ceiling. Okay, that last bit was added for dramatic effect, but you get the idea!

The biggest issue for a student was getting their patient to *attend* the examination. On the actual day, several students would always be let down by their patients not bothering to turn up. It wasn't the end of the world because you could still pass, but it meant that the *entire* exam would consist of that awful knots-in-the-tummy grilling because your work literally wasn't there to 'speak for itself'.

My patient, Mary Cooper, was a sixty-something-year-old lady with short, cropped hair and a kind heart. She diligently attended every appointment. She listened to my advice, improved her oral hygiene, and changed her diet. The results were textbook.

Throughout our year together, Mary had undergone several treatments including periodontics (deep cleaning to stabilise the gums), restorative (replacing old leaking/broken silver fillings in the front teeth with white ones), endodontics (root canal treatments), prosthodontics (crowns and dentures) and, finally, oral surgery (extraction of broken teeth). She was the 'unicorn' for dental student requirements – in other words, she ticked every speciality.

On the dreaded day, Mary arrived at the clinic early. As I walked into the exam room, she gave me a reassuring smile and mouthed *good luck.*

As soon as I saw the examiners, my heart sank. Dr Sanford *The Bulldog* and Dr Byrne. Both were the strictest tutors in the school.

Dr Byrne was a strange fellow. His face sported a tough stubble-cum-beard which was at odds with his height, build and manner – tall, reed thin, and a constant nervous energy.

What made him a tough tutor was his apparent knowledge of every evidence-based article in the history of restorative dentistry. For starters, he had read *Shillingburg* several times over. This was an ancient tome on dental crowns, some thousand pages in volume and scripted in a size eight font. So a student had to know their stuff or else they'd fail.

Thankfully, in my fifth year, I gave up all hope of having a social life and lived in the library. I, too, read *Shillingburg's Fundamentals of Fixed Prosthodontics* from cover to cover, although not multiple times. Once was hard enough. I had then picked my selected journal articles and hoped that this would be enough.

So, there we were. Mary, The Bulldog, Dr Byrne and me. The exam got underway. I resisted the urge to be punny and didn't refer to Mary's dental x-rays as tooth pics. Nor did I suggest that Mary had first visited me with her Smartphone because she had a Bluetooth. Instead, I responded to The Bulldog's barked questions with a number of respectful woofs, and returned Dr Byrne's encyclopedic knowledge of Shillingburg with my own impressive answers. I didn't even need to phone a friend.

After an hour of interrogation, it was over. I instantly felt a huge sense of relief. It had gone well. There had been no confrontation. No question that I couldn't answer. I'd quoted several studies and their sources. In other words, I was quietly confident.

Mary and I left the clinic and went into the waiting

room. She gave me a hug.

'Well done,' she said. 'You did brilliantly.'

'Thanks, Mary. Omigod, that was intense. I'm so glad it's now over.'

'I'll bet you are,' she agreed. 'I want to say thank you for everything you've done for me this year. I hadn't taken care of my teeth in a long time and, even now, can't quite believe the transformation.'

'You're very welcome. And I want to thank you, too, for giving me your time and trusting in me to complete the work. It wasn't a five-minute job and took a lot of appointments on your part.'

'It was nothing,' she assured. 'And as a token of my gratitude, I have a little something for you.'

'No, no, Mary,' I protested. 'You shouldn't have. There was really no need.'

'Nonsense,' she said, offering me an envelope. 'Please, take it. I'm so delighted with my treatment. Just... everything. When you start your job in the NHS, can you let me know where you are because I'd like to continue being your patient.'

'Yes, of course I will,' I said, accepting the envelope. 'Thank you, again.'

'Go on then,' she grinned. 'Open it.'

I peeled back the seal. Inside was a gift voucher for two people to enjoy cocktails at the Ritz. My eyes brimmed.

'You honestly shouldn't have, Mary, but thank you.'

'The pleasure is all mine,' she smiled, before bigging me a final farewell.

Mary was as good as her word. She continued to see me as her NHS dentist over the next several years, as did many of my other university patients.

I took this as a huge compliment. They'd put their trust in an unqualified student. But here's the thing that I learned: Humans are creatures of habit. We find someone we like or trust, and then we stick with them. For example, I ended up travelling, every three weeks, to a hairdresser over an hour away. Crazy, right!

Needless to say, I not only passed my finals, I also achieved the highest mark in the year for my case presentation. I was like the cow in that nursery rhyme. Over the moon!

❖

Graduation took place at St. Paul's Cathedral. Newly qualified doctors attended with the dentists as we'd all started together and then finished at the same time.

My mother, step-father, sister and grandfather attended on what was to be the hottest day of the year. My best friend, Joelle, and I had a picture taken together, standing on the steps of the cathedral. Later, there was the must-have classic shot of everyone throwing their mortarboard hats in the air. No one tells you how much they hurt when gravity takes over and they thwack you on the head!

When it was time, we all entered the cathedral. Graduates went one way, family the other, each consigned to their allotted seats. Later, we were individually directed to stand in the wings. And then I heard it...

'With honours and distinctions in his third, fourth and fifth year, dental society colours, best in Part B finals and the prize for best all-round student...'

There was a dramatic pause, and then my name was called. Everything slowed down. I honestly hadn't had the slightest inkling about this and couldn't quite believe it. I'd only gone and won the much-coveted prize for best student.

I took a deep breath and strode out on to the stage accompanied by loud cheers from my friends and colleagues, whoops from my proud family, and thunderous applause from all. I shook the Dean's hand and, basking in this incredible moment, took my certificate.

Dear reader, at this point I felt rather peculiar. Light... elevated... on a total high... as if I'd spent five years scaling a mountain but was now, finally, standing at the peak with huge satisfaction of completing that journey. I found myself briefly looking back... at rejections in applications to other universities, to this moment, here and now. I'd done it. I was ready to tackle the world. I felt optimistic. I felt *complete*.

I think *that* in itself is the problem. Kids are 'programmed' to work hard. To pass exams. Go to university. Achieve the qualification. But when it's done... after that incredible heady elation has dissipated... suddenly you're left feeling a little bit lost. Strangely empty. There is no further exam to study for. No more hurdles to overcome. There's just... *work*.

And that brings us to the next chapter. Discovering that dentistry would soon knock out of me all my previous post-graduation joy. Next stop, disillusionment, and disaster.

2

Foundation Training

Dental foundation training (DFT) (or vocational training if you're really old!), is your first year on the job as an NHS general dental practitioner (GDP).

This twelve-month post is salaried and combines a thirty-six-hour week plus a day of lectures and/or practical skills sessions. Throughout the training year, you must pass a number of assessments, complete assignments, meet certain requirements (for example, do a certain number of root canal treatments) and generally do 'enough' NHS work.

To understand this more, you need to appreciate how the NHS dental system works. To put it candidly, it doesn't.

To break it down to its most simple form. Every general NHS dentist in the UK is self-employed. The practice he or she attends is an independent business. The NHS has a contract or budget that it 'sells' to practices. This contract is worth a particular sum of money in return for the practice completing a certain amount of dental work. This dental work is measured via UDAs (units of dental activity). The NHS assigns different treatment values of UDAs. For example, an examination would be worth one UDA, while a filling would be worth three UDAs. So, let's say the NHS sells a contract with 10,000 UDAs to a practice, then that practice will sub-contract the UDAs to self-employed dentists who are technically hiring the facilities and a nurse from the practice. They may hire two dentists to do 5,000 UDAs each. Does that make sense?

Probably not, because it's bloody complicated and a shit system!

Anyway, as a foundation dentist (FD) one only had to do 1800 UDAs over the year (an average fully fledged dentist would be doing around 7000).

This low target was to take some of the pressure off because, as a newly qualified dentist, you're going to be slow!

Foundation training is about getting you quicker and more confident. It trains you to work like a conveyor belt: Patient in. Drill. Fill. Bye!

The NHS wanted its pound of flesh, and you were going to give it to them.

That said, my FD year was mainly enjoyable. I learned a lot. Also, luckily, the practice was supportive. So come closer and listen up. I'm now going to give you all the gossip about being a junior dentist.

❖

Everyone **knows everyone in dentistry.** My nurse knew not just my face and name but also my age, address, sexual orientation, car registration, national insurance number, favourite underwear brand *and* what I ate last night – and this was before I'd even set foot on the premises. This is because dentistry is a *really* small quasi-incestuous world.

To give you an example. Back in my university days, I attended a black-tie student event. A tipsy female tutor set her sights on my boyfriend. She staggered over and snogged him. Even worse, my sloshed boyfriend didn't push her away. Outraged – and not a little inebriated myself – I pulled them apart and then played tonsil tennis myself with the female tutor. In my alcohol-fueled state this made perfect sense to me – I was exacting revenge on both her *and* my boyfriend for having a snog.

Alcohol can really skew your perception of reality. God, I am cringing as I write this down. What a stupid thing to have done. She'd been a *tutor* for God's sake. But, fast forward. This woman also turned out to be the *wife* of one of the dentists at my dental foundation training practice. Groan. And yes, I can hear you groaning with me.

'So!' said Rachel, the nurse I was to work with. 'Nice to meet you.'

'Likewise,' I said politely.

'I hear you gave Layla a smacker last year,' said Rachel.

I instantly reddened. Oh *nooo*. How had she known about that?

'Oh, don't worry,' said Rachel, flapping one hand at me. 'Austin told everyone. He thought it was hilarious.'

Yes, Austin was the female tutor's husband. Austin was also a general dentist with a specialist interest in periodontics (that's gums to you and me).

By now my face was making a tomato look anaemic.

'Forget about it,' said Rachel, flapping her hand again. 'Austin used to be a tutor, too. In fact, that's how he met Rachel. She was a student and they ended up banging it out for extra credit.'

'Eh?'

'You know. Sex.' She regarded my blank face. 'In exchange for better grades.'

'Ah, right,' I nodded, dumbfounded.

Rachel led me into the surgery and showed me where everything was. She then booted up the computer and gave a demonstration on how the software worked, how to make appointments, digitally chart things, and how to print treatment plans.

It was now time to meet my trainer. Dr Paul Slater was a Brummie-turned-Southerner. His accent was faint until something really riled him up, and then he'd tell you to *quit aggin* (stop whinging). He'd been a trainer for more than ten years and his general approach was *hands-off*. In other words, get on with it. If you had an issue, he would generally help or, later, give you a tutorial. I rather liked this approach, although it meant my first few months were one of self-learning and self-evaluation.

'All right, mate?' said Paul upon our first introduction.

'Hello, Dr Slater,' I said formally.

'No, no, no,' he said, shaking his head. 'We're all equals

here. You're a qualified dentist. It's fine to call me Paul.'

I found it hard to start calling other professionals by their first name. At university, everyone had been conditioned to show respect throughout our clinical life, so this adjustment took time. Meanwhile, Rachel suggested I brown-nose the boss in order to curry favour, assuring that this was something she did this herself.

'Hi, Paul,' she cooed, batting her eyelashes. 'I've set up the computer and printed out the day lists.'

'Good work, Rachel,' he said, giving her a wink. He turned to me. 'Any problems, mate, give me a shout. Otherwise, have a good day.'

And that was that. I was alone with my nurse and the day awaited us. Rachel turned to me.

'I'm his favourite,' she said smugly. 'That's because I'm the best nurse here. Be careful when you work with Tami. She's an absolute bitch and a rubbish nurse.'

I was taken aback at Rachel's snipe. I'd not even yet met Tami.

The thing about dental practices is they're small, closed environments with hefty internal politics.

If the practice isn't run properly, dental nurses can be the source of almost all the dramas that take place. There are always cliques and there will always be a whisper in the dentist's ear about what he said/she said.

I learnt the hard way to stay out of it, but I'll tell you why later. For now, let's talk *crazy patient stories*.

❖

Medical emergency training is part of a newly qualified dentist's annual continuous professional development. This is in order to be compliant and provide emergency treatment to patients. Annually, someone attends your practice and delivers this training. This includes practical stuff, like: how to deal with choking; how to perform CPR; emergency drug administration for anaphylaxis etc.

The most common 'emergency' in dental practice is

vasovagal syncope – in other words, the simple faint!

Fainting happens because of a drop in blood pressure. The blood can't reach a person's brain, so they collapse. Once flat on their back, circulation is restored to the brain. Therefore fainting is the body's effective way of ensuring blood gets back to the brain.

So why am I harping on about faints? Well, there's a funny story about it. Although – obviously – it wasn't funny at the time!

A completely bizarre situation occurred. Ashleigh, a sixteen-year-old girl, attended my clinic for orthodontic extractions (the removal of two to four teeth to create space for braces and the correction of a crowded mouth). Ashleigh's mother had come along too, and it was obvious from the start that it was the mum who was terrified of the impending treatment.

My surgery was on the first floor and the stairs leading up to it were steep and narrow. Mum and Ashleigh came in, panting slightly. Together we discussed the procedure and signed the consent form. Mum then abruptly made for the door.

'Okay, darling,' she trilled to Ashleigh. 'Mummy is going to pop downstairs while you have this done. You don't mind, do you?'

Before Ashleigh could reply, Mum had clattered down the stairs and stationed herself in the waiting room.

'Do you feel okay about your mother not being here?' I asked.

Ashleigh looked apprehensive but nonetheless nodded and gave a nervous smile.

I applied numbing gel, warmed the anaesthetic to make the injection as comfortable as possible, and administered the LA. I then sat her up to have a rinse. Ashleigh had started to look a little pale.

'I feel weird,' she quavered.

'Shaky?' I queried. 'There's adrenaline in the anaesthetic, so that does sometimes happen. I'll get you some glucose – sugar – which will help.'

'No, no,' Ashleigh protested, her voice going up an octave. 'I need to go.'

And with that, Ashleigh stood up and ran out of the surgery. My nurse and I immediately made after her. Ashleigh got to the top of the staircase, wobbled alarmingly, and then swooned. Rachel and I managed to grab hold of Ashleigh as she collapsed. While Rachel cradled Ashleigh's head, I squeezed past, then raised up her legs to get the blood supply back to the brain.

All this commotion – a huge thump and shouting – had attracted the attention of Ashleigh's mother. She hovered uncertainly at the foot of the staircase, no doubt wondering why her daughter's head was in the grip of a nurse and a dentist was grappling with an upside down pair of legs.

'Is everything okay?' she warbled, wide-eyed.

'This is all part of the extraction process,' I joked weakly.

'Ah. Right. Jolly good,' said Mum doubtfully. Nonetheless, she made to go back to the waiting room.

'Come back,' I implored. 'I was joking. Ashleigh had funny turn and fainted. Did she have some breakfast earlier?'

Mum turned back and regarded me curiously, as if patients sprawled on staircases was all part of our standard care package.

'Er,' she said, her brow furrowing. 'I don't think she did. No, no, she didn't. I remember now. Ashleigh was too nervous to eat.'

'Ah,' I said. 'That explains everything.'

Ashleigh eventually came round and was very confused. I explained what had happened. We gave her the glucose. Due to being numb, she dribbled most of it down her front.

Her colour returned and she started to look better. We returned to the surgery, Mum reluctantly trailing us.

'I need you to hold my hand,' Ashleigh implored her mother.

'Oh,' said Mum, looking aghast. 'Er, erm, ah, I mean, er, yes, okay, of course, darling. But I can't look, okay?' she gabbled, now slightly wild about the eyes.

After checking Ashleigh was completely numb, I started

the extraction of her upper premolar. Mum was holding Ashleigh's hand, but her eyes were firmly on the ceiling. And then she started to sing.

'Baa, baa, black sheep,' she softly began. 'Have you any wool?'

My nurse and I exchanged *the look* (the universal code between every dentist and nurse when both believe someone is stark raving bonkers).

Meanwhile, Mum was getting in her stride.

'Yes, sir, yes, sir, three bags full,' she sang, her voice ringing out.

I'm a Little Teapot came next.

'Here's my handle' – Mum warbled, waving Ashleigh's hand about – 'here my spout!' Ashleigh's other hand shot upwards.

'Are you okay?' I asked Mum.

'Yes, yes,' she assured. 'Just trying not to pass out.'

The last thing Rachel and I wanted in the surgery was another swooning lady!

'Carry on,' I said.

And so, she did. We were all treated to rousing renditions of *Skip to My Lou*, *Here We Go Round the Mulberry Bush*, and Humpty Dumpty.

Finally, Ashleigh's tooth extractions were complete, and Mum shut up.

She dropped her daughter's hand, abruptly sat down and, breathing heavily, muttered, 'I did it.' Her head then whipped up. 'I mean' – she looked at her daughter – '*you* did it. Well done, darling!'

I winked at my nurse, who was desperately trying not to convulse with laughter. Mum and daughter were then given post-op instructions. Clutching on to each other, they finally left.

Since then, I've had many faints in the chair, but never one quite like that.

❖

Stunned silence... followed by a shocked exchange of looks between patients in the waiting room.

'You're such a cunt,' Tami screamed.

Yes, dear reader, this highly offensive label was directed at me.

The two of us were in reception. My mouth dropped open. I couldn't believe a nurse could behave like this, let alone in a public area and in front of patients. I swiftly removed myself from Reception, shocked and appalled.

So, what led to this moment?

Tami – the dental nurse that Rachel 'warned' me about – was proving to be a person who provided so many issues that I could write an entire book on the woman.

Let me select a few choice moments that attributed to the culmination of the *C word*.

Tami was a twenty-three-year-old dental nurse. She'd worked at Paul's practice since the age of seventeen. When she wasn't behaving like an asshole, she was a good nurse. At this point I'd ask you to bear in mind that a twenty-three-year-old newly qualified dentist – me – needed support. That included occasionally buoying me up and giving a bit of encouragement. Tami was the exact opposite. She loved to undermine... demoralise... discourage... dishearten... deflate... and any other adjective you can think of. Her sole intention seemed to be a desire to make me feel that I was a rubbish dentist. Even worse, she like to do all these things in front of a patient. Got the picture? Good.

For example, if I was giving a scale and polish, Tami would loudly say, 'You've missed a bit, mate. That spot there.' This would be followed by an eye roll.

'Thank you, Tami,' I politely replied on this occasion. 'However, I've not yet got to that section.'

There was another time when, upon removing an old crown (which requires *drilling* the old restoration off and – inevitably – removing a tiny bit of tooth in the process), she was loudly vocal.

'YOU'RE DRILLING THE TOOTH!' she screeched. In front of the patient! This was followed by the patient abruptly sitting up, completely panicked, and telling me I was obviously incompetent and to stop the treatment.

The final straw was Tami snatching the dental mirror out of my hand, mid-exam, apparently to confirm that I'd accurately found a cavity. Enough was enough. I retrieved the mirror and glared at her. She glared back.

'What's your problem?' she snarled.

'Nothing, Tami,' I said, my voice neutral. 'Thank you for your help. Could you now please finish the chart.'

She looked momentarily perplexed but did as I asked. As soon as the patient had left, I tackled her.

'Tami, you can't keep doing this,' I said.

'Doing what?' she retorted.

'Undermining me. You do it constantly. You're not the dentist. Because of the way you're behaving in surgery, my patients believe I'm incompetent and are complaining.'

'You're not a dentist,' she said airily. 'You're a *trainee.*'

'I'm a fully qualified dentist,' I corrected. 'This is my dental *foundation* year, not vocational training. Regardless, you need to stop.'

'I've been doing my job for five years, mate, whereas you've been doing yours for five minutes, so I think I know a bit more than you.'

'Tami,' I said evenly. 'I'm not standing for this. First, you're being disrespectful. Second, I might be newly qualified, but a nurse shouldn't behave this way in front of patients. It's demeaning for me and causes a loss of confidence for them.' She rolled her eyes. 'Third, stop rolling your eyes and behave more professionally.'

By now, Tami's eyes were rolling like a drunk trying to operate a pinball machine. Livid, she stormed out of the surgery. I went after her.

'Tami,' I implored. 'It doesn't have to be like this. Please, return to the surgery.'

'You're such a cunt,' she shouted.

We are now back to where this chapter started. In Reception. A stunned silence. Agog patients. The air fairly quivering with shocked disbelief.

I swiftly sought out Paul, my trainer. I had no choice

but to tell him what had just happened. Being the *hands-off* fellow that he was, he told me to sit Tami down and have a straight talk with her. It was my job to toe the line.

So, no help as such from Paul. I had to deal with Tami myself.

Until now, I'd never been treated with contempt. Somehow, I had to ask Tami to show a bit of respect. At just twenty-three, it wasn't going to be a given, unlike with our respective seniors.

I found Tami in the staffroom. She was chatting with a couple of other girls while sipping tea, and browsing social media.

'Tami, can I have a word in private?'

She gave me an insolent look.

'That ain't happening.'

'It is happening, and it's happening now.'

'Nah, it ain't–'

Oka*yyy*. Paul told me to sort it. Here goes.

'TAMI!' I boomed, startling her. 'We either speak privately, or I embarrass you in front of everyone here.'

It was evident from the look on her face that she was taken aback at the mild-mannered *kid* asserting himself. She opened her mouth, then shut it again. She then followed me back to the surgery.

'Enough is enough, Tami,' I began. 'Do *not* swear at me in front of patients. In fact, do *not* swear at me *at all*.'

Silence.

'I don't care what you think *you* know, or what you think I *don't* know. If you believe I'm doing something wrong, either write it down on a piece of paper and pass it to me or wait until the patient is gone. But under *no* circumstances do you undermine me in front of *my* patients. Do we understand each other?'

'Yes.'

And that was that.

Tami didn't talk to me for two weeks. However, she'd got the message. She never questioned or argued with me in front of a patient again.

It was a learning curve for me, this young dentist, in how to be assertive when someone was treating me like a mug.

It's the *only* time in my entire dental career that I have ever shouted at a member of staff, and I hope I never have to do it again.

❖

I've had my fair share of weird patients. My first encounter with one such was a lady by the name of Isabelle Chilblain.

Isabelle attended as a new patient along with her family –husband and two children.

'Oh, no!' she screeched, sounding not unlike Kathy Burke's character Linda La Hughes. 'He's not even a minger!'

This was Linda's... I mean Isabelle's... opening gambit as she entered the surgery, family trailing after her.

My nurse – Carly on this occasion – raised one eyebrow and we exchanged looks. Carly was my favourite nurse (although, officially, we don't have favourites! She was in her early twenties and had the same sense of humour as me. When we worked together, we were so in tune that we never ran late, and everything went like clockwork).

'Nice to meet you,' I said to everyone. 'So, who is going first today?'

Isabelle wanted to go last as she was anxious on account of not having had a dental check-up in six years.

Eventually, it was her turn to take the chair.

'My last dentist was a horrible man,' she said.

As the chair reclined back, she gave a series of facial contortions conveying the full extent of her horror at the hands of Mr Smith.

'He terrified me. His name was Mr Smith, and he was *really* old and *really* ugly, and that's the reason I'm now so scared. Isn't that right, Derek?'

She looked to her husband for confirmation. Derek was a man of little words – probably because Isabelle spoke for them both. He simply nodded but said nothing because Isabelle was off again.

'Oh, and you see this front tooth?' she pointed. 'It's a

veneer, so please be really careful with it.'

I reassured her. Carried out an x-ray. Completed the check-up.

'I'm delighted to say you don't need any work,' I said.

Her *veneer* was a post-core-crown (where a tooth is so badly broken that it is root canal treated, followed by a large metal point being cemented inside the root to hold a porcelain crown in place. This is, generally, a last attempt to keep the tooth before extraction).

I advised Isabelle to be careful with the front tooth as it was fragile.

'Yes, of course, my lovely,' she beamed. 'I'm always careful. I don't eat or chew or crunch on it.'

'See you in six months,' I said.

'God, I'm glad we're not seeing her for a while,' said Carly. 'She was a bit full on, wasn't she! And what was all that about you not being a minger?' she laughed. 'Because we both know you are!'

'Ha!' I grinned. '*Funny!*'

However, six *weeks* later, Isabelle was back. This time as an emergency.

She came into the surgery, covering her mouth and crying. Derek, the husband, silently shadowed her.

'I was walking along, minding my own business' – Isabelle sobbed – 'when I somehow tripped. I fell over and hit my face and now my front tooth has gone. Omigod, what am I going to do? I'm so ugly. Do you think I'm ugly? Omigod, you do, don't you!' she shrieked.

'Isabelle,' I soothed, guiding her to the chair. 'Sit down and then we can get you fixed up, and you'll be as right as rain.' I gave a reassuring smile. She complied and sat down. 'So how, exactly, did you fall over?'

'I'm such a ditzy cow,' she said, flapping one hand. 'I was drinking white wine with the girls and, gawd knows how, I stacked it up the kerb. I thought it was funny in the early hours. But when I woke up this morning, sober like, well I was in hysterics. And I don't mean laughing. You should've seen me. Screaming my head off, wasn't I, Derek?'

The hapless Derek nodded by way of answer.

45

I assessed the upper left central incisor, took an x-ray, and concluded that the tooth was ~~well and truly fucked~~ unrestorable.

Isabelle had knocked the tooth out of the bone. There was a vertical fracture where the post had ruptured out of one side, and the crown was nowhere to be seen.

'Unfortunately' – I said gently – 'I don't think we can save this tooth.'

Cue uncontrollable crying.

'But the good news' – I continued – 'is that I can get a false tooth made before the end of the week.'

She stopped bawling and regarded me with red, puffy eyes.

'I need to remove the broken root,' I explained. 'I'll do that now. Then I'll take some moulds of your mouth for the lab. They will make a baby denture with one tooth which you can wear while everything is healing. No one will ever know that you're missing a tooth.'

Isabelle looked momentarily relieved until panic overtook her.

'So, do you just rip what's left of the tooth out of my head?' she quavered. 'Or will you numb me up? In which case, what will you use? Cocaine? I don't really want to be drugged up. I'm already mental enough, know what I mean?'

'Don't fret,' I assured. 'We haven't used cocaine in dentistry since the 1800s.'

'You're wrong,' she said, wagging a finger at me. 'That Mr Smith used it on me. Tell him, Derek. I went loopy. Completely doolally. It was all part of Mr Smith's plan to have his wicked way with me. Wasn't it, Derek?

Derek nodded glumly.

'My goodness,' I tutted, privately wondering what planet Isabelle came from. 'Well, I promise that today I'll be using lidocaine which has no psychoactive effects. Okay to go ahead and numb up the area?'

Isabelle nodded and the tooth was duly extracted. I then took a couple of impressions of her upper and lower arches before we both agreed on a colour match for the new tooth. I then said I'd see her at the end of the week.

Friday came all too quickly. The denture was back and so was Isabelle.

She erupted into the surgery, rushed over to me, flung her arms round my neck, and hugged me tightly. Startled, I gently extricated myself and asked her to take a seat. The ever-silent Derek looked unmoved by his wife's outburst of affection, although my nurse flashed me *the look*. I turned to Isabelle.

'I have your new tooth,' I said. 'It's going to take a little time to get used to it. You may find yourself a bit lispy to start with.'

'Oh great!' Isabelle threw up her hands and gave me all the facial theatrics. 'So I'll seem even more of a tit.'

'You'll quickly get used to it,' I said. 'However, the tongue is a finely tuned muscle and isn't used to feeling a little bit of plastic. It might also rub – a bit like new shoes. If that happens, don't panic. It's quite normal. Just rebook and I'll ease where it's rubbing.'

'Ah, so I should come back to you for a rubbing, eh?'

Isabelle winked lewdly. Derek said nothing. I think he was in power-saving mode.

I gave an uncomfortable half-laugh before talking through the self-care advice. Finally, Isabelle left. As the door shut behind her, my nurse and I gawped incredulously at each other.

'You've got a right one there. Rubbing indeed,' she snorted. She bent over faux-seductively, through her head about and run her tongue over her front tooth, taking the complete mick.

'A case of rubbing the wrong way,' I winked.

❖

My first complaint happened in foundation year. University doesn't prepare you for things going wrong. It doesn't teach you the litigious side of dentistry, or the terrible emotional impact on you, the clinician. The hardest thing about complaints is that they're often personal attacks on you. More often they are unfounded and downright unfair – especially when you know you've done everything right.

This particular complaint came from a lady. It is now so long ago, I forget her name, but the sting of it remains. She wasn't even *my* patient! Usually she saw another dentist, but he was on sick leave (due to stress!).

On this occasion, the woman had fractured her lower left first molar and attended clinic as an emergency. She wasn't in pain as the tooth had been previously root canal treated.

I reviewed her notes and discovered that this was the third time the tooth had fractured. Her usual dentist had recommended a crown on each occasion.

She had now broken off three of the four cusps (the pointed 'prongs' of the tooth). This meant there was almost nothing left of the tooth.

I explained that there were two options. Either leave the tooth until it inevitably crumbled, or extract it. The patient begged me to save the tooth. She pointed out her previous dentist's advice – that it might potentially be saved with a crown. Could I not crown the tooth on this occasion?

I re-assessed the x-rays and commented that there was now very little tooth left. I said I could try putting a post in, build up the tooth, then crown it. However, this was a back tooth. Given that most of one's chewing happens here, it would likely crack and fail. My concern was that such pressure on the tooth would see it hardly lasting a year.

I still remember this conversation so vividly because, when it came to dealing with the complaint, it was all in the notes, in black and white.

I explained that it would likely fail. That if she got a year out of it, she would be lucky. I advised it would be done on the NHS and require two, maybe three, appointments. The patient said if she only got a year out of it, she would be happy. She also accepted that it was likely to need extraction in the long term.

I diligently completed the herodontics (the treatment you're carrying out as a last-ditch attempt to save a tooth).

The patient was happy, paid and left. Her normal dentist then returned, and her check-ups continued with him.

Eleven and a half months later, the woman attended an appointment with her own dentist. She complained that the crown I'd placed had become loose. An examination revealed that the tooth underneath had fractured.

That was when all hell broke loose. The patient's dentist spoke to me. He explained that she'd gone nuts in his surgery. She'd shouted that I was incompetent and not known what I was doing. She'd then demanded her money back.

When her dentist had explained that everything had been logged in the notes about the tooth's prognosis, the patient had then informed him she was going to call the GDC (The General Dental Council) and make sure I was struck off for malpractice and scamming patients out of money.

Bear in mind I was not even one year out of university. Immediately I felt a sinking sensation in my stomach. I also felt anger. Everything had been correctly documented. This wasn't *fair*. I'd managed to keep that tooth going for nearly a whole year when any other dentist would have taken it out.

It was a good lesson because it taught me:

Don't go above and beyond for a patient.
Don't be adventurous.
Don't try and help further than what is predictable.

I'm sad to say that, even now, this is what I adhere to.

I spoke about this patient with my trainer, Paul. He shrugged his shoulders. Said it was nothing to do with him. He told me I was my own practitioner and had to deal with it. Never had I felt so alone.

I had to call my indemnity (insurance provider) and send them all the notes and x-rays. We chatted for a few hours and spent several days going through the options.

In the end, one of the dento-legal advisors drafted a grovelling letter of apology and the entire cost of the treatment was refunded personally from my pocket (even though my trainer had taken half of the original fee!).

That was the end of the matter. It never went further. However, the cost to me was far greater than that refund. This was the pivotal moment where I stopped enjoying dentistry. Where I suffered anxiety while driving to work. Where I tossed and turned and had many a sleepless night.

It may sound like an exaggeration, but the stress of threatened litigation in our profession is mentally exhausting. Many a time I've wished it were possible to take out the patient's teeth, do the work, then hand them back afterwards – it would solve a lot of problems! Anyway, we live, we learn, and we *change*.

❖

Patients think you're their friend. Often, patients over-share or feel they can comment on aspects of you as if they're a close friend or family member. As a professional, you let a lot of it go over your head. Sometimes the comments are rather rude.

'How old are you, sonny?'

'When did you qualify – last week?'

'You look suspiciously like a student to me.'

'Do you truly know what you're doing?'

Sometimes, it can be hilarious. Take, for example, the eighty-year-old female who ticked *herpes* in her medical history.

I turned to her and, somewhat naively, asked for verification.

'You've ticked herpes on your medical. I need to check if you mean cold sores or… downstairs?'

She held up her hands theatrically.

'Upstairs. Downstairs. Darling, I'm riddled with it!'

Too much information!

One heartwarming story concerns a thirty-year-old lady by the name of Jane Palmer and her boyfriend, Chris Piper. Jane and Chris were two of my patients and both had additional needs. Jane worked at the local Tesco bakery while Chris was employed as a cashier at a nearby petrol station.

The pair of them had... well, let's just say, *unattractive* teeth! Chris had been missing several front teeth for years. They both had poor dental hygiene, never cleaned properly, and always needed fillings.

That all said, they were lovely people and no trouble as patients. Never rude. Always happy to see you. Nearly always over-sharing personal information!

Jane and Chris always attended appointments together. From what my nurse, Carly, and I had pieced together, the two of them had met while buying a meal deal at Tesco. They'd both reached for the last packet of Monster Munch at the same time. As their hands had touched, Chris had been so blown away by Jane, he'd asked her out to dinner that very night. She'd shyly accepted. Together they'd shared a bargain bucket at KFC, and the rest had been history.

One day, they burst into the surgery together. Jane was beaming away while Chris explained he wanted to replace his missing front teeth. He sat down in the chair.

'I know I've been missing front teeth for a while, but now I think it would look better to have something there. What can you do?' he asked.

I ran through the NHS option – a denture (because he was missing five teeth in the smile line). The private option would have been a referral for implants. Chris took the NHS option of a denture.

By this point, Jane was almost jumping up and down with barely contained excitement. Like a dam bursting, her words spilt out.

'WE'RE GETTING MARRIED!' she shrieked.

'Wow,' I said. 'Congratulations to you both.'

Jane grabbed hold of my dental nurse. One thing you should know about Carly is that she's a tomboy. She doesn't *do* frills or flowers or girly stuff. Also, being a little shy, she wasn't one to gush.

'Look at my ring,' burbled Jane. She shoved her sparkler under Carly's nose. 'We're *girls* so I know you'll want to see it.'

'Oh! Gosh. Yes. Erm, nice,' said Carly awkwardly.

I rushed to Carly's rescue with diversion tactics.

'How did Chris pop the question?'

'It was *sooo* ROMANTIC!' Jane squealed.

'Yeah,' Chris agreed. 'Jane was in Tesco's bread aisle. While she was putting away the Kingsmill, I went over to her with a jumbo bag of Monster Munch – just like when we first met.'

'And when I looked inside' – Jane continued the story – 'there was this plastic jiffy bag containing a RING!'

Chris grinned sheepishly.

'I got down on one knee. Right there. Amongst the wholemeal and sliced white. And I said, "Jane! Ever since I first laid eyes on you, I thought you woz the fittest thing I'd ever seen. I want to marry you."'

'And I said YES!' squealed Jane.

It was an incredibly sweet and touching story.

Carly and I congratulated them both again, and I promised to make Chris some great-looking gnashers in time for his big day. We were both invited to the wedding, but politely declined.

Patients may believe we're their best friends for life, but the relationship is purely professional. However, Jane and Chris shared a lovely moment, and it was a reminder that my work *did* make a difference – especially when Jane later showed me the wedding pics with Chris beaming away.

❖

Isabelle Chilblain, part two. Every time I saw her name on my list, my heart would sink. My nurse's heart would sink too.

'Right then, Doctor Not-a-Minger,' Carly mocked. 'Shall we get Isabelle in?'

I rolled my eyes.

'If we have to.'

'The quicker we see her, the quicker we get lunch,' Carly pointed out.

There was wisdom in those words. When we last asked

Isabelle to come into the surgery, she had hugged me. This time, she attempted planting a kiss on my mouth. I deflected it so that her lips touched my cheek. Carly gasped before struggling to contain a giggle-snort.

'Please' – I gestured hastily with my hands – 'take a seat.'

Derek, the husband of few words, entered silently. He stood in one corner, observing without comment or emotion.

Isabelle removed her denture and, spraying spittle everywhere, proceeded to hold it forth.

'On the whole, this ain't been too bad, has it Derek?' He nodded, possibly on the verge of saying something, but Isabelle was off again. 'However, I really hate taking it out, don't I, Derek? That said, it's made things in the bedroom a bit more interesting, know what I mean!' she winked, before laughing uproariously.

Derek remained mute. Carly and I were now mute too – from shock. I mean, I knew they'd had sex at some point because they had kids, but to contemplate the fundamentals of Isabelle and Derek's love life – especially since Derek had the personality of a damp cloth and the energy of a battery on the blink – was, well, I mean, *well really*!

'Er, right,' I said awkwardly. 'I'm glad it's not been too bad. The denture,' I hastily clarified, while inwardly cringing. 'So, what can I do for you today?'

'Well, it's been nearly three months innit, and I know you said I had to wait for everything to heal, and now it's healed I want something in the gap, so I don't have to wear this thing anymore,' she gabbled. 'Is that, like, possible?'

We ran through the options and Isabelle settled for a fixed conventional bridge.

This would involve preparing the other incisor for a crown and, from this, *hanging* a fake tooth to fill the gap.

Isabelle didn't want implants.

'They're too scary.'

Nor did she want a resin-bonded bridge.

'I worry it might fall off mid-wine'.

I advised Isabelle to continue wearing the denture for a

few more weeks until the lab had made the bridge. Reluctantly, she agreed.

After booking her next appointment, Isabelle left and, as she did so, I breathed a deep sigh of relief.

Carly shot me an incredulous look.

'Isabelle kissed you!' she exclaimed.

'Mate... don't even... it was just... too much,' I groaned.

'Yeah, I agree,' said Carly. 'She clearly has a thing for you. What do you reckon her husband makes of her behaviour?'

'No idea.' I shook my head. 'He just stands in the background. Always silent. He's like the Grim Reaper. So long as he doesn't come for me because he thinks I'm having an affair with his wife.'

'Perhaps he gets off on it,' Carly joked. I turned a pale shade of green.

A few weeks later, Isabelle returned for the bridge preparation appointment. Together, Carly and I had devised a plan to stop any further inappropriate behaviour. As she entered the surgery, Carly immediately positioned herself as a blockade between me and Isabelle. Undeterred, Isabelle powered forward – until Carly opened a drawer and immediately pretended to select instruments from within. Isabelle visibly deflated.

'Hello,' I chirped. 'Take a seat.'

It was only when Isabelle was safely in the chair that Carly moved. I stepped forward and explained today's procedure. Isabelle smiled and nodded.

'You're just so lovely,' she purred. 'Thanks *so much* for looking after me,' she added huskily.

And with that, she reached out and began rubbing my leg.

I stiffened – body, *not* crotch! – and took a swift step away from Isabelle's wandering hand.

Carly and I immediately shared *the look*.

Fortunately, the remainder of the appointment was uneventful. I completed the preparation, temporised the tooth, then sent Isabelle on her way with Derek the ~~carer~~ husband trailing behind.

I *almost* felt bad when Isabelle returned a week later.

Before taking the chair, she gave me a bottle of wine and a card expressing her gratitude. She thanked me profusely for all my patience following her drunken mishap.

Note I wrote *almost* felt bad. Wine doesn't make up for sexual harassment.

Carly once again acted as a blockade, and I took care not to wheel my dental stool so close to Isabelle that she could make physical contact.

'Right, let's pop the chair back and get you numbed up,' I said. 'And then we'll fit this bridge.'

'Oh, but you have such lovely eyes,' she cooed as the chair whirred backwards.

As Isabelle was staring straight into their depths, I resisted the urge to roll them.

I numbed her up, put the bridge in position, then handed her a mirror.

'Happy with the appearance?' I asked.

'Wow,' she gasped. 'You'd never even know, would you?' she said in delight.

I was distracted. Gazing at the bridge. Mentally patting myself on the back. That was when her hand shot up. She stroked my face.

'You've done *such* a good job,' she said throatily.

I absolutely HATE people touching my face. Also, I deemed this touchy-feely behaviour totally unacceptable. The next problem I faced was treading a careful line between professionalism while letting the patient know such behaviour should cease.

I switched to cool, robotic, nondescript mode. No laughs. No jokes. One could even say I *did a Derek*.

I then gave Isabelle a brief explanation of what I would be doing next, before once again proceeding.

Carly glanced at me. She could detect the change in my mood. From sunny to frosty. The vibe in the surgery had shifted. If there had been a thermostat on the wall, it would have registered a major drop in temperature. My nurse wisely said nothing.

I cemented the bridge, then gave the usual post-operative instructions – no food or drink for an hour – all the while making sure Isabelle was not within arm's reach.

Isabelle sat up.

'Thanks so much,' she smiled. 'I love it. I can't believe how good it looks. You're such a great dentist.'

'Thank you,' I said briskly. 'The girls at reception will sort everything else out for you.'

'Oh, right. Okay. I'm… I'm just so glad I came here.' Isabelle wasn't going. I didn't reply. I turned to the computer and started typing notes. 'Really glad,' said Isabelle, sounding rather desperate. 'Really, really, *really* glad, aren't I, Derek?'

Derek nodded, and still Isabelle hovered.

'Was there something else?' I asked.

'No, no, ah, *noooo*,' said Isabelle, looking flushed and flustered. 'Anyway, thanks again.'

'You're welcome,' I said, before returning to my notes.

I think, in that moment, Isabelle realised she'd overstepped the mark. She left, and never came back.

I occasionally saw Derek, the robotlike husband. Oh, and their kids. But never Isabelle, for which Carly and I were tremendously relieved and grateful.

'Do you think Derek has buried Isabelle under the patio?' Carly pondered.

'That would require a lot of blood, sweat and beers,' I winked.

❖

My trainer's wife, Jackie Slater, was the practice manager and also a dental nurse. That's how Paul first met Jackie. She was his nurse.

I don't think he'd necessarily meant to end up with her. However, when he was first training, they fooled around and… one accident later… a shotgun wedding ensued.

Jackie was now Paul's practice manager. All these years later, she still had an amazing allure – slim, long cascading curly locks, pouty lips and a curvaceous bod.

The two of them seemed like any other happily married

couple that worked together. You know what I mean. Regularly arguing. Jackie frequently rolling her eyes. Huffing every other minute. Paul yelling, 'SHUT UP,' in front of the staff. Truly idyllic stuff.

Anyway, Jackie wasn't the best practice manager. I wouldn't even put her in the top ten... thousand. She had her sidekick, Lucy. Lucy was also a long-term friend and – no surprise here – was also the head dental nurse.

They two women had done their dental nursing together. Lucy was next to useless and spent her days doing little nursing. Instead, she concentrated on winding up the other nurses and making sure drama followed in her wake – be that in staff rotas, spreading gossip or ordering incorrect stock.

One day, due to staff sickness, we were down two nurses. This meant that both Jackie and Lucy had to actually *do* some nursing. It was a shock to the system for all involved. Jackie tottered into my surgery in her high heels.

'Aren't you the lucky one!' she grinned, tossing back her mane of blonde hair. 'Today you have a pro in your surgery.'

'Great!' I enthused, feeling anything but.

Together, we looked at the day list – the patients that were planned for that day – and then got cracking.

Apart from having to ask Jackie for the three-in-one (the thing that sprays air and water on your teeth) for every patient, things went smoothly. That is, until the emergencies started.

In came a female patient I'd never met before. She complained of a raging toothache, a lingering sensitivity to hot and cold, and the pain coming in waves. Paracetamol and ibuprofen weren't touching the sides. She declared she was in agony.

A quick examination and x-ray revealed decay in the pulp (nerve) of the tooth.

Now, the thing with NHS dentistry is that it's time critical. A normal associate (i.e. has completed DFT training) would have ten to fifteen minutes to see an emergency in which he/she would get the patient's history, take x-rays, diagnose the problem, then get the patient out of pain. That is *not* enough time to perform highly skilled surgery. Indeed, this is often why *wrong* treatment is performed – namely handing out antibiotics like Smarties.

However, this is what Jackie was used to. To her, it was the norm. But now Jackie was nursing for me – someone in their training year. This meant I had thirty minutes to do all the above.

I explained to the patient that she had irreversible pulpitis, that the nerve in the tooth had been damaged so badly it would not recover, and the pain was due to the nerve dying. I explained that in the long term, the tooth would either need extraction or root canal treatment. Quite rightly, the patient asked if the treatment could be done today.

Jackie immediately reached for the prescription pad, a hopeful smile on her face. She was not up for a first stage root canal treatment. After all, there was a *lot* of equipment to sort out.

I returned Jackie's smile – along with the prescription pad and set about performing the patient's treatment.

Jackie's previously perky manner disappeared down the spittoon.

'Thanks for your help this morning,' I said to her later.

'Huh,' she huffed. 'Yeah, no worries.'

It was obvious she was livid at the amount of proper nursing she'd had to do. She flounced off to her lunch break.

As the afternoon got underway, it became more apparent that she wasn't pleased at how much work she had to do. She'd been hoping for an easy day with the foundation dentist.

Later, I overheard Lucy moaning to Jackie. They were in the corridor outside my surgery.

'Fuck me,' Lucy expleted. 'I've worked sooo hard today. One filling and only three tea breaks. I'm exhausted.'

Jackie gave Lucy a dark look.

'You think that's hard graft?' she snapped. 'Try working with the new kid!'

Remember what I said about dental practices? Basically, they're small environments and, just like a pressure cooker, can explode at any moment with internal politics.

Well, now it's time to explore that a bit further. But first, let me properly introduce you to the entire cast of my DFT practice:

Dr Paul Slater – practice owner (and my trainer).

Jackie Slater – practice manager (*un*-extraordinaire)

Lucy – head nurse (and headcase)

Rachel – nurse (and practice gossip)

Tami – nurse (who knows better than everyone else)

Carly – nurse (my fave)

Me – the world-renowned, highly celebrated, twenty-four-year-old *kid* dentist.

Put them all together and it will take just one spark to set the powder keg alight.

That spark came near the end of my DFT year, and in the form of an innocuous incident that became a game of whispers and finger pointing.

At the end of the day, one of the things a dental nurse oversees is the flushing of lines with disinfectant. This is to ensure that all harmful bacteria (like legionella) are killed.

Technically, and certainly from a health and safety perspective, the person doing the flushing should wear a visor or goggles to protect against splash-back. However, more often than not, the nurses wouldn't bother, opting to pour without protection.

Tami – who naturally knew better than anyone – certainly didn't bother with any eye protection. On this particular day, she opened the line and poured in the chemicals. Upon hearing an odd-sounding gurgle, she leant in to listen.

'That's odd,' she said to herself.

She then leant in further, ear next to the drain line. Suddenly, liquid regurgitated back up the line and splashed her square in the face.

'ARGH!' she screamed.

Startled, I looked up from my notes.

'What's happened?' I cried.

'Help! It's in my eyes. Omigod, I've gone blind,' she yelped.

'Shit,' I said, leaping to my feet. 'SHIT!

'H-e-l-*ppp*,' Tami wailed. 'Oh-God-oh-God-oh-God.'

'Oh-shit-oh-shit-oh-shit,' I said, panic stricken.

Hastily, I turned on the tap and, grabbing a patient cup, used it to repeatedly throw water at Tami's face.

'I'm drowning,' she spluttered, as I chucked the fifth beaker of water at her. 'For God's sake STOP!' she bellowed.

'But,Tami,' I panted, sloshing water everywhere. 'We need to clean your eyes.'

'It's okay,' she said shakily. 'My eyes are calming down. I think you rinsed the chemicals away.'

Tami blinked at me cautiously – a vision with red eyeballs and mascara-streaked cheeks. She then dried herself off before seeking out management (Jackie and Lucy) to talk it over.

Cue over-the-top fakery from both women.

'Oh my gosh, darling,' cooed Jackie, arranging her features into that of deep concern. 'Are you all right?'

'Tami, what are you like?' tutted Lucy. 'There's eyewash in the medical emergency kit.'

Tami did lots of sniffing and quite a bit of lip trembling. Eventually she pulled herself together and got back to finishing the line flushing. That should have been the end of the matter. But it wasn't.

The following day I was working with Rachel (practice gossip).

'Well,' said Rachel, puffing her chest out importantly. 'Lucy said that Tami behaved like an idiot.' It was obvious from Rachel's expression that she was relishing this office *scandal*. 'Lucy also said that Tami should have been wearing eye protection. And Jackie said that if staff can't follow health and safety rules, then they've only got themselves to blame. What do you think?' She eyed me beadily. 'Do you reckon Jackie and Lucy are right? Or are they simply being a pair of bitches?'

'Sorry?' I asked, looking up from my notes.

'Are Lucy and Jackie being bitchy?'

'Oh... I don't really know. I mean, I guess everyone should follow the rules. No one wants it happening again.'

Except that wasn't the end of it either. It transpired that Rachel went to Tami and Carly, intent on dragging me into it.

'He said that you brought it on yourself,' said a gleeful Rachel to the feckless Tami – in front of the other nurses. 'He said that he agreed with Lucy and Jackie, and that you got what you deserved for not following the rules!'

'That doesn't sound right?' said Carly (my fave).

'But you weren't there,' Rachel pointed out, hellbent on stirring. 'He said that Tami was always fucking up. And that she'd now fucked up *again*. He was so angry. I think it triggered him. You know, after that business earlier this year.' She looked at Tami. 'You called him a cunt. Remember? He certainly hadn't forgotten. He gave this strange smile and said what happened to you was *poetic revenge*.'

Tami looked confused.

'But that doesn't make sense,' she said. 'After all, he helped me. And he wasn't angry. Not at all.'

'Yeah, but since then he's had time to think about it,' said Rachel airily. 'Oh, and he also told me that Lucy called you an idiot and wished she could fire you.'

'Wh-*a-a-a-t*?' Tami gasped. 'How *dare* that lazy cow say such a thing. All she does is sit on her fat ass doing fuck all. HOW DARE SHE SAY SUCH A SHITTY THING!'

The following day, Lucy burst into my surgery.

'I've got Paul telling me not to get involved with nurses' gossip. Meanwhile, Tami wants to hand in her notice and Jackie says I've got to sort this mess out. How could you?' she roared. 'I thought we were friends. And after all the cups of tea I made for you this year.' And out it all tumbled. The latest version of *who said what and when and to whom.*

I took a deep breath.

'Lucy, just stop for a moment and listen. Do you think

61

this sounds like something I'd *really* say? As you just pointed out, we're friends'– we really weren't! – 'and I've known you for almost a year. When have I ever said a bad word about anyone?'

Lucy paused. Considered.

'You're right. So... where has this tittle tattle come from?'

'I'll find out,' I promised.

I messaged Carly and asked if she knew anything. She didn't text me back. Instead, she rang me.

'Look, I can't say much right now,' she whispered down the phone. 'But it was Rachel who said you spouted all this stuff. I did point out that it didn't sound like you, but she was very convincing. Did you really say that Tami deserved to go blind?'

What. The. Fuck.

I didn't waste a moment. I found her in the staff room.

'Rachel?'

She ignored me.

'I need to talk to you. In private.'

'No,' she said stubbornly, although she was visibly rattled. 'You can talk to me here.'

'We talk in private,' I said firmly. 'Now.'

I strode off. A few seconds later, she hesitantly came into the surgery. As she shut the door, I rounded on her.

'Why are you spreading lies?' I demanded.

'I'm not,' she protested. 'I simply said that *you* said that Tami hadn't followed the rules. I only said–'

'It's all filtered back to me, and you know perfectly well that I didn't say any of it.'

'You're a liar!' she shouted. 'And a bully. I'm not going to stand here and take this.'

As she went to open the door, I put my hand out, blocking her exit. She glanced up at me and I glared back.

A lengthy silence ensued. I continued to stare at her, while she began to fidget, unsure of what to do.

'It must be exhausting' – I hissed, my eyes not leaving her face – 'painting on two faces every morning.'

I removed my hand from the door, and she fled.

This was another great lesson in how to navigate the

inner politics of a dental practice. Never be led to comment on any matter relating to the nurses. Be neutral. After all, you're there to work, not make friends. As sad as that may sound, these people are work colleagues, not *BFFLs* (best friends for life). Certainly, I never made such a mistake again. I never made any comment, no matter how innocuous.

I continued to hang out at work events... Christmas parties... team building, and the like. But there was always a piece of me that held back.

I was glad this ridiculous bit of drama happened at the end of the DFT year when I thought I would soon be leaving.

It so happened that Paul Slater offered me a job there. To stay on! (I couldn't have been *that* bad if the boss wanted to keep me on). I accepted. However, it meant having to deal with some uncomfortable moments with Rachel. But hey, there's more drama, laughs and bitchiness coming right up in my NHS Associate Years.

If you're still with me, dear reader, the fun is just beginning!

3

The NHS Associate Years

The **NHS dental system is broken.** At the start of the (2) Foundation Training section, I touched on the UDA system, and the way that dental practices operate. Let's now re-visit this.

Almost all dentists in general practice are self-employed. That means they get paid only for the patients they see and the work they do.

It also means that if someone fails to attend for an hour's slot, they get paid zero.

Dentists who work in the NHS are paid per 'Unit of Dental Activity' (UDA) carried out. If the dentist carries out a check-up, that equals one UDA. If he does a filling, it will be a further two UDAs (so three in total).

A dentist is paid somewhere between eight and twelve pounds per UDA, depending on whether inside or outside the London area.

The reason the system doesn't work well is because the dentist gets paid the same amount for doing one filling for a patient, as they would be for a patient that needed seven fillings! You get the same amount of UDAs for one filling or seven.

If a dentist takes thirty minutes for one filling at twenty quid, that doesn't sound too bad. But if he must do *seven* fillings over, say, three hours (and remember, he's still only getting twenty quid), then suddenly he's taking less than seven pounds per hour – which is less than the minimum wage!

I'm not telling you this for a sympathy vote. Rather, to

better understand the NHS system and the pressures that come with it. When you know this, it makes sense why there are huge swathes in the UK where no NHS dentists operate.

There are certain hotspots in the UK where people need *more* dental work than others. This is complex and based on numerous socio-economic factors (which we don't need to go into here!). Locations that have higher needs will always show a shortage of dentists. Where patients have less needs, there is usually an abundance of dentists.

This raises a question: Would you work seven times harder than some colleagues, but be paid less per hour than them? No, of course you wouldn't! And that is why the current dental system doesn't work.

The British Dental Association has campaigned for years to persuade the Government of the day to change the system. However, other than tinkering with the outskirts of the system, no meaningful change has been made and certainly nothing has promoted the prevention of dental disease in the UK or balanced the health inequalities across the country.

Perhaps you've heard your parents and/or older relatives say, 'Dentists were paid per filling in my day – that's why I have a head full of metal!'

There is a sprinkling of truth in those words. Before this system, dentists were paid for the work they carried out. This meant, in the seventies and eighties, that there was less focus on prevention and more on restorations. This led to people having more work done.

Nowadays, the opposite is true. There is much more focus on prevention and *stopping* dental issues (decay and gum disease), thus minimising the need for treatment.

However, the NHS system has led to more of a *watch and wait* approach. This means that either people are not receiving necessary treatment, or treatment is delayed until a patient's teeth become more problematic.

Right, the above is all a bit heavy. However, it's important to understand time pressures and the way NHS dentistry works. Any questions? None? Good!

So, this next section is all about my first five years in general dental practice. I stayed on at my training practice as an associate (a fully-fledged self-employed dentist).

My boss, Paul Slater, offered me three days a week at the practice. The other two days were taken up with a variety of different things, like completing two Post-Graduate Certificates, lecturing at a university, and becoming a locum dentist (a temporary dentist that assists in practices struggling to meet their NHS targets).

In this section, I'll focus on the ups and downs of my NHS years at Paul Slater's dental practice. You're familiar with the featured performers already, so let's crack on with the main show!

❖

Clear, complete, accurate and contemporaneous notes are part of the GDC standards. Every patient has a digital record complete with charts of your teeth, x-rays, medical histories and notes written about a patient's examinations and treatment.

Not all dentists write notes the same. For many of the *old school* dentists, a detailed set of notes might say:

Exam done. E/O & I/O NAD. OH good. No x-rays.

Loosely translated, this means:

Extra-oral (outside the mouth) and intra-oral (inside the mouth) nothing abnormal detected. Oral hygiene good.

Not particularly detailed. Nowadays, newer graduates (although I may not be classed as one anymore now I'm in my thirties!) write detailed essays for patient notes – mainly because nowadays dentistry is so litigious.

Anyway, one of my nurses – Tami – tried to assist with my notes. I had a template that she would paste into the exam box and then complete as I went through the dental health check.

However, Tami – being such a judgmental person – based her notes on first appearance. Let me give you some examples.

If a well-upholstered patient came in, the section regarding the amount of sugar in the diet might say *likes to eat lots of cake and biscuits.* And in the section about fizzy drinks, Tami would likely record *drinks cola all day long.*

I then had to accurately rewrite the notes stating a simple *low/moderate/high.*

On one occasion, a rather whiffy patient came in. Tami completed the oral hygiene section in her own inimitable way:

Times per day brushing: *Likely none.*

Toothpaste: *What is this?*

Flossing: *See above.*

Mouthwash: *Needed urgently.*

Perhaps the best (or worst?) example would be when discussing treatment options.

I had a patient with a particularly *broken down* tooth. We ran through the options and discussed a possible root canal treatment versus extraction, including what might be put in the space if the tooth was removed.

It was a detailed conversation. Tami helpfully updated my records:

Tooth buggered. Needs to be binned. Patient happy to look like a toothless hag.

I did suggest to Tami that it would be more helpful to simply write bullet points of what had been discussed rather than log her interpretation based on face value.

Tami wrinkled her nose at this suggestion. In her mind, she was being incredibly helpful and going above and beyond her duties by making such notes.

In the end, I resigned myself to rewriting everything Tami had recorded. However, if nothing else it gave me a chuckle between the conveyor belts of patients that the NHS demanded. To be fair, every now and again Tami's observations did tally with reality!

❖

Beast. Defined in the dictionary as: *an animal, especially a large or dangerous four-footed one.* Sometimes, we may colloquially use this to describe something inhuman, or hulking, or difficult. For example: *Did you see the root on that extracted tooth? It was an absolute beast.* I certainly wouldn't use *beast* as a compliment or term of endearment.

However, one chilly morning, Mr Donald Jenrick decided this was the right compliment to give my nurse. Donald, a fifty-something man was short, overweight, but also distinctly weasel-like.

He entered my surgery for a routine filling in his lower left molar. His eyes darted around the surgery, then landed on Carly – my favourite nurse.

Donald darted towards the dental chair. As he sat down, he smiled, revealing a row of jagged, worn teeth. He tossed back his head, then ran a hand through his thinning hair, as if preening himself.

'Nice to see you, Sonny,' he said. His weaselly eyes then feasted on my dental nurse. 'And who is this beautiful *beast* working with you today?'

Carly and I shared *the look.*

'I-I'm Carly,' she stuttered.

'Carly. *Carly,*' murmured Donald, as if savouring a fine wine. 'And what a truly *captivating creature* you are,' he said before giving Carly an enormous wink. She gagged, then coughed to hide it.

'Right, Donald,' I said, attempting to move matters along. 'Shall we get this filling done?'

'Yes, of course. Carly, do you need a filling, or are you a good girl?'

Innuendo or what?

'Enough of that Donald. Lay back, please. Let's get you numbed up.'

Carly mouthed *thank you* over Donald's head.

Once I'd administered the local anaesthetic and Donald was suitably numb, I started to drill away the decay from his tooth. This was incredibly uncomfortable. Not for the patient, I hasten to add. Rather, for Carly.

Donald seemed to have the ability not to blink. He stared at Carly for the entire appointment. Even when I positioned the overhead light directly into his eyes in an attempt to dazzle him, his rodent-like eyes simply narrowed, and the staring continued.

'I'm now going to put in the filling,' I said, as Carly mixed the amalgam (silver material). I packed the cavity, condensed it, shaped it, then removed the excess while Carly suctioned away the waste.

'Okay Donald, that's all done,' I said. 'The filling will be soft for another hour or so, and the numbness will last for another couple of hours. In the meantime, no food or drink for at least the next hour.'

'Yes, of course, sir. Thank you for such a pleasant appointment. And a big thank you to this *alluring animal*' – he chortled while gesturing at Carly – 'for such excellent suck-tion.'

Carly immediately went bright red and I was lost for words.

'See you in six months,' I gasped, frantically propelling Donald towards the exit.

Donald paused before leaving. He turned, and for one moment his moustache twitched like a rodent's whiskers. He gave Carly a lingering look.

'Such a beautiful beast,' he sighed.

And then he was gone.

Carly and I heaved deep sighs of relief. I looked at her mischievously.

'Okay, my beautiful beast,' I said, mimicking Donald and giving her a lascivious wink. 'You'd better crack on and wipe down this surgery.'

'Stop it!' she shrieked, giving me a playful cuff.

'Ha! I think you've got yourself an admirer, mate. This is *your* Isabelle Chilblain!' (you will recall Isabelle as the lady who kept inappropriately touching me).

'Vom!' Carly yelped, making a puke face.

Unfortunately, unlike Isabelle, Donald Jenrick always promptly returned for his routine check-ups. And he always expressed his disappointment if Carly the captivating creature wasn't working with me on that day.

Some days everything goes wrong. Some days you go to work full of joy, but everything goes tits up. You run late. The extraction goes wrong. The patients complain. You're meant to emulate a robot!

I mean, who gives a flying fuck if you've just had the toughest patient of your life? Certainly not Mrs Jones, the eighty-five-year-old who, despite being retired, had people to see and places to be and couldn't possibly wait just ten minutes.

Most of the time it's just me beating myself up because, in my head, I'm not good enough – not smart enough not skilled enough, not charismatic enough. My God, I've had lots of those days.

One such day, a forty-five-minute extraction became ninety minutes. I kept my cool. I always do., I'm a good actor. Grace under pressure, even when my inner voice is screaming SHIT SHIT SHIT!

A new patient attended for an extraction. There was a large cavity in the upper right second molar (the tooth in front of the wisdom tooth). As soon as I saw the x-ray, I knew it was going to be a tough one.

I could see very little ligament space (the space between the tooth at the bone). This likely meant the tooth was slightly conjoined to the bone. However, I misjudged just how tough this exaction would be.

I soon discovered it would be a surgical. I raised a flap, removed the bone, and followed the usual protocol. As I elevated this pig of a tooth, a small piece of bone behind the bone began to also break down (remember, they were conjoined). This meant I not only had a semi-loose tooth, but also a separated piece of jawbone.

Okay, okay, I thought. *This isn't the end of the world.*

I carried on, following surgical protocol, dissecting it away, and finally freed the tooth. I then removed it, intact.

The bone remained behind, somewhat mobile. I sutured. Gave a steroid prescription (because I knew the patient would feel like crap the following day) and did the normal post-op instructions.

After it was all over, I felt like shit. I'd majorly overrun and was now incredibly stressed. The next patient immediately had a go at me for being late – even though they'd been forewarned and had chosen to sit and wait.

I apologised profusely, and explained the circumstances, but they told me they didn't care and that I shouldn't waste people's time.

After work, I popped into Aldi (yeah, not all dentists shop at Waitrose like some patients assume). I selected a bottle of wine at the humble price of three pounds and fifty pence, then drove home.

I then kicked back, with my glass of wine and chilled out. No, I'm not an alcoholic, although I know a few colleagues who have become high-performing alcoholics from the stress of the job. For me, it's one glass only – and only ever with my partner. I never drink alone.

Like many doctors and dentists, I sometimes suffer a touch of imposter syndrome.

You shouldn't be doing this, the inner voice might say.

Some days I feel like a dentist on top of his world, whereas on other days it collapses around me. There is a lesson here:

Dentistry is a form of *surgery*. We *cannot* always control biology. Also, *all* surgeries have risks. Dental surgery is no different.

I don't tell you this to mope or whine, but to let you know the realities when it comes to the stress this job carries. I often double guess myself. I'm left wondering if I'm good enough. I get a pit in my stomach worrying about all the *what ifs*.

Perhaps it's just me. I *love* the act of performing dentistry, but I *hate* being a dentist. The litigious nature of this career gets me down. There are often impossible expectations.

The human ego delights in remembering and flagging up every negative experience. Usually it's to do with one's survival instincts. However, this means every complaint stays with you, and the well-deserved compliments and positive reviews are forgotten about.

Consequently sleep can be problematic. Insomnia is often a visitor. Drifting off doesn't come easily – especially if you're a tooth grinder like me! I pop in my sexy mouth guard, close my eyes, and try to shut out the images of the day replaying on a loop.

Goodnight world.

Tomorrow is a new day.

A last thought floats through my mind, and it rings true:

I *am* a good dentist. I'm just not very good at *being* a dentist.

❖

Dentists are often seen as the carpenters of the mouth. I mean, after all, we are a practical profession. We drill. We fill. We use pins. We design restorations.

I can see how we may *look* like carpenters, but we are so much more.

As you read in my university years, we studied alongside the doctors. Consequently, we learnt a hell of a lot about medicine. Couple this with the fact that people see us regularly (as opposed to a GP who is only visited when you have a problem). This puts us the position of identifying issues that might not otherwise have been picked up.

One patient that I'd been seeing for some four years, had broken her upper premolar right down to the root. It was in her *smile line*. She was in her eighties and very nervous. She wanted to avoid an extraction at all costs. As the tooth wasn't hurting – and she was missing several back teeth – we discussed making a denture. The plan was to leave the root in and have a fake tooth sit over it.

The patient agreed. I made the denture, and she was very happy with it.

About a year later, she returned. She'd lost the denture and, as a consequence, didn't like the gap. Once again, we discussed the options. She wanted to remake the denture. I did this and, again, she was happy.

Three months later, she was back.

'I don't like this gap,' she said.

'Oh but... where is the denture?' I asked.

Lost. Again.

For me, alarm bells were ringing. I contacted her GP and explained his patient was having some memory issues and this might be a sign of dementia. I was shocked at the GPs response.

'I don't need some *dentist'* – said as if a dirty word – 'telling me how to do my job. If the patient is concerned about her memory, she can contact me directly. I suggest you stick to fixing teeth and stay out of proper medicine.'

Wow! That had told me.

So, I stuck to *doing my job*.

Meanwhile, as the patient kept losing her denture, I did some geriodontics (dentistry for older patients where medical issues mean compromises are required). I placed a few pins (very old school) in the tooth, then built up the tooth with white filling material, and kept it out of the bite.

The patient was overjoyed that the gap had gone and I was relieved that she wouldn't be returning missing a denture.

The most surprising part of this story happened a couple of years later. The same patient returned for a routine check-up. This time she attended with her daughter and an updated medication list. She was now on Donepezil – a dementia drug. I raised an eyebrow as I updated the patient's medical records. Maybe if that GP had listened to this tooth-carpenter's concerns, he could have done some *proper medicine* and improved that lady's quality of life!

❖

While we are talking about Dementia, it would be good to tell you another story that relates. After a few years in general practice, I'd now met several carers who had brought along patients living in care homes.

As a result, I found myself being regularly recommended for dementia patients requiring dental treatment.

I must tell you that it's incredibly hard and, at times, tremendously upsetting treating dementia patients. It is a skill.

Having witnessed my own grandmother's descent into Alzheimer's disease, I empathise with what families are going through, and employ the same strategies I use with my own grandmother when she's in surgery.

First, repetition.

I repeat what I'm doing. Over, and over again. As soon as I finish saying what I'm doing, I repeat it in a slightly different way.

Second, distraction. Numbing up a patient is the worst part of the job. Dementia patients cannot rationalise what is going on. They just know that I'm hurting them. They cry. They *beg* you to stop. It is so hard.

My adrenaline rockets up when administering the local anaesthetic, mainly because it feels like I'm performing some sort of torture. As soon as this is done, I distract. Crack a joke. Make them laugh. Move the patient on to a different topic. They quickly forget.

Third, timing. *Never* see a dementia patient first thing in the morning. Such patients need time to 'come to' and adjust to day-to-day life and settle.

Bringing a patient in first thing, usually rushing after a battle to get breakfast in them, makes them less receptive and gives a more difficult appointment.

With all this in mind, there are nonetheless occasions where appointments are both heartwarming and hilarious.

Mrs Audrey Smith, a ninety-one-year-old lady, had moderate-stage dementia. She was wheelchair-bound but could still communicate. Audrey had almost no recall, so whatever was said in the moment would be forgotten seconds later. However, she was always jolly when I saw her.

Audrey always attended surgery with both her daughter and a carer. On this occasion, she had some broken front teeth. Several had draining abscesses (although she hadn't complained of pain). It transpired that Audrey's granddaughter was getting married. The family wanted her at the wedding and smiling in the photographs. The family seemed to be more concerned about Audrey's appearance rather than her gross dental infections.

Regardless, my protocol was the same as always – those broken infected roots needed removing. After healing had taken place, only then would I make a small upper denture for the patient.

I *always* discussed the proposed treatment with a patient, no matter their mental capacity. Even though the daughter had a medical power of attorney, that didn't mean a patient was treated like a non-person. Audrey agreed she would like some new teeth, so we all agreed a plan of action.

Numbing up Audrey was awful. She cried (I nearly did too). She screamed (ditto). Finally, she settled. Indeed, she started to laugh about how she was now feeling. She became flirty. *Very* flirty. I now had a ninety-one-year-old lady blowing me kisses and telling me where she was taking me for a sherry afterwards.

When this sort of thing happens it's handy because I can easily employ *distraction*. So while I remove Audrey's upper central incisor, I'm chatting about where we might go drinking and clubbing.

It transpired that Audrey was up for visiting the iconic Koko Club in Camden, couldn't wait to swing me round the dance floor in her wheelchair and have a cheeky G&T or three.

'You're an awful flirt, Mum!' said her daughter, faintly horrified at this chit-chat.

'Go away!' sprayed Audrey through her numb mouth. 'I saw him first.'

'I only have eyes for you, Audrey,' I reassured. 'Now then. Shall I remove this last tooth? Then you can have some new glamorous gnashers.'

'Oooooh,' she cooed. 'Yes, yes, indeed, young man. After this, I must get my face on. You're such a lovely young man,' she sighed. 'Lovely. Just *lovely.*'

I winked at her daughter who snorted with laughter. At

the end of the appointment, she thanked me.

'My own dentist wouldn't see Mum, so I just wanted to say thanks for how you handled her. I could tell it was hard.'

'It can be, especially when numbing up someone who isn't able to grasp why you're doing that.'

'I had to close my eyes for that bit. Anyway, I'm really grateful.'

'No problem,' I smiled. 'See you next week when we get the dentures sorted.'

I said goodbye to Audrey, who promptly got the hump that I wasn't taking her for a night out in London.

Over the next few months, I saw Audrey several times and completed a set of dentures for her. She was very happy with them but didn't realise they weren't *real* teeth. So I had to show her daughter and carer how to remove them at nighttime.

When the daughter tried to practice removing the denture, Audrey playfully tapped her hand away.

'Get your own teeth,' she grumbled. 'These are mine!'

Her daughter rolled her eyes, but took her hand away.

Audrey is a reminder of the good a dentist can do and the gift of a smile they can give. I definitely felt all warm and fuzzy when – at the review appointment – I was shown the wedding photos. There was Audrey, beaming away, and beside her the granddaughter in a gorgeous white gown.

❖

Never treat your family. And if you do, treat them like any other patient. This includes charging them for treatment.

This was a mistake I made. I treated my family for free. Family feel they can comment on what you're doing, even though they have no idea what they're talking about. Family is far more demanding, and their expectations are colossal.

What makes things worse is if the family member is a

nervous wreck – like my mum. Valium was required. Also, an hour of deep breathing and meditation before the appointment. And that was just for me!

My mum's fear was borne from a dentist she saw as a young adult. His name was Mr Payne. Yes, the irony of his name is not lost on me. Mr Payne was apparently a brash Australian with the patience of a lit stick of dynamite and a bad attitude. Incredibly, he was a *private* dentist. Even more incredibly, my mother kept coughing up to see him.

'Why did you keep going back to him?' I said,

'Because my Mum said he was the bee's knees, so I presumed I was in good hands.'

One of the worst stories she told me about Mr Payne was when she had a throbbing toothache and suspected abscess. The receptionist gave Mum an emergency appointment – which instantly irked the charmless Mr Payne – and took the chair. However, Mr Payne simply thought my mother was being dramatic and making a fuss about nothing.

'I'm going to drill into this tooth and a load of blood is going to erupt over your pretty white blouse,' he snarled.

By this point my mother was in such pain she couldn't have cared if Mr Payne had extracted the tooth without anaesthetic.

He promptly drilled into the tooth. But instead of blood pouring out, pus exploded everywhere and stank out the room.

'Shit!' Mr Payne swore. This was in the days when dentists didn't have to wear masks. 'Oh, god! What a STINK!' he roared, flapping a hand in a futile attempt to fan the smell away. 'Nurse! Open the window. I think I'm going to hurl.'

Mum silently chuckled to herself, absolutely delighted that this bullying dentist was having a most unpleasant time.

Anyway, years later, my mother had a toothache. Mr Payne had long gone. And I (unfortunately) was now her dentist.

I completed the examination of her lower right premolar which included temperature testing, tapping the tooth to check for infection and taking some x-rays. I concluded that the nerve was starting to die due to an old and very large filling being present. I suggested removing the nerve (the first stage of root canal treatment) and then rebooking to finish off once everything was calmer. She agreed, but I could see the fear in her eyes.

I applied numbing gel to the area that would be injected with LA. I'd barely rubbed the gel into her gum, when she announced that her throat was closing up. She believed she was having an allergic reaction and started choking. She sat bolt upright and started to spit and dry-heave into the sink.

Tami – my nurse for that day – glanced at me and rolled her eyes. On this occasion, I agreed with Tami's reaction.

I reassured my mother that she was fine and that it was just the sensation of the gel. She settled down and I continued. Upon numbing up the area, Mum's arms and legs flailed about, as if her limbs had strings upon them being worked by an amateur puppeteer.

She then slumped back in the chair complaining of feeling faint and hot. She pat-patted one hand around the sink, picked up a cup of mouthwash and promptly threw it in her face.

Tami looked on incredulously. I was definitely with her on this one.

'Er, Tami,' I murmured. 'Can you fetch a glucose drink.'

Tami rolled her eyes again but went to the emergency box for the glucose.

Mum drank it and said she felt better.

'I don't think I'm numb,' she then declared, despite now drooling. The right side of her lip had stopped working. It appeared to be dangling around her chin. 'I'm not numb,' she repeated.

'Yes, you are,' I assured.

'No. I'm not. I need more,' she lisped. 'I NEED MORE!'

'Okay,' I sighed, and topped it up. 'Better?'

By this point her teeth were snuggling into her lip.

'I'm not sure,' she said, dribbling everywhere. 'Maybe a bit more.'

'Let me test the area first.'

78

'Noooo,' she bleated. 'I'M SCARED!'

'For goodness' sake, Mum!' I snapped. 'Calm down.'

My patience with the patient was running thin. Her hysteria of the unfunny kind had caused a huge delay, and I was now running late.

Reluctantly, she allowed me to poke the area with my probe. No response. The area was definitely numb.

I picked up my handpiece (drill) and sprayed water above the tooth. At this point no drilling had taken place.

'ARGH!' she screamed. 'That drill really hurts. I can feel it hitting the nerve!'

'That's peculiar. Because I've not actually drilled anything...'

'What? Oh.' She had the grace to look sheepish.

'Indeed. So stop being so melodramatic.'

Finally, she let me drill the tooth. And there was no flinching. No flying hands. No screaming. In fact, from that point on, it was the best she'd ever been in the chair.

I took out the nerve, temporised, and gave post-op instructions.

'Bye, darling,' she said, picking up her handbag.

'Bye,' I said. 'Oh, and Mum?'

'Yes?'

'When you come back, less theatrics next time, please.'

Now it was my mother's turn to roll her eyes at me.

'I'm not *that* dramatic,' she sniffed.

'Whatever you say, *dearie*,' I grinned, then gave her my own eyeroll.

Between me, my mum, and Tami, I reckoned we'd rolled our eyes enough times to make someone watching spectacularly dizzy.

Treating my mum has never got any easier. It's pretty much the same high drama performance *every* time. Luckily, I've managed to palm her off to the hygienist for the routine cleanings – makes my life easier!

❖

I **had been seeing Albert and Agnes for nearly five years.** Both were in their eighties and longstanding patients of the practice.

They always visited wearing their smartest clothes, as if attending job interviews.

Both were deaf and I believe they'd always been that way. They signed to each other. They were also devoted to each other and inseparable.

Their faces were etched with the lines of a long life, but their eyes still held an undeniable spark of youth and mirth. From my interaction with the two of them, I figured that Agnes was best at lip reading. When it came to Albert, I had to write everything down, because I cannot sign.

Over the years, I had repaired their teeth with several fillings and crowns.

On one occasion, Albert fractured his front tooth. I'd pleaded with the dental lab and managed to get a bridge made within a week for him. He was ecstatic because he'd not enjoyed being out and about with a missing front tooth.

When I'd fitted the bridge, he'd sat up, waved at Agnes, then pointed at the new tooth. She'd pushed her glasses up the bridge of her nose, then scrutinised the colour, design, shape and fit of the tooth. She'd then nodded and given me a thumbs up – her seal of approval.

This story confronts two parts of dentistry that we have yet to properly touch on. As a dentist, you see patients come and go. Some like you and stay. Some love you and hunt you down, even travelling across counties to see you (true story!). Others can't stand you and don't come back (and often you're glad about that too!). And then there are the folks in between – they don't like you but, for some unfathomable reason, they keep coming back and are vile at the same time! But my next story is a bit different.

One bright May morning, I studied my day list. Agnes was on it. She was marked for an examination. Just Agnes. No Albert. This was surprising. They came as a pair. Always together. Could it be that Albert was a bit under the weather?

Carly, my nurse, gave me an anxious look.

80

'You don't think...?' she trailed off.

My mouth compressed.

'I hope not.'

Agnes entered the surgery. Her posture was hunched, rather than upright. Her normally bright eyes were dull. Despite the warmth from the sunshine streaming through the surgery windows, it felt like the room had suddenly dropped in temperature.

Agnes didn't make eye contact. She sat in the dental chair, eyes fixed firmly on her feet. I rolled my saddle-stool over to her so that I could look directly at her, and she could lip read.

Agnes looked up in anguish. Her eyes brimmed. It was like a dam about to break.

'Albert?' I said.

I had to ask. To ignore the fact that he wasn't there when she was so distressed would have been unacceptable.

Her chin wobbled. She opened her mouth to speak.

'Gone,' she managed to croak.

And then the floodgates opened. I took her hand. Squeezed it tight and my own eyes brimmed.

'I'm so, *so*, sorry,' I said.

She lunged forward and hugged me hard. Automatically, I hugged her back. And then Agnes cried. Her guttural cry and jagged breathing was that of a broken woman.

Eventually, her breathing regulated, and she dropped her arms. Her eyes were bloodshot, but brighter. She gave my hand a final squeeze before letting go. I wiped my own tear away. Gave her a gentle smile. And then we returned to our more usual professional relationship and completed the dental examination.

Before leaving, Agnes paused. She looked at me.

'Thank you,' she said.

I nodded and she quietly shut the door behind her.

To be clear. The two parts of dentistry we haven't touched upon are *human connection* and *death*.

In dental school it's drummed into you not to touch patients. It could be misconstrued as battery – unlawful touching – and/or being inappropriate.

Professionalism can be cold and unyielding. Sometimes you simply need to be *human*.

As for death, well, it's a normal occurrence. It happens every day. I still don't know what took Albert and I never asked.

Death is personal to the people involved. I am not a mortician. I have no business with the details. Like all of us, I've experienced loss. In my case it was the death of my father while still a child. However, experiencing the death of a patient was different – but still tremendously sad. I had got to know Albert over several years. Completed work that was impactful upon his wellbeing. Seen him every six months or so. A cheerful chap of whom, admittedly, I was fond. And suddenly he'd gone.

That evening, I raised a glass to Albert.

❖

Do you ever get bored at work? Certainly, dentists and nurses do! I probably shouldn't tell you this, dear reader, as you may think less of me but – oh what the heck! Warts and all, yes?

So, you've heard that school exam invigilators used to play games to keep themselves entertained during kids' exams? You might remember, on Capital radio, a few years ago an invigilator went on air and admitted to playing games like *Pacman* where one invigilator is the ghost and the other chases them down the aisles. Well, dentists do games too! *Pacman* isn't possible in the surgery, but here are some of the games that have kept us sane:

Game 1: *Fit or Shit*.

This was a simple one. If we were expecting a patient who was thirty-five-years or younger, my nurse and I would make a bet predicting if the patient would be hot or... not! The loser had to make tea. It wasn't all blind judgment. We would assess the patient's name, their chart (for example, how many fillings they had), x-rays and the area where they lived. Then we'd simply wait for them to cross the threshold. Cue sharing *the look* which was either one of triumph or disappointment.

Game 2: *Use the wrong name.*

I'm not quite sure how this game started. One long twelve-hour day, Carly and I were about to begin a root canal treatment (an hour long epic). The patient's name was Helena Foster. I looked at my nurse.

'Carla, pass me the patient's file, please.'

She caught on immediately.

'Yes, of course.' Carly handed me the file then smiled at the patient. 'Are you comfortable, Helen?'

I noted Carly using the wrong name, but the patient nodded. We continued.

'Cathy, what is the working length, please?'

'Hannah's root length is twenty-one millimetres.'

'Perfect. Thanks, Claire. Can I have some Milton's?'

Carly handed me the Milton's solution. Her shoulders were starting to shake with suppressed laughter.

'A little more suction, please, Carl.'

That was it. She desperately tried to stifle a snort. At this point I was trying not to crack up myself.

'Just going to check your x-ray, Heather,' I managed, before quickly turning away. Carly and I slumped over the worktop and silently convulsed. Poor Helena Foster was bewildered.

Game 3: *Get reception to call the wrong name.*

When we were ready for a patient, we would send an instant message on the computer to the reception desk asking for the patient to come to the surgery. For example, 'John Smith to surgery three, please'. Reception would then call this out and the patient would come to the surgery. Very often Reception wouldn't bother to check if the person actually existed, so they'd proceed to yell out to phantom patients. Carly and I would have hysterics listening to Reception hollering names like Hugh Jass, Ivana Tinkle, Benny Dover, Justin Case and Anita Bath. One receptionist laughed like a drain. The other was not amused. We may have been told off. This would deter Carly and me... for a week or two!

So, as you can see, a dental practice is full of mature staff and professional clinicians, and every single member is respectful and abides by all the rules.

❖

I've worked at some bad practices in my career. Places where the principal dentist was a bully. Where health and safety wasn't properly observed. Where shortcuts were routinely taken. In other words, places where you'd walk in but want to turn right round and walk straight out.

When I started at Paul Slater's dental practice, I didn't know any better. It was my first job as a dentist and – as he was a trainer – I presumed *everything* would be up to code.

The reality of the situation was that Paul would do the bare minimum to keep things running. He was tight with money and didn't spend unless he *really* had to.

The longer I worked there, the more I noticed it. Like… suction tubes splitting at the seams and being fixed with duct tape. When the x-ray machine stopped working, instead of fixing it, we had to use an ancient analogue machine where you cranked a handle and then waited half an hour for the film to process – a bit like old cameras.

But the worst thing – and the most unforgivable – was the dental suction pump. There was a central pump in the practice, that all the surgeries were linked to. This powered the suction, which is essential for dentistry. When we drill teeth, we use a lot of water to help cool the tooth and stop injury/damage to the nerve from the heat that drilling generates. This water needs to be removed to stop you, well, drowning! Hence suction.

Many of Paul's associates, myself included, raised an issue over the suction, stating that it was getting weaker. Often, I'd pick up the suction, but there would be a delay before it kicked in. As the weeks passed, this delay got longer, and the suction weaker.

Eventually, the suction became so weak, one particular

patient of mine – Mrs Jones – had to sit upright to spit out the water every three seconds (a pet peeve of mine because Mrs Jones was a big spitter!). It was at this point that suction reached critical failure.

Paul finally had to act. He instructed the practice manager (his wife, Jackie) to get some quotes to have the central unit checked and repaired.

After a number of weeks with virtually no suction and struggling to perform our duties, Paul finally ~~repaired the suction unit so we could get back to work~~ found an incredibly dodgy portable suction unit on eBay that he had shipped over from China.

This *single* suction unit was meant to be wheeled between surgeries. That's right! *A single suction* was to be used between six surgeries. Just to be absolutely clear here, we're talking five dentists and a hygienist all sharing a single suction.

This made reception's job ten times more difficult. They had to ensure that no one had any overlapping restorative work. Actually, forget that. What I should say is that it made reception's job *impossible*.

Even worse, the suction was extremely difficult to empty. Being portable, it wasn't plumbed into the mains and had to be manually emptied. This required two nurses and a dentist to physically lift this heavy-ass machine to tip its contents down the sink. Its sheer weight and bulk meant it was impossible to fully empty, meaning there was always a considerable residue of dirty water left behind. Grim!

Paul had now managed to achieve disgruntled dentists, riled receptionists, narked nurses and hacked off hygienists. The only thing missing was pissed off patients. But trust me. They were coming!

So, back to my Mrs Jones. She'd returned for a filling. Mrs Jones was annoying at the best of times. She always had a complaint about something. The air conditioning was too cold. Now the room was too hot. The toilet's loo paper wasn't soft enough. The waiting room had ancient magazines. The television showed BBC instead of ITV. You get the picture.

On the day of this unfortunate incident, the fiery Tami was my know-it-all nurse. After our spat in my DFT year, things had settled somewhat, and we mostly got along fine (to the point where she even asked me for a reference – instead of Paul Slater – when she left years later).

However, right now, in surgery, I had two volatile individuals. My nurse and my patient.

I numbed up Mrs Jones, then ran through the plan of action, namely repairing a broken tooth that had never been filled before. There was also quite a bit of decay in it. We got cracking.

Tami picked up the portable suction nozzle and I began to drill. It was a huge cavity and at one point I thought we might end up in Australia. Tami's eyes widened.

Suddenly, Mrs Jones sat bolt upright. She put her hand to her mouth. Perplexed, Tami and I glanced at each other. Mrs Jones now had her fingers in her mouth. She retrieved a piece of amalgam (silver filling) and handed it to Tami.

'Is that one of mine?' asked Mrs Jones.

My mouth dropped open. Where the hell had this amalgam come from? Meanwhile, Tami had turned rather green.

'Well?' demanded Mrs Jones. 'Did you knock out one of my fillings?'

'Er, I don't think so,' I said carefully. 'However, if you wouldn't mind laying back, I'll check.'

Mrs Jones obeyed. There was no missing filling. I reassured her and suggested it might have come from the one we were working on (I was second-guessing now as I'd been certain that tooth had not had any filling).

We continued. I kept my eyes peeled. The suction went back on – and out came another piece of *something*. I grabbed it with the tweezers and put it to one side.

It appeared the portable suction had regurgitated *someone else's* filling back into my patient's mouth. For one horrible moment I thought I might throw up.

Tami and I exchanged *the look*. We were both feeling more than a little queasy. I quickly finished the filling and bade farewell to Mrs Jones.

Tami and I then rocketed down to Paul's surgery.

'Paul,' I said urgently. 'You need to repair the central suction unit and get rid of this portable one.'

'I'm not forking out any more money,' he protested. 'There's nothing wrong with what we've got.'

I handed Paul the piece of amalgam.

'The suction regurgitated this into my patient's mouth. This was *not* part of her tooth.'

Paul didn't turn green. Instead, he went bright red.

Before the week was out, engineers had fitted six brand new individual units to power each surgery.

Luckily, Mrs Jones never put two and two together, which was a huge relief.

This incident highlighted to me what to look out for when assessing a practice – whether to accept work there, or decline. I understand dental equipment is costly, but when the principal dentist (i.e. the owner!) is taking more than fifty percent of your earnings, they have a responsibility to ensure everything is up to scratch!

❖

Play-Doh. **Do you remember it?** It's the modelling material that kids have fun with.

In dentistry, we have something similar. It's called *alginate*. Like Play-Doh, it comes in many different colours – purple, green, blue, white, etc. *Unlike* Play-Doh, it goes in the mouth, which no one likes. To make it more palatable, alginate comes in a variety of flavours, such as: plain, hint-of-mint and barely-berry (basically they taste like nothing).

In summer, alginate sets very quickly (heat accelerates the chemical reaction, so it sets within thirty seconds), but in winter the process is more like ninety seconds. I know that doesn't sound like much difference, but for Mr Max Magnum it was an eternity.

I've always found men to be worse in the dental chair than women (a huge generalisation, I know!).

Men are complete wusses, far less pain tolerant, more

likely to try and grab you when you're numbing them up and simply more melodramatic.

Max Magnum was a vastly overweight man in his late thirties. He had a big beard, a bald head, and a bad attitude. He didn't like being told something was wrong. He disagreed with all given advice. Any information was taken as a criticism, and he was aggressive with it.

Max had been forewarned about reducing his sugar consumption, the fact he looked like he was grinding his teeth, the reduced bone support holding his teeth in due to smoking and that, in the near future, it was likely he would likely lose his front teeth without intervention. Of course, this was all nonsense from the 'NHS dentist who just wanted to make a tonne of money from him' (yeah, that is a quote from Mr. Magnum).

Just three weeks after Max's check-up (and 'telling off') he returned as an emergency. My patient burst through the surgery door in a complete state.

'MY FRONT TOOTH HAS BROKEN!' he howled loudly.

Carly – today's nurse – and I shared *the look* and then I asked Max to sit down. He didn't oblige.

'WHAT ARE YOU GOING TO DO ABOUT IT?' he ranted at top volume.

'Max, please,' I soothed. 'Take a seat.' I indicated the dental chair with one hand, keeping it outstretched in the vain hope he'd sit down and cool his shit.

'NO!' he screeched. 'I'll stay STANDING! Your SHODDY dentistry has done this. YOU SHOULD HAVE WARNED ME THIS MIGHT HAPPEN!'

I raised my eyebrow. My hand was still outstretched, indicating he take the chair.

'Take a seat,' I said firmly.

He finally obliged and lowered his vast backside. The chair creaked alarmingly.

'Max,' I began. 'For the past three years, I have warned you about your grinding, about your diet and your cleaning and the long term impacts on your teeth.'

'No, you did not,' he protested.

'Oh yes he did,' Carly interjected, taking me (and possibly herself) by surprise. 'I was present at your last check up and you were told this would happen if things didn't change.'

'Who the hell are you?' Max demanded.

'Please don't talk to my nurse like that,' I said. 'And she's quite right. Everything has been documented in time-stamped notes over the past three years since you've been seeing me. The notes are locked and cannot be edited.'

There was a silence while Max's diminished braincells tried to come up with another reason why his broken tooth was my fault. His mouth opened and closed, much like a fish out of water. Finally, he conceded.

'Fine,' he said through gritted teeth (maybe that was why one had broken?!). 'What do I do now?'

'There is a fracture at the gum level,' I observed aloud. 'This means the remaining root will need extraction and then you'll require something for the gap.'

'Like what?'

'Options would include doing nothing, a denture, a bridge or an implant. However, on the NHS, we can only provide what is clinically necessary. As discussed previously, because of the other issues ongoing in the mouth, the only option I can offer you currently is a denture. If we can get the other bits up to scratch, we could look at a bridge longer term.'

'You fuckin' *what?*' he hissed.

'Swear at me again and I'll ask you leave and then you'll have nothing for that gap.'

Max gave me a sullen look but went quiet. I was reminded of a child. A spoilt brat at that.

'A denture can be made within a week,' I continued. 'Moving forward, we can complete the other outstanding work. A better oral health regime means you can work towards a fixed-solution. What are your thoughts?'

'Okay,' he grunted.

'Great. Shall I start now?'

'Okay.' Another grunt.

'Carly, please can you put together a treatment plan for an extraction and denture?'

My nurse wrote out the same which Max Magnum

begrudgingly signed. She then fetched the alginate.

'I shall now take some moulds of your teeth,' I said. 'Both upper and lower. This is so the lab knows how your jaws meet and can make an immediate denture.'

Another inaudible grunt from Max Magnum.

Carly's mouth compressed. She was visibly annoyed. She began to mix the alginate adding more water than normal. I frowned. Gave her an enquiring look. She smiled sweetly, then loaded an extra-large tray with the sloppiest mix of alginate I'd ever seen. She placed it in my hand. The expression on her face spoke volumes. She gave me a *fuck this guy* smile. I understood.

'Right then, Max, bit of a mouthful now.' And in the upper tray went. Cue Max gagging and flailing around. He grabbed my hand, indicating I take the tray out.

'Max,' I said firmly. 'If I take this out, it'll be much worse because the mixture hasn't yet set. There will be a lot left in your mouth.'

Max wretched again, then yanked out the tray of slop. Needless to say, most of the material stayed in his mouth and almost none came out with the tray. His gagging continued. He shoved his fists in his mouth attempting to rid himself of the alginate. Carly beamed at me. What a vindictive little minx. God, she was great.

The alginate was now in Max's beard. The purple material had started to set. Max now resembled something between a clown and Father Christmas.

'Oh dear,' I said, affecting sympathy. 'We'll have to start again.' I turned to Carly. 'Mix another alginate, please.'

I handed Max a tissue and gave him a look. *Don't piss off the nurse.* I think he got the message.

❖

I stayed at Paul Slater's practice for five years, working in the NHS – until I found out he was paying the other dentists twenty percent more than me. I went to Paul and asked to be paid the same as everyone else. He said it *wasn't the right time* and *things are too uncertain with Covid.*

I'd invested heavily in myself and already undertaken two post-graduate certificates (further accredited training with university certificates) in dental education, meaning I could teach foundation dentists.

The second considerable financial outlay had been in dental implantology. Paul had refused to invest in any equipment to provide implants to patients and told me that if I wanted to do implantology then to *fork out* for it myself. Which I had done – to the to the tune of seven-thousand pounds!

'Paul, I've paid seven-thousand for all the kit to be able to provide *your* patients with implants. I think it would be fair to change our split of the fees to help cover this, so for the first twelve months, for implant patients, could I take home 60% of the costs rather than 50%, to help off-set what I've had to personally invest.'

'No.'

Underpaid. Overworked. Staff dramas. Equipment failing (remember the suction?). I was starting to feel disillusion with Paul's practice. What was I doing working my ass off for him with no proper support or interest?

I handed in my notice. I didn't have a job lined up, but I didn't really care. I wanted out. Of course, once my notice went in, Paul offered a pay increase and better working conditions, but I declined. He'd had the opportunity to do that beforehand.

He wasn't a great boss. It had been a good place to start my career, given me a space to work, but this was not where I wanted to live and die.

During my notice period, I went job hunting and found a great demand for my skill set. I ended up in a fully private practice, but that will come later in the book.

My next few chapters are about the other bits I did throughout my five years at Paul's, working as a university lecturer and NHS locum dentist.

I hope you're still on this journey with me, dear reader, because things are about to change scene.

4

The Professor

Ok, fine, I wasn't a professor. I was a university lecturer.

I taught dentistry for a year while obtaining my post-graduate certificate in dental education. Why did I decide to teach for a year? Well, because I actually really enjoyed teaching. In fact, when I was a sixth former, the head of year tried to encourage me to go into teaching instead of dentistry (maybe I should have?).

In my head – and maybe naïvely – I thought that teaching *adults* would be easy. As in, they were grown-ups so would *want* to hear what I was teaching, right? Except they didn't. I don't think it helped that the majority of my students were older than me. Some were double my age.

That said, I still really enjoyed it. University lecturing is far less stressful than practicing dentistry, hands down. When I taught, I actually looked forward to going to work, rather than rocking up some days with a pit in my stomach – as was the case with the dentistry. Also, I was able to easily balance my time in the office to lesson plan and complete my post-grad certificate assignments in school time. That was a win.

So why did I stop teaching after a year?

Simple. The pay was shit.

After considerable travel expense into London, I was taking home around eighty quid a day. That was fine when I was renting, but I'd since bought a diddy flat with a not-so-diddy mortgage and needed to make ends meet. However, If I ever won the lottery, I'd quit dentistry in a heartbeat and go back to lecturing.

Teaching dentistry made me feel like a sheepdog. It was like trying to herd a group of rambunctious toddlers through a maze of sharp instruments and intricate procedures. It was a constant case of patience, persistence laced with humour to stop the students turning the dental clinic into a scene straight out of a slapstick comedy.

Imagine, if you will, dear reader, a room filled with eager dental students, their white coats barely containing their excitement. Having memorised tome-like textbooks, they're now armed with mirrors and probes, ready to tackle the world of teeth. But amidst the sterile environment and serious subject matter, I made sure there was always room for a little bit of lightheartedness.

As I don't wish to be sued, I won't name the university that I taught at. This section of the book will instead focus on the stories that derived from teaching wannabe dentists, dental therapists, and hygienists. So, let's visit dental school again, but this time from the teacher's perspective!

❖

In the beginning, I was just as nervous (or should I say excited?) about starting uni as if I'd been as a student.

I think I felt a bit of an imposter, having started teaching only three years into my career. I mean, what did I really know about dentistry? I'd barely scratched the surface of the beast, and here I was testing students' knowledge and telling *them* how to perform different procedures.

The uni staff were lovely. It was a relatively small department. There was just six of us in our office. It felt more like a bunch of friends working together. We all got on well. We often went to lunch together. Or met up after work for a drink. It helped me settle in quickly.

There were a few oddballs, but then there always are in teaching. Let me introduce you to my team.

John. He was Head of Department, in his early forties, and sported a mid-life-crisis ear piercing.

Elon (real name William). He changed his name by deed-poll because he loved Elon Musk. This guy had seven rodents, still lived at home with Mum and rocked up to work in baggy tees and sweats.

Janet. She was in her seventies and walked with a cane. Everyone tried to avoid any extended conversation with her, because it was painfully slow and turned into a lecture on how dentistry wasn't like *the good old days*.

Claire. Late thirties. Strict in class. Chill in the office.

Flo. She was the closest to me in age and really good fun.

Me. The best of the bunch (just kidding).

My orientation week involved a load of *must do* training that nobody ever used – like *display user operator* (taking ten-minute breaks every hour to give one's eyes a rest). Then there was all the guff about the university's policies, how to use the online lecture/assignment tools, and so on. It was a nice and gentle easing into things at the start of this school year.

The real work kicked off in our Start of Year meeting. Here, all the lecture topics were set out on large whiteboards (and there was an awful lot of the bloody things).

'Right,' said John, the head of department. 'Who wants what?'

Elon jumped up.

'I want *research methods*' – he wrote his name under this topic – 'and *work-safety issues*.'

They sounded so dry, and I was glad not to have them. Feeling a little nervous, I cleared my throat.

'I'm happy to do *local anaesthetics*, *prevention*, and *cavity preparation/design*,' I said timidly.

'Great,' said John.

At the end of the meeting, anything unassigned was randomly shared out amongst the staff. If we really hated a subject, we could swap with each other.

In all honesty, there were some lectures where I hoped I'd never get asked questions. Some were deeply complex, and I'd be winging it (naturally it was Sod's Law that I'd find myself being asked every question under the sun!). Other lectures were a breeze. But that is the nature of the beast…

❖

One lecture where I was *way* out of my depth was particularly relevant to hygienists.

My training in periodontics (treating the supporting structures of the teeth, e.g. gums) comprised of an ultrasonic scaler (the one that sprays water during the clean) and two types of hand scaler (in other words, scrapers). The *sickle* was used above the gum, and the *curette* for below the gum. Go figure, because there are, like, a hundred different types of scaler!

Luckily, I was about to share a practical session with Flo, who just happened to be a qualified hygienist. Prior to the lecture and while still in the office, I went through her prepared lecture slides.

'What on earth is a *Montana Jack*?' I pondered aloud.

'Some sort of gum gardening instrument,' Elon hooted.

Claire's feathers were instantly ruffled.

'Gum gardening?' she said haughtily. 'You no longer practice dentistry, Elon,' she snapped, swiftly rising to the bait,

'What's that got to do with the price of fish?' Elon goaded. 'It doesn't change the fact that hygiene is just a bit of cleaning.'

'Oh, go back to your rats, mummy's boy,' she spat.

John's head appeared round the door.

'Kids, behave!'

His manner was mild enough, but it instantly shut down the start of any commotion. Claire sulked and Elon smirked.

I sidled over to Flo.

'I have no idea what any of these hand scalers are used for,' I whispered.

She chuckled.

'Don't worry. I'll handle the lecture slides. You stick to monitoring the students.'

'Okay, that's a deal.'

We then headed off to the practical together. Flo set up the instruments. I looked at what she'd chosen and tried to familiarise myself with what was in front of me (clueless!).

Together, we applied curry paste over plastic teeth in phantom heads (these are the plastic *faux* humans that students practice on).

The hygiene students filtered in. They sat at their allocated spaces and Flo commenced the lecture. I'd stationed myself at the back and was listening intently. Soon I'd have to check that the students were using these instruments correctly!

'It is now time to do a practical session,' said Flo. 'You have thirty minutes. Use the instruments to remove calculus (limescale deposits that form in the mouth) from the model in front of you. We will be checking your technique,' Flo smiled.

Oh fuck, I silently thought.

The students picked up their scalers and set to work removing curry paste from the plastic teeth.

As I wandered through the rows of students working on the phantom heads, I avoided all eye contact. If I could just get through the next thirty minutes without a single question, no one would be any the wiser.

In front of me, a student raised her hand.

Oh fuck. The second silent expletive.

I went over and sat down, smiling with a confidence that was inwardly missing.

'Sir?'

'Yes?'

'Is this the Gracey #13 shank?'

'It is.' (No idea.)

'Am I angling it correctly?'

'Show me.'

I watched as she awkwardly removed fake calculus from the plastic teeth. Her angle looked quite odd and the whole thing was something of a struggle.

Right, I told myself. *This must be simple logic. Surely, I can work out how to use this instrument by holding it and then determining what feels 'right' against the teeth.*

'Let me help you,' I suggested.

We swapped places. I positioned the instrument against the tooth. It felt like the right angle. I did a few strokes by way of demonstration, hoping I was correct (probably not!).

'Thanks, Sir. That's really helpful!'

'Glad to be of assistance,' I replied, fervently hoping that would be it.

Unfortunately, it wasn't. Up went another hand. Flo was with another student. I went over, hoping I could wing it again.

'Sir, please can you show me how to properly use the Quétin furcation curette?'

I stared at the student, momentarily dazed.

What the fuck is a Quétin furcation curette? I silently screeched. *Okay, think, THINK! Furcation is the where the roots split out from the tooth. So... so this instrument must be used to clean an area of severe gum disease. But how do you actually USE the damn thing?*

'Right,' I warbled. 'I must be honest. Before today, I hadn't heard of half the instruments that are being used here today. As a dentist, I know of the ultrasonic, sickle and curette. That's it! I think Flo will have to help you on this one.'

I signalled Flo who immediately took over, thus saving both my bacon and embarrassment. I was beyond grateful when the session ended.

'Learn anything?' Flo teased.

'Yeah,' I nodded. 'That I'm not a bloody hygienist.'

She laughed.

'Come on,' she said, patting my shoulder. 'Let's get a coffee before the next class.'

'Damn right, I flipping need one!'

'Oh, and mate...?' She trailed off and promptly dissolved into giggles.

'What's so funny?'

'There's curry paste on your collar.'

After this session, I had a new respect for hygienists. Their work was a lot more complex than I'd been led to believe. Meanwhile, I kept my fingers crossed that I'd never have to bluff my way through such a session again.

❖

When the opportunity arose to teach *local anaesthetics*, I jumped at the chance. I knew exactly what to do. I would emulate Dr Bowman, the lecturer that taught me at uni. The teaching was split into two sessions: theoretical and practical (the bit everyone was nervously excited for!).

In the theory lecture, we discussed the different types of anaesthetic (amides versus esters) and the history/dev-elopment over time.

We recapped the anatomy of the skull, the muscles, bones, and attachments. We discussed what internal landmarks to look for in the mouth and how best to administer LA – which I will tell you here and right now: Put simply, it goes behind the last molar, at the back of the mouth. When a patient *opens wide,* an upside-down triangle forms between the side of the jaw and a small piece of tendinous tissue and the top molar. The needle should be aimed at the mid-point of this triangle.

After showing several diagrams, answering many questions, and giving a lot of reassurance, the theory session finished.

In due course, the students would return to the clinics at set times for their small-group practical session. It would be here that they would administer LA to each other.

My first group of ~~victims~~ students, shuffled into the bay, looking slightly terrified. I stood quietly to one side, waiting for everyone to settle. Then, the theatrics started.

'Right, who's volunteering for some pain?'

I glared at the panic-stricken students. No volunteers.

'You!'

I pointed to Greg, a twenty-one-year-old student. He

was almost six feet tall. A pair of worried brown eyes were framed in an angular face. It was then that I noticed his ear piercing.

'You're obviously fine with needles,' I joked.

He gulped.

'Take a seat.' I indicated the dental chair, and he sat down. 'Okay, everyone. Gather around.'

I picked up a pair of latex gloves and then did my best impression of Dr Bowman, snapping them on as if in a horror film. I then assembled the long gauge needle, right in front of poor Greg, who now had white knuckles from gripping the chair's arm rests. I waved the needle up in the air, squirted out some anaesthetic – ensuring it shot upwards in scary-movie style. I hit the foot pedal and Greg shot backwards. 'Open up!' I said, possibly now emulating Jack Nicholson in *The Shining*. 'This is gonna hurt.'

There was a smattering of nervous laughter as I advanced toward Greg with my ginormous needle. Greg screwed up his face and squeezed his eyes tightly shut.

'And... that's how you *don't* do it.' I said, as Greg went limp with relief.

I spent the rest of the practical running through the best techniques to ensure a patient stays calm and is provided with effective anaesthetic. I discussed using numbing gel, how to hide the needle so a patient can't see it, even suggesting that a patient close their eyes, and so on.

At the end of the session, each student left the clinic droopy and dribbly (their mouths, obvs!) having successfully given each other an injection. Before leaving, Greg approached me.

'I honestly thought you were going to hurt me,' he said with a relieved smile.'

'Never, Greg.'

'I'll won't ever forget this session, that's for sure,' he grinned. Well, half-grinned, because he too was droopy and dribbly.

Mission accomplished. *Thank you, Dr Bowman,* I said to myself as the next group came in. I greeted them, my snappy latex gloves at the ready!

I **always found it beyond incredible** when a student turned up late to a lecture, or fell asleep, or was busily texting – in other words, not paying attention.

I mean, each student is paying (at the time of writing) approximately nine thousand pounds a year for an education that they can't be bothered to turn up for, or fall asleep halfway through, or zone out thanks to the distraction of smart phones. Why? To me, it seems completely peculiar not to *be present* for what you're paying for.

Remember my nurse, Tami? She was the hothead who'd called me a rude name in front of a waiting room of patients. So, guess what? She applied to university to study dental hygiene, and got in.

The relationship of dental nurse and dentist is one of symbiosis. As a dentist, you're very reliant on your nurse. As such, you're equals in the surgery.

However, the student-lecturer relationship is very different. A lecturer needs to hold the attention of some fifty-odd students. It goes without saying that if one student pushes the boundaries, the rest will follow.

It wasn't long before friction occurred between Tami and me. At the time, I was lecturing on dental prevention – fluoride varnish, oral hygiene, diet, etc.

I'd split the lecture into six working groups. They would then present back to the class (self-teaching). It was then that I spotted Tami chatting away on her phone. She wasn't engaged in either the lecture or her group.

I walked over.

'Hey, Tami. Put the phone away, please. Focus on the task.' She looked up, gave me an eyeroll, and carried on with her telephone conversation. Presumably a mystery suitor was on the other end of the line.

'Yeah, babe,' she cooed. 'You treat me to a new Gucci bag, and I'll send you some snaps.'

I raised an eyebrow (I could do that before Botox).

'Okay, babe. I'll wear the lacy red one. I know it's your

fave,' she giggled naughtily.

'Tami,' I repeated. 'Hang up, please.'

She put her hand over the receiver and glared at me.

'I'm busy!' she hissed.

'You're in a lecture,' I reminded. 'You need to focus.'

'Listen,' she said cockily. 'Don't make this into a battle, because we both know who will win.'

'You're so right,' I agreed. 'Me.'

And with that, I deftly confiscated her phone.

'HEY!' she loudly protested, as I put her phone to my ear.

'I'm so sorry but Tami can't talk right now,' I said to the surprised suitor. 'She's learning about prevention.'

'Eh? You mean, like, condoms and stuff?'

'That's right,' I said sweetly, before hanging up. I turned to Tami. 'You can have this back at the end of the lecture.'

She folded her arms across her chest looking both angry and embarrassed, before lapsing into a major sulk.

I moved away, walking around each group, checking to see how they were getting on.

After five minutes or so, Tami stopped pouting and decided to engage in the task. Her group's subsequent presentation was excellent. Tami even took the initiative and elected to explain her group's work to the rest of the students.

At the end of the lecture, as the students were filing out, Tami came over to me. I returned the phone.

'I'm sorry,' she said.

Tami didn't do apologies, so I tried not to show my shock at getting one from her. I knew it had cost her a lot, so I could afford to be generous.

'That's okay,' I said. 'Your work today was good. *Really* good. Keep it up.'

'Thanks,' she said sheepishly, but clearly delighted. 'See you next time.'

And with that, she left. Our relationship changed that day. Not in a bad way. Just... different. Well, from a former colleague to a student! In due course, Tami became a qualified hygienist and thus a colleague once again. But that was later. This was now.

The dynamics with adult students is a delicate one. It's about treading a fine line between being friendly and approachable, while also maintaining respect.

❖❖

Some students were a total pain in the ass. Bethany Malark, one of my dental students, was such an individual.

Bethany was *always* late. She was *always* on her phone. And she was *always* talking. She had a bad attitude and loved to argue. Throughout my year at the university, we had several run ins.

The first was quite early in the academic year. She was fifteen minutes late to the lecture. At this point I didn't know her, or her patterns of behaviour.

I let this initial lateness slide and indicated she quickly take a seat. Her response was to stick her nose in the air. Moments later, she was on her phone, texting and taking selfies. I watched her do a pouty face to camera, followed by a peace symbol. She then began chatting with – and disrupting the concentration of – the student sitting next to her.

I stopped the lecture.

'What's your name?' I asked.

No response.

'Hello?' I waved one hand.

Finally, she looked my way.

'*Me?*' she mouthed, looking appalled.

'Yes. You. You who keeps talking and using your phone instead of focusing on the lecture.'

'*Excuse* me?' she said incredulously.

'What is your name?'

'Bethany.'

'Bethany what?'

'Malark.'

'Well, Ms Malark. Put the phone away.'

'Why are you picking on me?' she demanded. 'Loads of

other students have their phones out.'

'Put the phone away or leave the lecture.'

Bethany glared at me. For a moment, there was a silent stand-off. She then put it away and the lecture continued without further incident.

The second episode with Bethany happened a few weeks later. She'd now been late to a lecture four times. On this occasion she was twenty-five minutes late.

She entered the lecture hall, and I immediately stopped the lesson.

'You're late.'

'So?' she retorted.

'So, you're interrupting the students and me.'

'And?'

'Bethany, leave the lecture hall. If you can only be bothered to arrive halfway through a lecture, there is no point in you being here at all.'

'I'm not leaving,' she declared.

Here we go, I said to myself.

I sat down at the front of the lecture hall and stared at Bethany. She was now standing in front of the entire class, looking somewhat awkward.

'I'm not willing to continue this lecture with you here.'

Chuntering broke out. Some of the students were getting annoyed. But not at me. Rather, her.

'BETH, JUST GO!' shouted one.

'YEAH, FLIPPING LEAVE!' another jeered.

'I'm going to report you,' Bethany snarled at me, before storming out.

The lecture continued and, on this occasion, Bethany didn't report me. However, her veiled threat prompted me to start logging her attendance and disruption, which was duly fed back to John, the head of year.

The third locking of horns was in a practical session.

It was 'small group teaching' meaning there were only ten students in this set. It was a *shared clinic* situation, meaning other students in the clinic were dealing with patients – so practicing basic examinations and scaling on each other.

Bethany arrived ten minutes late to clinic. Instead of

wearing her uniform (tunic and smart trousers) she was dressed in joggers and a sweatshirt. My nine other students looked first at Bethany, then me. They knew what was about to unfold.

'Ms Malark,' I said. 'You're not wearing your clinical uniform.'

'And?' she said flippantly.

For fuck's sake, I inwardly screamed.

'And you're on a patient clinic. Do you think your clothing is appropriate for the clinical setting?'

'We're not treating patients though,' she countered. 'We're treating each other.'

'Bethany, there *are* patients on this clinic–

'But we're not seeing them,' she interrupted.

I'd had enough of her lip. This was a twenty-one-year-old woman behaving like a brat.

'Get off my clinic,' I ordered. 'Now.'

'No,' she retorted, chin jutting.

'If you don't get off my clinic, I will fetch Security to escort you.'

I didn't shout. My voice was quiet. My tone, level. But I could tell that my threat was having an effect.

Bethany glared at me.

'You. Wouldn't. Dare.'

'I said *now*.'

She went. Straight to John, the head of year.

❖

John and I subsequently had a meeting about Bethany Malark. She'd made a formal complaint about me.

The complaint stated that I picked exclusively on her. That I singled her out without any due cause. That I had a personal vendetta against her. That I was a bully. As I read the statement, I rolled my eyes. Oh, brother.

'Look,' said John. 'I know this is all bullshit. However, because it's been done in writing, I must now follow the protocols in place. This means that I must investigate the complaint. I need your written statement on the matter, plus any evidence to refute it.'

'Yeah, of course,' I replied. 'Not a problem.'

'I will also have to ask two other students from the group for statements regarding Bethany's behaviour. Do you have two students who can support your version of events?' I gave John two names, and he approached those individuals for accounts, which corroborated mine.

I made available all the weeks of reports, which included attendance history (students had to sign in to lectures and this was time-stamped) along with numerous warnings that Bethany had received. Bethany's attendance history in the first semester showed nine unattended lectures, over four hundred minutes of late attendance to lectures (not just mine, but across the board) and even warnings from other lecturers. It transpired Bethany was a truly model student. Not!

Once the evidence had been collated, a meeting was arranged with Bethany, John, and me. We duly sat around a table and ran through her allegations.

'So, Bethany,' John began. 'You claim to have been victimised and picked upon without any due cause.'

'Yes,' said Bethany. 'I've been bullied. No one else ever got into trouble or was refused the opportunity to learn. Just me.' Bethany glared at me.

'I've examined your attendance records,' said John. 'You have been consistently late to every one of your lectures by an average of twenty-two minutes. A lecture is fifty minutes long, so you're actually attending lectures midway through. Is that not cause for reprimand?'

Bethany stopped glaring at me and turned to John. Her face registered shock. She was visibly rattled that he wasn't siding with her.

'Furthermore, I've collected statements from other students in your year group,' he continued. 'Anonymously,' he added. 'Let me read one of them: *Bethany is disruptive in lectures and argumentative with it. She is distracting and always on her phone or Snapchat. I find it difficult to concentrate if I'm near her in the hall.*' John glanced at Bethany, who was now mouthing like a goldfish. 'Do you think such behaviour is conducive to effective learning?'

'Someone in *my* year said that?' said Bethany, in disbelief. 'Who?' she demanded.

'I cannot give you that information. But the fact remains that you're accusing this lecturer of treating you unfairly. However, it seems to me that your behaviour to *him* and fellow colleagues is anything but fair,' said John.

'Other students used their phones, and were never told off,' she growled.

John looked at me for confirmation.

'Untrue,' I said. 'I have confiscated phones for durations of lectures on three occasions from other students.'

Bethany was livid. She'd also turned purple and was starting to make a beetroot look anaemic.

'Anything else to add, Ms Malark?' asked John.

'No,' snapped Bethany.

'Good. Based on my findings, you will receive an official warning. If you are late to any further lectures, I will be forced to escalate this to a fitness-to-practice board.'

Bethany instantly paled. Fitness-to-practice meant the university deemed a student's behaviour so poor they would not be able to continue their studies and would require independent investigation and legal counsel.

'Do you understand, Ms Malark?'

'Yes,' Bethany whispered.

'Good. In which case, you may leave.'

She abruptly stood up and flashed me a filthy look. I gave her my warmest smile. Sticking her nose in the air, Bethany stalked off.

'Right,' said John. 'I'm glad that's sorted. You coming to the pub tonight?'

❖

You probably thought that was the end of **Bethany Malark**, right? Wrong!
However, this time, I almost felt sorry for her. I

said *almost*! What am I referring to, dear reader? The end of year exams.

This included a face-to-face *viva* exam (*viva voce* is an oral examination where the student presents a case, and the examiners ask questions based on what the student has presented to defend the treatment and planning).

This particular viva was conducted by two tutors together. For fairness, the vivas were assigned to tutors at random.

Bethany Malark was lucky (or unlucky?!) to have Flo and yours truly as her examiners.

Flo gave me an impish grin.

'Be nice,' she said.

'Hey, I'm always nice!' I smiled, while privately wondering how I could make this exam horribly uncomfortable for Ms Malark.

Together, Flo and I entered the box room where the exam would take place. There was a small desk within. On one side were two chairs for the examiners. On the other, a single chair for the student. There were no windows within. This almost cell-like room was illuminated by a single overhead fluorescent fixture. The walls were painted a nondescript cream, and the floor was covered in a cheap charcoal carpet. As I stepped over the threshold, it was like entering a prison's meeting room.

When it was eventually Bethany's turn to take the seat opposite Flo and me, I saw her swallow hard. Her complexion had gone from pink to ashen.

'Bethany,' I greeted. 'Come in. Sit down.'

She almost collapsed onto the chair.

'So,' I continued, ignoring her discomfit. 'The way this examination works is that you have fifteen minutes to present your patient case to us, show us your x-rays, the treatment you completed and the rationale behind your planning. There will then follow thirty minutes of questions from Flo and myself.'

Flo then spoke.

'Do you have any questions before we start?'

Bethany shook her head.

'In which case, your time starts... now.'

Visibly flustered, and horribly nervous, Bethany began.

She struggled to make eye contact, preferring to mostly address the table. She spoke quickly, gabbling to meet the timed deadline. Her planning was reasonably competent, and her work had been carried out to an acceptable standard. She was able to quote a few studies to back up her work with an evidence basis. Once her presentation was over, I leant in and began to grill her.

'So, you referenced *Mayfield et al* for your justification of periodontal treatment. What type of study was this?'

A brief pause from Bethany.

'It was a systematic review?'

'Is that a question or an answer?'

Underneath the table, Flo kicked me.

'An answer,' said Bethany quickly. 'It was a systematic review.'

'Why did you go with systematic reviews instead of, for example, a random controlled trial?'

'Systematic reviews are the gold standard in evidence-based medicine. They're meant to be rigorous and unbiased. They're also based on multiple other studies being analysed.'

'You also discussed using a porcelain bonded crown on a molar, rather than a metal based one. Can I ask your justification of this, because I can see multiple wear facets on this patient's teeth.'

'Yes, the patient had cracked tooth syndrome, so a crown was indicated. I discussed a metal crown as the best option but the patient was an actor and concerned about the appearance. Therefore, we opted for a porcelain bonded one and ensured it wasn't heavy in his excursive movement.' (Excursive movements means when a patient grinds.)

'Can you tell me how you arrived at the diagnosis of cracked tooth syndrome?'

'I took a full clinical history; sensibility tested the tooth using a tooth *slooth* and had a positive response.'

I had to hand it to Bethany. She knew her shit. After a heavy grilling from me, I let Flo ask a few questions. I then leant back in my chair.

'Thank you, Bethany,' I said. 'This concludes your exam.'

She stood up and practically fled from the room.

Flo tutted and then looked at me.

'What do you think?

'I think she did very well,' I said.

'Me too. So, you'll pass her?'

'Of course. I'm not unfair!' I rolled my eyes. 'Let's look at the grade boundaries.'

Together, we checked Bethany's understandings and responses. She passed with distinction. So, even though she'd been a complete prat in lectures, she had bothered to do the work after John's bollocking.

A few weeks later, it was exam results day. This was when students and lecturers celebrated together in the pub.

Bethany sought me out. She was a bit drunk at this point and lurched over.

'You were really hard on me,' she complained.

'And yet you passed with distinction.'

'Yeah, but you weren't very nice to me.'

'You weren't very nice to me either.'

'I suppose,' she said, regarding me blearily. 'Well, thanks for passing me.'

'Thanks for finally doing some work.'

She flashed me her trademark filthy look before opening her mouth to say something, but the words suddenly died on her lips. She clamped her hands over her mouth, then legged it towards the loo. Unfortunately, she didn't make it and vomited all over Elon.

Oops.

Perhaps *a bit drunk* was an understatement. More like *plastered*?!

❖

Not all the exams ended with smiles and cheers. Throughout the year, we assessed students' practical skills. These could be assessments on

109

phantom heads, or actual patients in the clinic.

We didn't grade students there and then. Rather, results would be either directly emailed or anonymously posted on the year noticeboard (with the student number alongside).

Some students were extremely put out at failing. One comes to mind. She was incandescent with rage at failing her practical *Simple Extraction Gateway* exam.

I received a long and furious email from this student demanding to know why she'd failed... where I "got off" on being able to fail someone... how was I even qualified to make such decisions (erm, several dental implantology qualifications plus numerous referrals to remove impacted wisdom teeth)... concluding with a diatribe that basically blasted me for failing to recognise she was God's gift to dentistry.

I sighed and took a gulp of my black coffee, fighting the urge to email back a sarcastic response. Surely it was too early in the morning for this shit.

Dear Bhavisha,

Thank you for your email.

First, I would remind you that both the Student Code and the General Dental Council guidelines advise treating people with care and respect.

Second, regarding your recent examination, I am happy to organise a meeting with both the head of year and me in order to further discuss.

Kind regards.

I received an immediate response from Bhavisha demanding a written explanation as to why she'd failed.

Dear Bhavisha,

Thank you for your second email.

It is more for your sake, than mine, that the reason for failing your exam is not put in writing. I have organised a meeting at the office for noon tomorrow.

Please attend.

Kind regards.

Cue radio silence from Bhavisha. Well, until the scheduled meeting...

The following day, at the appointed time, John and I awaited Bhavisha's attendance. Her arrival was precipitated by a hammering on the door. I opened it. Initially ignoring me, she strode in.

John and I exchanged looks. Bhavisha was invited to sit down.

'Well?' she demanded. 'Why did you fail me? Are you jealous of me or something?'

I suppressed a snort of laughter. Jealous of a fourth-year dental student that managed to...?

I won't spoil the surprise. Keep reading.

'Thank you for attending, Bhavisha,' I said. 'John is here to document our meeting.'

'Hello,' said John pleasantly.

Bhavisha ignored him.

'Let's hear it then,' she demanded angrily.

'Before I give my feedback' – I began – 'can I ask how *you* thought the examination went? Talk me through it, please.'

'Fine,' she shrugged. 'The exam was to carry out a simple extraction, which I did. I took out a woman's front tooth.'

'Was there anything that didn't go according to plan during this... *treatment*?' I asked.

Bhavisha paused to consider.

'Nope,' she said eventually. 'Everything went fine.'

I sighed and took a deep breath.

'Okay, Bhavisha. I observed you from start to finish. Apart from the key matter of neither confirming your patient's date of birth and name, nor introducing yourself, you failed to consent the patient to extraction. You didn't even explain what you were going to do. You also made a blunder administering the LA (local anaesthetic).'

I paused and regarded Bhavisha. She was quiet now but sullen. I continued.

'Upon giving the patient an infiltration, you slipped. You went through her lip and then her nose.'

John's head turned sharply, looking at me with alarm and shock – not quite believing what he heard.

'At this point, I was hoping you would have retracted the needle – having realised you'd exited the oral cavity through the nasal passage. You didn't. Instead, you attempted to deliver the anaesthetic. This resulted in LA being squirted through the patient's brand-new nose piercing... at yourself.'

Bhavisha shifted in her seat.

'Yeah, but I still took the tooth out without breaking it.'

'Well done,' I said sarcastically.

'Yeah, exactly. Well done! I should've passed.'

Meanwhile, John's bald head turned a dark purple reminiscent of a beetroot. His jaw was tense and teeth gritted.

'I'm going to ask this question once,' he said. His voice was dangerously quiet. 'Consider your answer carefully before answering. Do you think you conducted yourself to a professional standard deemed safe in general practice?'

There was a long silence.

'No,' Bhavisha admitted.

'That is the correct answer,' said John. 'You are extremely lucky that there haven't been further consequences. I suggest you apologise and go on your way.'

'Sorry,' she said curtly. She stood to leave, then paused. 'The patient did say she was considering a nose piercing, so, you know–'

'OUT!' John roared.

Bhavisha didn't wait to be told twice.

John turned to me, aghast.

'Did the patient *really* end up with a nose piercing?'

'Yes,' I said, trying not to laugh. 'Just think. If Bhavisha's hand had slipped further, the patient might have ended up with a nipple piercing too.'

❖

Graduation was at the height of summer. The day was glorious. The sun shone. Students smiled. Robes were draped over smart suits and glamorous dresses. Mortarboards flattened quiffs and curls.

The day passed in a haze of good cheer, nervous excitement, and tipsiness from the nonstop champagne.

I inhaled deeply. The air was warm and smelled sweet. For a moment, I felt like I'd travelled back in time, to my own graduation.

Throughout the day, many students came up to me. They wanted to introduce me to their parents who shook my hand and thanked me.

Imposter syndrome really kicked in at this point. Why were all these people thanking me? After all, it was only five minutes since I'd graduated!

I told the little voice to shut up, then enjoyed a glass of fizz. Some students clapped me on the back. I did the same back, congratulating them on their success. For a select few, I passed on my personal number in case they needed some guidance in the future.

At around one o'clock, everyone filed into the large graduation hall. The staff sat together on the stage. John came in dressed in full ceremonial regalia. He looked a bit like a grand magician from a bygone era, although his mid-life crisis earring rather spoilt the illusion.

One by one, the students were called on to the stage to collect their diplomas. The auditorium was packed. As each student shook hands with John, family and friends would erupt with cheers, applause, and the occasional whistle. This was a glorious day for every one of these newly qualified practitioners. I don't think they realised how proud we – their teachers – felt too. It is quite something to see someone you've mentored not only complete their training but also walk, with confidence, into the next stage of their lives.

The ceremony eventually ended and everyone shuffled out again, back to the bright sunshine.

An official photographer then arranged both graduates and staff over some large stone steps. The teachers then moved away, and the photographer counted everyone down to throwing their mortarboards in the air. It was like a scene straight out of an American high school film. The photographer snapped away, capturing the moments in digital pixels that would later adorn the walls of proud parents and graduates alike.

Flo, one of my fellow lecturers, tapped me on the shoulder.

'Someone has suggested we grab a few drinks around the corner and see where the day – and maybe the night – takes us. Want to come?'

'Yeah, sounds great,' I agreed. 'But shouldn't we dump the garb first?'

'Mate,' she grinned. 'We're as trendy *AF*.'

Nonetheless, I slipped off my robe, removed my tie, then undid the top button of my shirt preferring to look more like a city businessman than a Hogwarts wizard.

We headed into a small pub, where the rest of the staff had already got several drinks on the go. Elon was now smashed and trying to show everyone pictures of his pet rats.

A few of my students chose that moment to come through the door. They looked around uncertainly. I waved at them, and they came over.

'Hi,' said one, timidly. 'We just wanted to say thanks again for everything over the last year. We all chipped in and got you something.'

'Oh, you really didn't need to do that,' I said, genuinely surprised at the lovely gesture. 'It's been my absolute pleasure.'

'We insist,' said another student.

He handed me a padded envelope. Inside was a voucher

for two people to enjoy a slap-up meal at a fancy London restaurant. I was so taken aback I began to tear up. I gulped and hastily composed myself.

'Thank you. So much. All of you. This is so kind.'

We all shook hands, then I bought them all a drink to toast their future.

'Here's to health, wealth, success and, most importantly, happiness.'

❖

Saying goodbye to my university colleagues and friends was unbelievably sad.

We all went to the local pub and had a few pints. Several students came along too. They said they'd miss me, and that they'd enjoyed my teaching (a huge ego boost).

My year of teaching had not only helped me gain a post-grad certificate in education, but also taught me practical skills in *how* to truly teach.

Only a few years earlier, when I'd been a student myself, lecturers had predominantly been didactic droning ancients, mumbling away in a dusty hall.

My teaching experience had shaped and enforced that this was not the way to lecture if you wanted your students to *learn*! Instead, I'd dared to do a complete about turn. I'd been hugely interactive, incorporated group self-teaching, and successfully made the driest topics somewhat more bearable.

As I said at the start, I loved teaching. I had liked it so much, that when I later worked in the NHS, I took on a foundation dentist of my own (and we are still in touch to this day). It is so rewarding to see how you have helped shape someone's career/practice.

I think my final takeaway on this subject is this:

Teaching dentistry is a balancing act. It's a delicate dance between the seriousness of the profession and an occasional foray into the realm of the absurd. It's a career that requires not just expertise and knowledge, but also the ability to embrace the occasional dental mishap with humour.

I'm still waiting for that lotto win. And when it happens, I'll toss aside the drill and immediately don my mortarboard. Hey, a guy can dream!

5

The Locum Tales

What is a locum? A locum is a temporary dentist. One who wafts upon the winds, going wherever he or she is needed, and staying a while before eventually moving on.

Locums are hired to fill gaps in staffing, for example if someone is on maternity leave, or long-term sick. Some posts are short – weeks or months – while others can last years.

I spent five years as a locum in various places. My longest stint was three years at once practice. Here, it became a running joke that I was the permanent locum.

The great thing about being a locum is the fixed day rate. This means I never had to chase NHS UDAs (remember those *units of dental activity*?) and had less stress over end-of-month earnings because they were always consistent. The flip side to being a locum was being let go with only a week's notice.

Back then, I didn't worry too much about being served notice. Practices that require locum dentists generally struggle to retain permanent staff. Certainly, I never thought (probably somewhat arrogantly!) that I'd ever be given a week's notice after being a locum for three years...

But I did! With a week's notice and no chance of finding a new post. The reason? Covid hit. The CQC (Care Quality Commission - one of our burdensome overlords) shut dental practices. Dental practices are businesses at the end of the day, and with no possibility of maintaining income, overheads needed cutting. Dentists are self employed. Cut them.

This example sums up the risk/reward balance of being a locum. You will earn more, you can pick where you go, and you can leave at your own whim. However, you risk being dumped at a moment's notice.

Anyway, this section of the book is not to discuss Covid (although we will get there later, I promise, and don't groan!). Instead, let's chat about some of my experiences as a locum dentist.

I locumed at several practices over a five-year period including two fully private practices. One was *ruled* by a tyrant principal (and former used-car salesman!), and the other was a fully NHS practice in a very high needs, poverty-stricken area.

Most of these tales will come from the NHS practice, although I can't wait to tell you about the dictator dentist and his dastardly dealings.

Despite all the dramas, each experience helped shape my understanding of this crazy career. It taught me about small business, and small-minded businesspeople!

I learnt what to look for in a good practice and, conversely, what to spot in a bad one. I found out how to stand my ground and speak up. It gave me confidence in my own skillset. Oh, and I can tell you with absolute certainty that working as an NHS locum gave me the ability to work efficiently, fast, and effectively.

I discovered that a nurse could make or break your day. At the NHS post, my nurse was a young Nepalese lady named Nea. In the end, when we worked together, it was almost as if we had psychically bonded. Our workflow was seamless. She knew what I wanted before I even asked and was set up ready for a procedure before I'd even voiced a plan of action was. I will forever be grateful to Nea for all her help.

So, without further ado, let's get to the nitty gritty, the commotions, turmoil, and tantrums! Stay close, dear reader, because these locum tales are wild...

❖

I want to start with a lone story about a private practice I once locumed at. This was in an affluent area in Greater London.

The practice had three surgeries. The principal dentist worked between two of these surgeries. In the third surgery, days were split. A specialist endodontist (someone who performs root canal treatments) worked for two days, and a hygienist was there for three days.

I think the most interesting part of this story is that I kind of knew the principal (owner) of the practice.

Many, many moons ago, I'd been at primary school with his son. Indeed, we'd been mates. We had enjoyed the occasional sleepover. Even days out together. Our friendship had eventually fizzled out when we went to different secondary schools. It turns out his son is now a doctor.

Anyway, let's talk about this principal. His name was Wayne Adams. He was a large, red, angry man. He had all the charm of a child's tantrum in a crowded supermarket.

Before being a dentist, Wayne had sold used cars for a living. This was fairly apparent by his no-frills, no-bullshit attitude. Wayne was a *bloke* and had no redeeming features.

His wife, Sally Adams, was also the practice manager. Middle-aged, she had veneers whiter than the porcelain throne you'd park your derriere upon. She was also so full of shit, she'd make the toilet jealous.

Together, Wayne and Sally inspired a regime of discipline and fear in their staff (patients too, for that matter).

So, how did I come to work at this fabulous pit of despair? Well, Sally found out that I was a qualified dentist. She sent me a message via Instagram asking if I'd like to come for a trial.

I thought this was a great opportunity (hindsight is a wonderful thing!) to get into some private dentistry. I went along to the practice. There, I was asked to complete an extraction for Wayne to observe. This I did. I was then offered a job. Not by Wayne. Rather, Sally.

I started officially a week later, with the promise of a

full book of patients.

I arrived to find that I had only been booked two patients for an entire day. To put this into perspective, in a private practice I would usually see around fifteen patients a day and, in the NHS, *thirty* patients!

Never mind, I told myself. *Everyone must start somewhere.*

So, I did my check-ups, treatment-planned any work required, and booked patients' return appointments. One lady needed two crowns, so I booked her in for the following week to get them sorted.

Unfortunately, when that day rolled around, I discovered that Wayne had moved this appointment to his own book. I was shocked. Politely, I asked his reason for doing this.

'Listen, lad,' he said. 'You're new to this. You need to do more courses. Patients here are paying *privately.* Understand? You just ain't got the experience.'

'I've completed plenty of crowns, Wayne,' I reasoned. 'And, with respect, I had treatment-planned this case.'

'I'm not arguing with you, mate,' he said gruffly. 'This is *my* practice, so I'll be seeing the patient.'

That was that. I was mighty pissed off but heeded his advice and booked an expensive digital crown course in CEREC (computer-aided design and milling). I told myself that, at the end of the day, I was only three years out of uni, so perhaps he was right.

I instead spent the rest of that day overseeing some emergency patients. I had so much empty space in my diary that I offered any required treatment there and then. I remember doing a couple of extractions and a filling.

At the end of the day, Wayne called me into his surgery and treated me like a naughty schoolboy.

'What on *earth* do you think you're doing?' he shouted.

'Sorry?' I said, taken aback.

'THIS!' he yelled, waving about an extraction consent form.

'Well, obviously that details the risks and benefits of the extraction,' I said.

'No,' he countered. 'It *scares* the patients. You do *not* tell patients what can go wrong. You just do the treatment.'

'At uni, we were taught to discuss the pros and cons in order to obtain valid consent.'

'Well, this is private dentistry. You don't do that.'

'But surely I have a duty to explain risks so people can make informed decisions.'

'You clearly aren't a professional,' he said disdainfully, before dismissing me.

The following week, I continued to do what I normally did. I made sure to stay out of Wayne's way as much as I could. You may be thinking, dear reader, why did I stay at all if it was such a bad environment? There were two reasons. First, I thought it would be good experience and look impressive on the CV. Second, I'm a stubborn bastard.

The following weekend – in my own time – I went on the crown course. On the Sunday, just as I was completing the course and receiving my certificate, I had an email from Wayne.

You're not a good fit for this practice. I don't want you back.

Regards
Wayne

My heart sank. Here I was being fired with a zero-notice period. I felt a rush of emotions. Initially, I wanted to give him what for. Next, I felt relief. And then I was bloody annoyed. After all, I'd just forked out a large sum of money on a course I needn't have done!

I wrote back.

Dear Wayne

My service agreement states a one month notice period unless I violate the terms of the agreement. To my knowledge, none of the clauses have been violated. I therefore expect to work my notice period.

I am a competent dentist. I have also personally invested at considerable expense – and at your request – in a course to improve my digital delivery of dental treatment which includes crowns.

Regards.

This didn't bring a response from Wayne. Instead, Shitty-Veneers-Sally replied.

The practice will transfer the cost of your course and you will not return for the notice period.

Sally

I cut my losses and accepted. I'd managed three months as a locum at that practice. It had taught me to stand up for myself and value myself as a clinician. Remember, private is not always better, and you get unethical individuals in all walks of life.

❖

Let's move onto something more lighthearted! The next practice that I went to as a locum was in an impoverished high needs area.

I am not exaggerating when I say that every patient required at least five fillings and the average age of a person needing a denture was twenty-seven. This town had a record of soaring crime, high unemployment, and a ton of violence.

Despite these daunting facts, I stayed at this practice as a locum for more than three years. The team were decent, the staff good, and the nurses worked their butts off. It was a nice place to work, despite the clientele being very different to those under private care. There are many bizarre tales to tell from those years, none more uncomfortable (for me at least!) than one young mother and her adult daughter.

Chardonnay was in her early twenties. Her mother, Zinfandel, was in her mid-thirties. I'd seen Chardonnay several times in the past. She'd been over the moon with a denture I'd had made (due to missing some front teeth). Today Chardonnay was accompanying her mother in a supportive role. Zinfandel had only three teeth left and wanted to do something about it. However, she was very nervous.

'Don't worry, Mam,' said Chardonnay. She patted her mother's hand. 'The dentist is well nice. It's all fine.'

'Yeah, Chards,' said Zinfandel. 'I'll be okay, babe. No worries.'

I smiled at them.

'Nice to see you both.' I indicated the dental chair to Zinfandel. 'Take a seat.'

'Oof,' said Zinfandel, sitting down heavily.

'What can I do for you?'

'Well, aren't you lovely,' she said, looking me over. 'You married?'

'No, I'm not married. So, tell me. Are you having any trouble?'

'I might have trouble keeping me hands off yer,' she said, giving me a gummy grin.

She winked at me and stuck her tongue out of her toothless mouth. I was a little sick in my mouth, but disguised it by clearing my throat. Nea, my nurse, flashed me *the look.*

Zinfandel tore her eyes away from my crotch. 'Me tooth has gone all wobbly.' She pointed to her last front incisor and wiggled it with her fingers.

'I see.'

'I want it out. I'd like some plastic teeth, like Chards.'

'No problem. Let's take an x-ray and see what's going on under the surface.'

I took the picture and gave it to Nea to process. While she was out of the room, I turned to my computer to type up some notes. That's when I heard Zinfandel stage-whisper to Chardonnay.

'Corrrrrr! Look at his ARSE!'

123

Chardonnay giggled.

'I told yer he was fit.'

I froze, hunched over the keyboard. Dear Lord. This was Isabelle Chillblain all over again. (Remember her? The fruit loop who'd wanted to snog me at Paul Slater's.) And anyway, how could she work out what my backside looked like? I was wearing scrubs!

'So, you're single, eh?' Zinfandel cooed. 'Want to come back to mine later? I could show you what an experienced woman can do.'

Chardonnay immediately chimed in.

'Or you can have someone younger with more teeth.'

'What truly... lovely... er, offers,' I said, red with embarrassment. 'However, I don't think it's appropriate to ask your clinician such questions.'

'I won't tell if you don't!' Zinfandel winked.

'I think it's best we keep things professional ladies,' I demurred.

Thankfully Nea chose this moment to return to the room with the x-ray. I took it from her like a drowning man seizing a lifebuoy and concentrated on studying it intently.

'That tooth definitely needs to come out. Okay, let's get you numbed up.'

'Oooh, lovely,' leered Zinfandel. 'A prick in my mouth.'

Chardonnay snorted.

'We love those, don't we, Mam!'

For one surreal moment, I wondered if I might faint. Nea swiftly crossed the room and opened the window. A gust of reviving cold air blasted the room.

Needless to say, I'd never worked so quickly in order to get those sex-obsessed women out of my surgery.

In due course, I made a set of dentures for Zinfandel. She loved them. When she popped in her new plastic gnashers, she said she felt like she was twenty-one again.

'Are yer sure I can't take yer out for a drink?' she asked. 'I'd like to say thanks.'

'Your smile is thanks enough,' I replied diplomatically.

Zinfandel looked momentarily crestfallen at not having her offer taken up. I have a sneaking suspicion that she and Chardonnay were hoping that I might provide either one of them with a little Malbec in nine months' time.

❖

FTA. **Failed to attend**. This is when a patient doesn't turn up and when you call them to chase where they are, there's no answer. It is a universal sign, in *every* dental practice, that it's time for a tea break.

Sometimes, FTAs are a godsend, especially in a busy day. They let you catch up, have a breather and replenish motivation (and also stops an aggy nurse from giving you daggers).

Equally, some FTAs are a complete inconvenience and pain in the ass. The annoying no-shows are those that were booked for treatment, like an hour-long appointment. It puts the entire clinic out of sync because everyone is sitting around twiddling their thumbs.

If an FTA happens at the end of the day, that's different. Everyone celebrates getting out of surgery early. But in the middle of the day? Well, there's nothing to do but wait.

We hear all sorts of reasons why patients miss their appointments. Some are serious – emergency hospital attendance... broken down car... road traffic accident. Others are a little *stretched* and some are downright farfetched.

Let me tell you some of my favourite stories. Well, *favourite* might be the wrong word. *Most interesting* is probably better.

The Tale of The Troublemaker
One wintery morning, twenty-seven-year-old Jordan attended clinic for a routine check-up. He seemed like a nice guy. He was missing his upper lateral incisor (the tooth just to the side of the front one). Jordan explained that the tooth had been 'hit out' in a fight a few years earlier.

'Listen, boss,' he said. 'I want the new tooth in gold.'
I frowned.

'You want a gold front tooth?'

'Yeah, man. It'll look *sick*!'

'I see.' I cleared my throat. 'Unfortunately, this material is incredibly expensive, so I won't be able to provide a gold bridge on the NHS. However, we could do it in silver. Would that work?'

'Silver?' he repeated. 'Hmm.' He thought about it for a moment or two. 'Yeah, I reckon that could work. But I want, like, a zig-zag design. Right down the middle.'

'If you draw the design, I can ask the lab to make copy it.'

'Cushty, man!'

So, we got to work. Jordan drew the must-have artwork across the front of the new tooth. I then took impressions and detailed out the design with the dental lab. They were somewhat bemused, but obliged and created a nice-looking piece of work. The bridge came in three weeks later. However, Jordan didn't. He FTA'd the appointment.

Well, that was disappointing. I'd been quite excited to see how this unusual piece of dental work would look.

We tried to contact Jordan, but the phone didn't connect. In the end, we closed his course of treatment, and the bridge was put into storage along with his casts (models of his teeth).

Over a year later, I spotted Jordan's name in the diary. He was back for a check-up.

'Hello, sir,' I said. 'Long time no see. You never came back for your bridge.'

'Yeah, sorry about that, boss. I went to prison. I only got out last week.'

Oka*yyy*, I guess that's as good a reason as any!

'You still got that bridge, man?' he asked. 'If so, you can put it in today.'

And so, we fitted Jordan's bridge. He was delighted. In fact, we both agreed that it looked pretty damn *sick*.

The Last of the Late Comers

Sometimes, a patient FTAs but then turns up very, *very* late. One such individual, who shall remain nameless, turned up for his appointment three hours late and just as we were packing up to go home. I'd been aware of some background shouting, but my mind had been elsewhere, like what to cook for dinner once home.

There was a knock on my surgery door and Joan, one of the receptionists, came in.

'You okay?' I asked, continuing to put things away.

'Not really,' she said, looking apprehensive. 'A patient has turned up. However, their appointment was three hours ago.'

'And?'

'And he wants to be seen. Now,' she added.

I glanced at the clock on the wall.

'I know,' she said. 'However, he's really angry.'

'Is that who I can hear shouting?' I asked. Joan nodded miserably. 'Offer to reschedule his appointment. If he kicks off, call the police. We don't take abuse from anyone.'

'Okay,' she said.

Thirty seconds later, all hell broke out. The patient was yelling at Joan. He knocked over a display of healthcare leaflets. Bits of paper flew about like something out of *The Crystal Maze* (if you don't understand this reference, you're either ridiculously young, or I'm ridiculously old). He then stormed outside, only to peer through the windows trying to work out which was my surgery. However, without a ladder he wouldn't have sussed it because I was on the first floor.

At this point, Joan locked the front door and called the police. We were safe! But not for much longer. Having been locked out, the man was incensed. This *gentle*man started to violently kick the door to get back inside. The door groaned against his blows, but thankfully held. At this point, two officers who had been patrolling locally, turned up.

From my window, I overheard one of the policemen.

'Whoa, fella. Whoa! Hey, calm down.'

'Who the fuck are you?' came the angry retort.

'We're coppers, buddy. You need to stop battering that door.'

'I want my dental appointment!' the patient screamed.

'Mate, we hear you. But you were apparently three hours late. You missed it. If it's this practice's policy to then not see you, there's nothing you can do about it.'

'Oh YEAH?' the enraged man spat. 'Well, it's *MY* policy to break down their door!'

'That ain't going to happen,' said the other cop. 'You've got two choices. Either you walk off now, or we arrest you. What's it going to be?'

Sensibly, the patient took himself off.

There was a lot of paperwork to do after the incident including writing to the local area team about why we were blacklisting the patient, as well as informing other practices in the area.

At times, working in this particular town felt like another world. Joan and I heaved a sigh of relief that it was all over.

'Well done for keeping so calm,' I said.

She gave me an eyeroll.

'Yeah,' she dead panned. 'I have a lot of *patients*.'

The Belated Blondie

Mrs Blondie, aged sixty-two, was, unlike her name, a grey-haired lady with a mole on her cheek that had sprouted a full head of hair.

Mrs Blondie was always late. It was often a lottery on *how* late. It could be anything from two minutes to *twenty-two*. I always tried to accommodate her if her tardiness didn't exceed this time frame.

She always had some story or other about why she was late. Like… she ran out of petrol (despite living only a five-minute walk away). Or, just as she was leaving, her cat had meowed in such a way it had sounded like *hello* causing her to try to get the animal to repeat it on film (which had, naturally, made her late). Or even the time she'd left all the Christmas presents on her bed and had to rush home to quickly wrap them.

Yes, all genuine stories. Most of the time, I laughed off her funny excuses. However, on this day, Mrs Blondie was forty-seven minutes late. I declined to see her as I would have ended up running very late. I asked reception to rebook her.

A week later, Mrs Blondie turned up bang on time (a miracle). When she came into the surgery, it was immediately apparent that she was angry.

'You refused to see me last week!' she scowled.

'Hello, Mrs Blondie. Please sit down.' I indicated the chair. A trick I had learnt a while back was to keep your hand outstretched in the direction of the chair. Eventually the person will sit down and their desire to stand and shout suddenly dissolves.

She continued to stand for another moment or two, but then it became awkward for her. She sat down.

'I'm not happy,' she whined. 'I came all the way here!'

Yeah, five minutes away, I silently muttered.

'I hear you, Mrs Blondie. Unfortunately, you were nearly an hour late.'

'I was barely forty minutes late,' she protested. 'And anyway, you've run late before.'

'Indeed,' I agreed. 'That's because I always try to accommodate those that turn up late. However, I have a limit as to how late I can run. I set that at a maximum of twenty minutes.'

'You don't even have any sympathy for *why* I was late,' she howled.

I said nothing. There was a long pause during which she hoped I'd say something. Mrs Blondie took this as her cue to continue.

'I got my toothbrush stuck,' she said woefully. 'But it wasn't in my mouth.'

I really didn't want to hear where Mrs Blondie's toothbrush had been or how she'd removed it.

'Enough of that,' I said firmly. 'You're here now. So shall I continue making your denture?'

'Well, yes, okay, but–'

'Perfect,' I said, cutting Mrs Blondie off. 'So, today, we are at the stage where you can put the teeth in and make sure you're happy with the colour and position. If all's good, I'll send them off to be finished in plastic.'

The rest of the appointment was uneventful.

'See you next week for the finished denture promptly

at a quarter to one.'

'You will,' said Mrs Blondie, before taking herself off.

Nea, my nurse, looked at me with wide eyes.

'Where do you think her toothbrush got stuck?'

'God knows,' I said, shaking my head.

'Gives a whole new meaning to *bristle* brush,' she snorted.

I started to giggle.

'Maybe she fancied a brush with fun.'

'Omigod,' Nea laughed. 'I'll bet it was an electric toothbrush!'

'Would that still be classed as oral hygiene?'

We convulsed.

❖

Being a locum in a deprived area meant I often saw things that weren't common in day-to-day dentistry. There were higher incidents of the weird and not-so-wonderful.

I'm talking about cancers and large cyst-like conditions that can cause havoc in the mouth.

Oral cancer is devastating. If diagnosed early, the prognosis is generally good. Unfortunately, only about a quarter of oral cancers are diagnosed early. Those diagnosed late yield a poorer five-year survival rate.

In areas of higher deprivation, patients are much less likely to regularly attend check-ups. They are also much more likely to smoke or engage in risky behaviours, like drugs. And more often than not, their diet is poor.

These inequalities across the country are stark. You cross a county border, and it's like entering a different world. Even East London, where I did my training, was starkly different to West London.

I think one of the biggest unspoken scandals of our time is *dental inequality.* As a locum, I saw children with rampant decay, young adults with severe gum disease and the elderly with no teeth at all. All dental diseases are preventable. Yes, there is a genetic component, but even with this, prevention can offset any genetic component. Tooth loss is *not* part of the aging process.

This is not a political memoir, so I will not get on my soapbox. However, I will say that successive governments (on both sides of the divide) have failed to invest in NHS dental services and let them languish to the point of collapse.

There should be far more prevention steps being taken – like dental visits to schools for fluoride programmes, education on the causes of dental decay, *Bring Your Toothbrush to School Day*, fluoridated water, and so on. The public health options are endless.

Anyway, one day, a forty-year-old patient called Patricia attended for an emergency appointment. Patricia hadn't been to the dentist for sixteen years. She'd previously had multiple loose teeth, and when they became troublesome she'd simply removed them herself with pliers. However, this time, she'd been unable to do it. She'd tried and been left in agony.

'This is the bastard, Doc,' she said.

She pointed to her lower left premolar and wobbled it to show it was loose. As she did so, there was an awful rancid smell.

Dentists smell all sorts of things. Decay. Abscesses. Periodontal (gum) disease. They all have very distinct and foul smells. This was like nothing I'd ever smelt before. It was truly putrid.

I popped Patricia back in the chair and looked in her mouth. The tooth was indeed mobile, but it was the surrounding gum that alarmed me. There was a huge and deep ulceration with rolled borders. It was hard to tell where healthy gum stopped, and the ulcer started. It was one vast necrotic mess. And by god, the cadaverous odour that sprang from Patricia was something that I could never forget.

I did my due diligence. Took an x-ray. Checked the lymph nodes (which were matted and raised). Took clinical photos. There was no doubt that this was oral cancer. More specifically, a particularly nasty oral squamous cell carcinoma.

'Patricia,' I said softly. 'I think there's something else going on here.'

'Yeah? An' what's that?' she squinted at me.

'There is a particularly nasty looking ulcer surrounding the tooth. I think you should be urgently seen at hospital.'

'Nah,' she said. 'It's just an abscess. Take the fucker out. It'll clear up.'

This was hard. All my uni training started to swim around in my head. I could remember what one of my profs had said.

You can't tell a patient they have cancer, because you do not know without a biopsy.

However, there was also a fundamental need to give honest advice. That and a referral system with a tick box saying you'd told the patient there was a possibility of cancer.

Deep breath.

'Patricia,' I said gently, looking directly into her eyes,

'Oh God,' she said, staring back. 'It's something serious, isn't it?'

'I cannot tell you for sure, but I don't like the look of it.'

'Oh God. Oh God. Oh fuck. Oh shit. Fuck.'

'Patricia.' I took her hand. 'Take some deep breaths for me.' She did. 'I'm going to call the local hospital's *maxfax* team.' Maxillofacial surgeons are the guys who do facial reconstructions and deal with cancer referrals. 'I'll get them to see you today, okay?' She was very shaken, but nodded. 'Give me a moment.'

I left the room, leaving Patricia with my nurse, Nea. I immediately called the local hospital and spoke to the on-call registrar. I said I would send over the referral digitally but felt the two weeks wait time wasn't quick enough.

The registrar agreed to see Patricia immediately. She was grateful and headed straight off to the hospital.

Nea looked at me.

'Is it cancer?' she asked.

'Almost certainly,' I said.

We were silent for a bit. Then the reality of the NHS system kicked back in. We had to crack on. There were check-ups to do. Teeth to fix.

Three weeks later, I received a letter from the hospital. It was a reply to my referral. Patricia *had* been diagnosed with oral squamous cell carcinoma. It had been very advanced and unfortunately metastasised (spread) throughout her body. The prognosis was poor. Patricia had been put on end-of-life care with palliative chemotherapy.

Patricia passed away a week after that letter. Her family telephoned the practice to let us know. They said she'd been comfortable and her passing peaceful.

This was the first time I'd seen an oral cancer that wasn't in a textbook. It was also the first time I'd been confronted with a dental-related death. It was terrifyingly ordinary. One minute the patient was there. And then she wasn't.

It was a stark reminder of the fragility of life. That things can change in the blink of an eye. Having met Patricia, I'm sure she would have later told her family something like:

'Fuck it. Pour me a vast brandy. If I've gotta go, then it will be with a belly full of booze and heart full of cheer.'

She'd be right, of course. It underlines that we should all embrace the day, because you never know what tomorrow might bring.

❖

As a locum, I saw more than my fair share of weird shit. The patient population of my locum practice was very *casual*. This meant that they only came along when they felt there was something wrong. They weren't routine attenders.

I tried to instil the importance of regular attendance. Routine check-ups minimised fillings and so on, but more often than not my advice fell on deaf ears.

Take Jake (I didn't mean for that to rhyme!). He was a twenty-five-year-old chap with a ruddy complexion and patchy beard. He came into surgery wearing a hoodie, joggers, with some Nike shoes and a snapback cap. I did a double take because he was wearing the hoodie as a cape! The arms of the sweatshirt were wrapped around his chin, fully covering his neck.

Was this the latest style? Was I witnessing some sort of cutting-edge fashion in my surgery? Perhaps I was not keeping up with the times. After all, I'd recently entered my thirties and, according to my little sister, I was only a decade away from being positively ancient.

'Hello, Jake,' I said. 'Nice to meet you. What can I do for you?'

'Yeah, hiya, mate. I just want a cleanup. My teeth are a bit stained.'

'I see,' I said, indicating he take the chair. 'And when was your last check-up?'

'Not since I was a teenager,' he admitted. 'I'm scared of dentists.'

At this range, what I'd thought to be a ruddy complexion was starting to look like something else. The left side of his face was very red, specifically where his cheek met his jawline. However, everything was obscured by the hoodie-cum-cape.

'Please could you remove your cap and hoodie?' I asked.

'Yeah, sure,' he said, immediately obliging.

As he did so, my eyes widened. All was revealed. Namely, an enormous red boil. It looked very angry. I'm not exaggerating when I say it was the size of an egg. It was attached to his jawline and pressing into his neck. The skin was so shiny, taut and stretched, the whiskers in that area had ceased growing.

I regarded it in horror, momentarily lost for words. Nea, my nurse, surreptitiously kicked me.

'How long have you had this swelling?' I asked, shocked to the core.

'Dunno,' Jake shrugged. 'Maybe a couple of months?'

'A *couple of months*!' I boggled. 'Jake, did you not think it was a problem?'

'Well, no. Not really. Why? Is it?'

'Blimey,' I muttered. 'Er, yes, Jake. Yes, it is definitely a problem.'

'Oh,' he said, unperturbed. 'Can I still have my teeth polished?'

'Not today,' I said faintly. 'In fact, I'm going to call the max-fax team at the local hospital, and you are going to A&E.'

'What?' he squawked.

I telephoned the local team, explained that my patient had a large facial swelling, and that I was extremely concerned about risk to airways. They agreed to see Jake immediately.

Shaken, Jake did as he was told and left.

A month later, he was back. The hideous egg had gone, but his beard hadn't regrown – but maybe he was just late to the puberty party. Anyway, in he came.

'How are things now?' I asked, as he sat down.

'Yeah, good, thanks. I've got a letter for you. It's from the hospital. They took out seven teeth. They said you'd sort out the rest of the problems.'

Fuck me, I thought. *How many other bloody problems remain if a twenty-five-year-old has already had seven extractions?*

I looked at the letter. There was also an attached panoramic (full mouth) x-ray. Jake's mouth was a mess. It transpired he needed a further six fillings and some intense deep cleaning.

I shook my head imperceptibly.

'Do you understand the seriousness of this situation?' I asked.

He gave me an embarrassed look.

'Yeah,' he said sheepishly. 'I do now.'

'Okay, listen. I'll get you fixed up, but you *must* come and see me regularly. You also need to clean twice daily *and* make some lifestyle changes. Chiefly, your diet. Is that understood?'

'Yeah,' he nodded.

Over the next six weeks, Jake's remaining broken teeth were repaired and filled. Gums were cleaned and intensive oral hygiene instructions given. His diet was assessed, and meaningful changes suggested.

I thought I'd got through to him, and that he would

continue along this new path and hopefully not fall into old habits.

Jake didn't return for his six-month check-up. In fact, throughout my subsequent five years as a locum at this practice, I didn't see him again. I can only hope that if he ever did deign to turn up again, he wasn't wearing his hoodie as a cape.

❖

It may surprise you (or maybe it won't) that some **people do not brush their teeth**. Like, ever. Cross my heart, I'm telling the truth.

I'm always surprised when some patients confess to only brushing once a day. There seems to be a heavy trend of people avoiding night-time brushing. If you're one of them, then be warned. It is the most important time to brush. Food stagnates in the mouth. Also, your saliva rate drops. This leads to a perfect environment for dental decay.

My locum practice, as we've established, was in a high-needs area. This meant I saw the worst of the worst. I had to work *very* quickly and efficiently. Consequently, my tolerance for bullshit was low.

Cue Andrius, a thirty-nine-year-old man with a bad attitude and dreadful oral hygiene. Andrius attended the practice as a new patient. His chief complaint was that he didn't like the gold crown he had on his upper second left premolar. He wanted it changed for porcelain. The crown was clinically sound (no decay). During the check-up, I took x-rays and charted the work that was required.

'And how often do you brush?' I asked, making notes.

Andrius started to laugh. I stopped writing and looked at him. What was funny?

'Twice a day?' I prompted.

'No!' He laughed harder.

'Once a day?'

More laughter.

'Once a week?' I suggested queasily.

'Maybe once a month,' he said, convulsing.

My nurse and I glanced at each other, stunned. When he'd finally stopped splitting his sides, he looked at Nea and me. Our expressions were stony.

'What?' he said.

'I don't find this funny,' I said. 'So let me get this straight. You've attended here, expecting the NHS to provide cosmetic work for you, yet you can't even be *bothered* to look after your own oral health and clean your teeth?'

Andrius shrugged.

'You will change this crown for me, yes?'

'No.'

His eyes flashed.

'Why not?'

'It's cosmetic. The rest of your mouth looks dire, but *this* tooth is fine. The NHS provides what is clinically necessary. In your case, that is a deep clean, intensive oral hygiene instructions and five silver fillings.'

'I don't want silver.'

'I can do them in composite – white material – but it will cost one hundred pounds per tooth.'

'No,' he snapped. 'I want it for free.'

Herein lies a major problem with NHS dental care. It creates a two-tier system. In other words, those who pay, and those who are exempt.

It is a broad characterisation, but I've found that those who are exempt from payment are far less likely to value their teeth, be far more demanding and far more likely to complain. If a patient doesn't have any penalty for not looking after their teeth, then why bother? Certainly, that was Andrius's attitude.

'There is no argument,' I said. 'You have three choices; one, do nothing. Two, the NHS will provide what is clinically necessary. Three, you can pay privately for cosmetic fillings and crowns. Please let me know which you'd like to do.'

After much huffing and puffing, Andrius opted to let the NHS complete his treatment.

Over the next few weeks, I rectified everything, then

went through oral hygiene. His bored expression told me he wasn't going to heed my advice, which included returning in six months.

He took his leave. No word of thanks or even a goodbye. As he went out the door, I silently said, *and good riddance to you*!

❖

Andrius returned nine months later with a new problem. He'd lost his front tooth. It had previously been an old crown secured with a post into the root system. This had now fractured. All that was left was a small fragment of root that couldn't be saved. He told me that the tooth had broken three weeks earlier. He was in no pain. And he still wasn't cleaning his teeth!

'I want an implant,' he demanded.

'The NHS only provides dental implants in very rare circumstances,' I explained. 'For example, severe trauma from a road traffic accident.'

'No,' he argued. 'I want an implant on the NHS and I don't want to pay for it.'

Fuck me, I thought. *How do I get through to this dickhead?*

Nea flashed me *the look*. She was obviously thinking the same as me!

I took a deep breath.

'Andrius,' I said levelly. 'The NHS will *not* be providing you with this treatment. Nor do I know any private dentist who would consider doing it for you given that you smoke cigarettes and don't clean your teeth. Any implant would likely fail.'

'What can I have then?' he said sullenly.

'There are two options. First, a denture. You can take it in and out. Second, a bridge. This is fixed to the tooth next door. I'm happy to make a fixed solution but will not do so unless you're cleaning your teeth twice a day. If you don't keep it clean, it will fail, require extraction, and then we're back to square one.'

'Okay,' he nodded. 'I want the bridge.'

'That's fine. I'm going to book you in for two weeks' time. That gives you time to get cleaning and have those gums under control. If you can do that, I'll make the bridge. Are we in agreement?'

'Fine,' he snapped.

A fortnight later, Andrius strolled in. He gave Nea a cocky look and chucked his jacket onto the floor. She picked it up and hung it on a coat peg. Adrius flopped down on the dental chair. He gave me a toothless grin,

'Right. Bridge, please.'

His insolence was quite breathtaking.

'Okay,' I said. 'To recap. How often are you brushing your teeth?'

'Dunno,' he shrugged. 'Maybe once a week.'

I was confounded. Not even an attempt to lie. Just total arrogance.

'So, no bridge,' I said. 'Instead, a denture.'

'No. I want a bridge.'

'Two weeks ago, you agreed to clean your teeth twice daily otherwise I wouldn't make you a bridge.'

'Yeah, but you do what I say, not what you say.'

'No. I do my job.'

'Yeah, do your job then.'

'I am doing my job,' I said, struggling to keep my patience. 'You are an adult. I gave you the opportunity to have a bridge, but only if you cleaned your teeth twice a day. You made the decision not to clean your teeth. Therefore, you've opted not to have a bridge.'

'Well, I don't think that's fair.'

'Okay,' I shrugged.

'What do you mean *okay*?'

'I mean, it's okay if you don't think it's fair.'

'Eh?' he frowned. 'So, I'm meant to walk around with a gap? You're an evil man!'

'I'm happy to make you a denture. You are highly likely to lose more teeth, so they can be added easily when this happens.'

'No.'

139

'Okay,' I shrugged. Two could play this game of *whatever*.

'So?' he demanded.

'So you've made your choice.' I said.

'I'm not happy about this,' he roared. 'This is fucking out of order.'

'Okay,' I said.

This conversation was going round in circles. Enough!

I stopped engaging. Instead, I turned around and began typing up my notes, all the while ignoring the barrage of abuse being hurled my way. After a while, he went silent. I glanced his way. He was still in the chair, face thunderous.

'You're free to leave,' I said, before turning back to my notes.

He snatched up his coat and stormed out, never to be seen again.

'Well!' Nea gasped.

'I pity the next dentist he visits.'

'Let's hope he *brushes* up on his manners,' she said. 'Brushes up... get it? Because he doesn't brush his teeth!'

'That's *bad*, Nea,' I grinned. '*Really* bad.'

'But not as bad as Andrius's teeth,' she chortled.

❖

Sometimes, I'm lost for words. Sometimes, I don't even bother arguing. It isn't worth it. You won't be able to change someone's opinions.

As dentists, we've all heard the same anecdotes from patients. We've given up trying to dispel the myths. Instead, we give a fake laugh and move on.

The most frequent old chestnut I hear is:

The dentist had to put his knee on my chest to get my tooth out.

This is one hundred percent utter bullshit.

Whenever I hear these words, I mentally roll my eyes, give the fake laugh and then politely explain that extractions are never pulled. They are pushed!

Removing a tooth is all about applying pressure to dilate the space between the root of the tooth and the bone. This allows the tooth to pop out. There is *never* any pulling involved.

Another great one is:

When I got pregnant, the baby sucked all the calcium out of my teeth, and that's why they're full of decay.

Stuff and nonsense!

Once your teeth are formed, nothing can remove minerals from the teeth. Decay happens due to bacteria in the mouth which is then fed by sugar. Acid is produced as a by-product which then breaks down the teeth.

However, one old wives' tale that I'd never heard before was courtesy of a fifty-year-old hypochondriac by the name of Lois Lunabin. She was one of the most eccentric personalities I'd ever encountered.

When I first clapped eyes on Lois, she was sitting in the waiting room with a carpet sample under her feet (you know, those small tiles you take away from shops to ponder whether you like the texture, colour, and so on.)

She spotted my quizzical expression.

'It's for my bad back, chuck,' she explained. 'If I put my feet on it, it helps lessen the pain.'

'I see,' I said, none the wiser.

She followed me into my surgery and took the chair.

'Right, love,' she began. 'I'm here because my last dentist told me I need to have all my teeth out. He also said I needed veneers because I'm grinding. He then quoted fifty thousand pounds for four teeth. I can't bloomin' well afford that! So, can you do it on the NHS, please?'

'Er...'

There was a lot to unpack here. First, I would have been very surprised if such a price had been quoted – unless the dentist had been trying to get rid of her as a patient (quite possible!). Second, regarding veneers, well, that wasn't possible if everything had been extracted!

'Um, why don't we start with a full check-up?' I suggested.

'Okay, chuck,' she agreed. 'But I must warn you. I can't

go back very far in the chair.'

'No worries,' I assured. 'I'll recline you gently. Tell me when to stop.'

I'd barely touched the button when her hand shot up.

'That's far enough.'

Nea and I gave each other *the look*. Lois was still upright.

'Er, I need to put you back a little further.'

'Okay,' she nodded. 'But only a taddy.' She held up a thumb and forefinger by way of demonstration.

Once again, I pressed the button and once again her hand shot up.

'That's... fabulous, Lois,' I said. She'd reclined back by, ooh, a whole five degrees.

I proceeded to do the check-up contorting my back into the most ridiculous and spasmodic of angles. Afterwards, I 'sat' her back up and explained my findings.

'Okay, so you grind your teeth. There's a loss of surface enamel on the front teeth. In terms of repairing them, I could do crowns or build ups. However, these would likely fail without a specialised night-guard. Unfortunately, the NHS doesn't cover cosmetic work, so they won't cover the cost of crowning the teeth. However, the NHS *can* provide you with a protective guard.'

'A *guard*?' she spluttered. 'Oh, dearie me, no. No, no, no! I couldn't put that in my mouth, love.'

'Is that because you have a bad gag reflex?'

'Gag reflex? No, no!' she chortled. 'My husband will tell you that's not the case at all!'

Way too much info, Lois!

'Nah, it's nothing like that.' She shook her head. 'Rather, I can't put plastic in my mouth because that shit causes cancer, love. That's why I don't store food anymore in Tupperware.'

'Er, right. Do you use ceramic bowls then, and store leftovers in the fridge?'

'The *fridge*?' she said incredulously. 'Good God, no way! Refrigerators cause cancer too. I don't use anything like that. I use paper bags and then pop everything in the cupboard.'

Somehow, we'd gone off topic.

'Right, Lois,' I said, attempting to get back to the matter of the cancer-causing plastic guard. 'It would seem that I can't help you.'

'That's orright, love,' she said. 'I'm going to Thailand soon. To a special retreat. I'll ask the Shaman to remineralise the tooth enamel for me.'

'Ah, righty-ho,' I said. 'Good... idea. Best of luck.'

'Thanks, love. See ya!'

And with that, Lois (and her carpet) left the surgery never to be seen again. I looked at Nea.

'Did that really just happen?' I shook my head, flabbergasted. 'Plastic? Fridges? Paper bags? A shaman!'

Nea flashed me a mischievous look.

'What do you call an incredibly insensitive shaman who is also weak and suffers from perio?' (perio is gum disease)

'Uh-oh. Is this another of your terrible jokes?' I rolled my eyes. 'Go on. Tell me.'

'A super callous fragile mystic plagued by halitosis!'

❖

It was never boring working in my locum practice. I can say that with true conviction – although perhaps not always for the best reasons.

One of my most 'exciting' moments (or should that be terrifying?!) was finding myself caught up in some local gang warfare between two filling appointments.

I had just finished Mrs Smith's filling and was bidding her farewell. As she opened the door to leave, she was almost knocked over by a scruffy young man.

'Well *excuse* me!' she snapped, as he shot into my surgery. She slammed the door behind her to convey her annoyance at this guy. He had wild eyes, messy hair, and his clothes were covered in mud. I had no idea who he was. Certainly not a patient! Nea and I regarded him in surprise.

'Er, can I help you?' I ventured.

'Listen, bruv. I gotta hide. They're looking for me.'

'Sorry?'

'Shut it and do me a check-up, bruv.'

And with that, he leapt on the dental chair and snatched the safety specs out of Nea's hand.

'Quick, put the chair back, man!' he said urgently.

I found myself automatically doing his bidding and jettisoned him backwards.

'Are you registered here?' I asked, desperate to gain a sense of normality. 'I need to open your file to do a check-up.'

He waved a hand in frustration.

'I'm Stanley Brown. Now hurry up, bruv.'

Feeling increasingly uneasy, I quickly found Mr Brown in the system and opened up his records. A quick scan of the notes showed he hadn't been for a check-up since the age of fourteen. He was now twenty-one.

I picked up my mirror and started the examination. Midway through charting, there was a furious hammering on the surgery door.

'Come in,' I called.

In bowled another young man. Except this one was holding a small switchblade.

Shit.

My heart rate instantly skyrocketed.

'I'm looking for Stanley,' he said.

'Well, whoever Stanley is, he's not here. Now if you don't mind, I'm in the middle of a patient exam.'

I was amazed at how calm I'd sounded. Mentally I was cacking myself and I didn't dare look at Nea to see how she was holding up.

'Please leave,' I asserted.

'Nah,' said the delinquent, slowly shaking his head. He began to advance towards the chair. 'I think your patient is the man I'm looking for, bruv.'

Stanley instantly rolled sideways and catapulted out of the chair, snatching up the metal tray of instruments alongside him. They flew through the air before clattering down to the floor. The delinquent's knife lunged towards Stanley. He swiftly smacked it away with the metal tray.

Meanwhile I was hemmed in directly behind Stanley, and unable to move. I risked a quick glance at Nea to see how she was coping. Badly, it transpired. Her mouth opened and suddenly she was shrieking her head off. I was in two minds whether to join in!

Fortunately, Nea's screams attracted the attention of other staff in the building. Unfortunately, it also alerted further gang members.

Staff and gang members alike burst into the room as Stanley and the delinquent proceeded to engage in a messily choreographed knife-and-tray scenario.

'Call the police!' I shouted to no one in particular.

I didn't dare take my eyes off the violent tango going on in front of me. All my concentration was on keeping out of the way, frantically ducking and side-stepping like an out of time salsa dancer.

I have no idea what happened next. I think shock and adrenaline had kicked in because suddenly Nea and I were out of the room leaving the entire gang going for each other.

The police swiftly arrived and restrained the rival gangs by snapping them all into handcuffs. Patients were agog in the waiting room. One of the officers took me to one side.

'What happened?' he asked.

'I-I don't really know,' I stuttered. 'Stanley burst into my surgery, demanded a check-up, and then the other fella came in with a knife, and the rest is a blur.'

'Right,' he nodded. 'These are two warring gangs. They've been fighting for weeks. It's all over tagging each other's turf. It's rather unusual for it to come to a head in a dental practice,' he snorted. 'Anyway, I'll need a statement from you and your nurse.'

Nea and I complied and did the necessary paperwork with the officer. I also cancelled my clinic for the rest of the day. After that bit of drama, I needed a bloody stiff drink.

Like I said, working in my locum practice was never boring and by the end of my time there, I'd met the local police force several times over!

When **I was a locum,** I was in my twenties. I ended up growing a beard because people kept asking if I was old enough to be a dentist – which implied I either looked inexperienced or was inept! The beard did help, but I still found myself on the occasional receiving end of comments.

One such patient was a cantankerous sixty-something by the name of Owen Peterson. He'd been the patient of another dentist at the practice but hadn't liked what she'd had to say. He rejected her clinical diagnoses on the grounds of her being unqualified to give him advice!

Cue reception booking him in for a second opinion with the youngest dentist in the practice. Yup. Me!

Mr Peterson entered my surgery and hobbled over to the chair. He sat down. He ignored my greetings and pleasantries.

'I saw that Jan dentist,' was his opening gambit. 'She was bloody awful. She told me I needed three extractions. I was *not* happy.'

'I'm sorry to hear that,' I replied.

'And so you should be,' said the charmless Owen. 'Now then. You look very young. Do you know what you're doing?'

'I should hope so.'

'In which case, I want you to save the teeth that Jan said needed extracting.'

'Why don't we start with me having a look in the mouth and reviewing the x-rays. Would that be okay?'

'I suppose so,' said Owen grumpily.

I popped him back in the chair and had a look at the car-crash that was his mouth. Jan had been right. In other words, *everything* was fucked.

I hummed and hawed, as if considering, then sat Mr Peterson back up. I reached for the x-rays that Jan had taken. There were huge holes through the roots of three teeth. They looked like trees about to be felled while someone shouted *TIMBERRRRRRR*! There was no

146

question of being able to save any of them.

'Did Jan show you the x-rays?' I asked.

'No. She merely said I needed three extractions. And I am NOT having those teeth out.'

'Okay. Can I show them to you?'

'I guess so, yes.'

So, I showed the grumpy Owen Peterson his pictures, explaining that the shadows were holes and infection was at the end of the roots. I explained that the teeth would likely soon fracture and advised what replacement options were available if the teeth were removed. I said he could leave them alone, but they would likely break within six months. By the end of the appointment, he'd somewhat calmed down but wasn't budging over extraction.

'I shall leave them until they break and then return for treatment.'

'That's fine. Give us a call when you're ready.'

'Can I ask – do you do this without supervision?'

'You mean dentistry?' I frowned.

'Yes.'

'Well, I have my nurse working alongside me,' I joked.

'Ah ha!' said Owen, having some sort of lightbulb moment. 'Your nurse keeps tabs on you. That makes sense. That said, you are very clear and concise for a student.'

Nea sniggered.

'I'm not a student, Mr Peterson,' I said gravely.

'Really? So... newly qualified?'

'Nope.' I shook my head. 'I qualified more than five years ago. In fact, you're talking to an implant surgeon.'

'You can't be,' Owen spluttered. 'You don't look old enough to have hairs on your chest, boy!'

'I'll take that as a compliment,' I said lightly, although actually I was starting to feel a taddy miffed. A little bit offended. Sometimes I was annoyed at not being taken seriously, and today was one of those days. In fact, I just wanted this old man to leave my surgery!

'Right, I'll be off,' he said, creaking upright.

'All the best,' I said.

A second later Owen Peterson had gone.

'Do you want a cuppa?' Nea asked.

'Yes, please,' I said.

She had a mischievous look on her face.

'Come with me. I'll teach you how to boil the kettle. You don't look old enough to do it without supervision!' she teased.

I rolled my eyes.

Obviously, I'm a few years older now and my face has (thankfully?) aged a little. To be honest, I was more upset when I stopped getting ID checked for buying alcohol, than when patients ceased assuming I wasn't qualified.

❖

Building bridges is better than burning them. Now that is some stellar advice! I definitely built some excellent bridges while working at this locum practice. Even later, when I went fully private elsewhere, I always had the offer to go back for a few sessions at this practice. I appreciated this. Especially when times got tough – and sometimes they did. After all, contrary to popular belief, dentists don't drive around in Porsches or jet off to the sun every other weekend.

I learnt many lessons being a locum. I think the most important one was how to say no, and to stand my ground.

I discovered how lucky I was to have had a mum who supervised my own teeth cleaning and regularly took me to the dentist.

I discovered my sense of self-worth - having worked in some truly awful places over the years where I was treated like shit.

It was refreshing to now be called upon and be told, "I know I can count on *you* to deliver the targets."

During this time, I learnt how to work quickly and effectively. I now understood some major truths about the healthcare system. Primarily, Government would prefer to turn a blind eye to a broken system with no real intention to fix.

A locum's work schedule is fast-paced, tricky and exhausting. Despite that, I look back on that time with fondness. I made lots of wonderful friends and many of those friendships stood the test of time. Indeed, years later, some were guests at my wedding.

Being a locum provided a sense of ease. Of not having to worry about the work you were doing. There was something almost soothing in those rhythmical drill-and-fill days.

A locum is the one who plugs a hole in a sinking ship. That ship is NHS dentistry. It is still sinking. However, the locum slows that sinking *dramatically*.

For anyone considering being a locum, the only thing I would flag up is the risk versus reward considerations. As a locum, you can be let go with just one week's notice (whereas a permanent dentist's notice period is three months). As a locum, you often find yourself drifting from one place to another, never fully settled, never fully being *yourself* with the staff, because you know that soon you'll leave.

When I stayed at this high-needs area as a locum for more than two years, I thought they would never let me go. They were so far behind on targets. They *needed* me, not the other way around. Life has a funny way of correcting such conceptions!

6

Covid Strikes

In late December, a headline from the Telegraph dominated our work-place discussions: *Mysterious Pneumonia-Like Illness Cases in Wuhan Emerge as Health Officials Investigate.*

One of my colleagues read the article to us.

'It sounds like that iPhone game,' he said. 'You know, where you have to try and get a disease to spread across the world before humanity cures it.'

'You're right,' I nodded. 'That's rather scary.'

'I don't think it'll ever happen in real life,' he chuckled. 'Don't worry about it.'

Famous last words. The following months saw the first case arrive in the US combined with China going into lockdown, all airplane travel ceasing and global markets crashing.

Then the rumours started. There were whispers of an imminent lockdown in the UK. Patients had started to ask if we were going to remain open and if we knew things that they didn't. We didn't know anything. Something felt fundamentally wrong. I had a sense of foreboding. My stomach had a constant knot in it, as I fretted and worried about what may or may not happen.

The UK Government kept the country open until 23rd March 2019. On this day three things happened:

1. Prime Minister ~~Bumbling~~ Boris Johnson announced we should ~~go to work~~ stay at home and the first lockdown got underway.

2. The CQC (Care Quality Commission – a UK agency

with Godlike ambitions) announced that dental practices should close and focus only on tele-diagnostics (emergency care via the telephone only).
3. I received a termination notice from my locum practice that read:

Unfortunately, I am serving you one week's notice for locum services. I hope this is not a permanent measure. However, only a skeleton staff and emergency clinic will be running. When we are once again fully operational, we will reinstate your contract. This will change week by week depending on NHS England guidelines. I will keep in touch. Sincere apologies.

A part of me had known this was coming, but it was still a blow.

When non-locum colleagues had previously moaned about my day rate being better paid them, I'd always reminded them of the pitfalls and risks of not being a permanent member of staff.

They'd given me all the replies. Like:

'Risks? *What* risks?'

And:

'They'll never close NHS dentistry!'

And:

'There's always a shortage of dentists. It'll never happen.'

Ha! Just goes to show that you never know what's lurking around the corner.

I had always balanced what I perceived as locum risks by working three days a week as a permanent (associate) dentist at Paul Slater's practice. But, if the CQC closed dental practices then how would I earn any income at all? Remember, dentists are self-employed. No work, no pay!

It's a funny old world. You work your arse off. Long for the day you can take a break. Hopefully go on holiday. Retire.

But when you're *forced* to stop, the reality is so different. It's anxiety provoking, stressful and unnatural. Perhaps, as humans, we are conditioned to work and be target/goal driven.

I think it is the balance of work and relaxation that makes the time off so treasured. For me, not working takes me out of balance. It isn't remotely relaxing. Rather, it's totally stress inducing.

So, this section of my book is about my experience of the pandemic. It's from a dental point of view, and from that aspect gives all the crazy stuff that happened as a result of Covid.

❖

Numb. **Panic. Despair.** Those were the initial sensations that I felt upon reading the termination email. Meanwhile, over at Paul Slater's practice, our WhatsApp Group Chat was going berserk.

'Paul what are we doing?? Are we coming to work tomorrow?' One of the associates asked.

'What about us nurses, are we still going to get paid?!'

'Guys, we need some calm' Paul typed, 'For now, everyone come in tomorrow and we will have to maintain an emergency service via telephones only.'

I looked at my partner and just started crying.

'How are we going to pay the mortgage?' I asked,

'It'll be ok, look, let's call the mortgage company and ask for a holiday.'

'But what about all the other bills? If I'm not earning anything, we're fucked!'

'Breathe,' said my partner. 'Somehow we will muddle through.'

Together we went through the finances, every loan went onto a holiday (car, mortgage, etc) and cancelled absolutely everything that wasn't necessary (gym, Netflix, Prime, etc)

I then scoured the internet for a job. Any job. I applied for anything and everything that I could realistically do – a hospital cleaner, a supermarket worker, a pharmacy assistant, an administrator – you name it. I sent my CV to hundreds of places. All were met with silence or rejections as they were flooded with people all doing the same.

To make matters worse, I had a family member who was a conspiracy theorist. In other words, a nutcase. I was bombarded with messages. Covid was simply a nasty cold. That the vaccine would give you a microchip… and also HIV. Oh, and that it had been invented to cull the population. However, good news. You could avoid Covid by howling at the moon with an onion stuffed up your bum and then dancing to Barbra Streisand singing *Enough is Enough*.

Family fruitcakes aside, it was a time of great turmoil, uncertainty and dark clouds. For dentistry, it personally felt like a backward journey and return to the dark-ages. For NHS dentistry, it was the final nail in the coffin of a truly fucked up system.

❖

Paul Slater had contacts within the NHS system. And sometimes, it really is all about *who* you know and not *what* you know.

He ensured that his practice was highlighted to LAT (the Local Area Team – which consisting of people who distribute funds/contracts in a certain area).

However, let's go back a moment. In the beginning, no one knew what was going to happen. We were told to go to work. So we did. But then what?

The reception team were kept busy on the phones, cancelling the next four weeks' worth of appointments, listening to a ton of abuse and having to apologise profusely.

The nurses (employed) were put to work organising the filing systems and clinical records. But what to do with the dentists?

That morning, Paul called the dentists into a private meeting where he explained his plan to move forward.

'Right,' he said, throwing his hands in the air. 'I don't have a bloody clue about what's going to happen. I know you're all self-employed, but I have no idea how to pay you to work here. Hopefully we will get some guidance from the NHS. Until then, sit tight and help me set us up as an emergency dental service.'

'So, we won't get paid?' someone asked,

'Not immediately, no,' he said. 'But when the NHS gives us an update, hopefully anything owed will be given out as back pay.'

'What exactly will this emergency service provide?' I asked. 'I'm confused, because currently we aren't even allowed to see patients.'

'To start with, the receptionists will screen calls. If someone is in pain, their details will be passed over to one of you guys. It will be a rota basis – to triage and give advice, also prescribe antibiotics to help with pain.'

And so it was. The first two weeks were triages and dish out antibiotics like smarties, often knowing that they would so sod-all to help the pain. Indeed, the CQC issued an amnesty on antimicrobial resistance and basically said give everyone antibiotics!

During my time on triage, I was on the receiving end of much swearing and verbal abuse.

'I'm in fucking agony,' screeched one caller. 'I've got fucking toothache so why the fuck won't you see me?'

'Because we are not allowed,' I explained.

'You're a fucking prick, you know that?'

Cheers mate.

There was an awful lot of such diatribe during the early days of the pandemic. Unfortunately, the Government had closed everything without properly considering healthcare. At that point, there was no plan for dentists to help the nation's toothaches.

Within a month, designated dental emergency centres were set up. These were normal dental practices that had managed to get the local area team (LAT) to allow them to see patients.

There were perhaps four or five centres per county, meaning that some patients had to travel two hours to get to a centre.

Guidelines were issued on a local basis. Some of it was

ridiculous. Like, *a patient must have had two failed courses of antibiotics and had no relief from pain to be seen at an emergency centre.*

As a dentist, I knew antibiotics would not fix many of the issues we were triaging. A patient with decay into the nerve and severe lingering sensitivity was not going to respond to antibiotics because it was *not* an infection. It was the nerve dying. Yet, we still had to prescribe antibiotics knowing full well it would do fuck all.

The profession was tipping into anarchy.

❖

In the early months of being an emergency centre, we eventually started seeing patients again.

However, most other practices were not able to do this. Instead, they had to send referrals over to us that we then triaged and booked in.

New guidelines on *fallow* time came into effect. Basically this meant that, after treating a patient, the surgery could not be used again for another hour (although this was later changed and only occurred after an aerosol-generating procedure, like drilling).

These timings meant that clinic slots were severely limited. It reduced patient capacity to a maximum number of twenty per day across a four-surgery practice (versus the normal one hundred or more that we would've otherwise seen).

Furthermore, adequate PPE (personal protective equipment) was not available. There was a national shortage. At the time, all PPE was being used in hospitals. This meant that we were NOT allowed to drill because it generated an aerosol that could *potentially* spread to the dentists and pass on Covid. So, if someone had a toothache, and the dentist couldn't drill, what options were left? Endure the pain or extract!

As I said earlier, those months felt like a return to the dark ages. Extracting teeth that could otherwise have been saved simply because we hadn't been provided with

PPE was almost soul-destroying.

Dentists are trained to save teeth. To prevent disease. To minimise disability from tooth loss. Yet here we were taking out teeth that could have so easily been saved.

For the patients who lost front teeth, we couldn't even provide dentures or bridgeworks, because it was emergency treatment only. It went against all our training.

Oh, and at this point, we still didn't know if we would ever get paid for the work we were doing. We were, effectively, working for free and hoping that we would be remunerated at some point.

Eventually, the NHS made an announcement. It would pay all NHS dentists (not locums) at eighty percent of their normal contract on the proviso they continued their triages services.

We all knew we'd be fucked over when we came out of Covid but, for now, we took our payments and did the best we could.

Eventually, we were sent some PPE. I remember receiving a single box of protective equipment. It included a bright red hazmat suit that covered you from head to toe (except your face), along with some FFP3 paper masks (that contained a filter to stop viral particles from entering). They were *six years* past their date of use stamp.

I'm not quite sure how a mask deteriorates. According to Dr Google, air, light and moisture can affect the integrity of the filter qualities after the expiration date. Anyway, onward.

The good thing was that we could finally start saving teeth and picking up our drills (even if we had to leave the room afterwards for an hour). It was almost too good to be true.

We started booking patients in for AGPs (aerosol generating procedures such as root canal treatments, fillings, and so on). Our joy was short lived.

Three days later, the NHS demanded this single box of PPE to be returned. Apparently, it was required for more essential services!

Eventually, practices took matters into their own hands. They ordered reusable FFP3-esque masks that were available at places like B&Q for non-healthcare environments (e.g. builders who came into contact with debris/dust particles etc) and plastic gowns that could be donned as necessary.

Practices were forced to invest in special ventilation systems that helped decrease the original hour of fallow time.

All of this came out of the pockets of the business owners, not from the NHS. The pure disregard that the Government had for NHS dentistry became ever more evident throughout this time. Indeed, it was one of the driving factors in me leaving NHS dental care. Why was I working so hard trying to help people when the Government didn't give a shit about me and *my* health, never mind my patients and the entirety of dentistry?

It was at this point I made a plan: get through the pandemic then get out of the NHS.

❖

Despite making this decision, there were still some light hearted moments along the NHS path. Nothing hysterical. No crazy patient stories. No laugh-out-loud moments. Instead, genuine warmth and pleasure in simple things.

The isolation of Covid, the reduction in working days, the inability to go out, meant that moments with work colleagues became one's social life.

Going to work and being able to chat, have a laugh, and forget about the world outside the surgery walls, suddenly felt so amazing.

Like most workplaces, we had weekly Zoom quizzes (do you remember those?). Also, because the weather was *so* wonderfully dry and sunny during that time, we'd enjoy outdoor lunches, or webcam chats from our respective gardens, and always with a little tipple (although never in work hours)!

We laughed about how terrifying we looked dressed in huge gowns with accessorised ventilator masks, like some sort of Victorian plague doctor. The hours of fallow time gave us all a chance to chill and have a good chinwag over a cup of tea.

In between the stress of losing a job, and the struggles of making ends meet, there was also hope, warmth, rest and reset.

After six weeks of trying and failing to secure any sort of extra work, I had resigned myself to the job loss and spent the free time drawing, lazing in the sun and putting on weight! At the end of the final lockdown, I was the heaviest I'd ever been, having put on some thirty-five pounds!

❖

Tele-dentistry became the norm during the pandemic. This involved telephone calls, Zoom-based consultations and a whole lot of very blurry pictures of the mouth and teeth taken by iPhone cameras.

I was currently working through a triage list of thirty patients. I paused to look through the window, appreciating the glorious sunshine filtering through the trees and freckling the pavement. The world was still outside, but it was different. I could hear beautiful bird song that would otherwise have been drowned out by traffic. The scene was idyllic. I sighed with contentment, then turned back to the computer.

My next patient was Mrs Anne Smith, a forty-six-year-old woman complaining of a broken tooth and pain. I picked up the phone.

'Hello,' I said. 'I'm responding to your request to see an emergency dentist. This is your triage phone call.'

'Oh, yes, hello! Thanks for calling me. Okay, I have this tooth that's so sharp, it's cutting my tongue to buggery.'

I resisted typing *tooth performing buggery*.

'Can I first confirm I'm speaking to Mrs Anne Smith, and

that your date of birth is the thirteenth of February?'

'Yes, and yes.'

'Perfect. So, tell me more about this tooth.'

'Well, it's really sharp. It's one of the back molars on the lower left side. It broke two days ago. I can't eat without it cutting my cheek. I now have a huge ulcer and am living on Bonjela.'

'That sounds very uncomfortable,' I sympathized. 'Do you have any toothache, like sensitivity to hot or cold, or any deep throbbing, in addition to the tooth cutting the cheek?'

'No toothache. Just ulceration.'

'Do you have Zoom on your computer or phone so I can take a look at the tooth?'

'Yes,' Mrs Smith confirmed.

These were the days when many of us stayed in pyjamas because we had nowhere to go. So when Mrs Smith and I connected on Zoom, I wasn't too surprised at what I saw, although Mrs Smith was oblivious to the fact that I could see her sitting there in her bra and knickers.

'Hello again, Anne. Could you use your phone's torch to show me the broken tooth, please?'

'Of course,' she said.

Mrs Smith leant forward giving me a screenful of ample cleavage but none of her mouth.

'Er, I think you need to adjust the camera.'

'Oh dear, sorry,' she apologised.

She said as she repositioned the camera to her mouth instead of her boobs. A dark cavern blurred into view, with a few strands of green vegetation (what I assumed may be rogue spinach) between some of the molars.

'Can you put the torch on?'

'Bugger,' she swore. 'I don't think I can do both. Hold on, love. Let me get my husband. JOHN!' she bellowed. 'JOHN, LOVE! COME AND HELP ME!'

I waited, hoping that John wouldn't appear in *his* bra and knickers. Luckily for me, he was wearing a string vest and shorts.

'John, love,' Anne continued. 'Hold this camera and help the dentist see my broken tooth.'

John duly obliged and brought the problematic tooth into stunning HD. Anne had fractured her first molar. It didn't look like there was any decay present, although it was hard to be sure over a Zoom call.

'Thank you, both,' I said. 'Okay, Anne. So, what I need you to do as a first point of call is smooth that rough edge off with either a nail file or emery board. I'd also like you to pop in on your local chemist and ask for some temporary dental filling material. You can roll this with your fingers and pack it into the crack to stop it being so sharp. If that fails, we may be able to bring you in to smooth it, but we won't be able to properly repair the tooth at the current time due to the guidelines in place.

'Okay, love,' she said cheerfully. 'I'll give it a go.'

'No problem,' I said. 'Have a good day.'

With that, Anne stood up and turned to her husband, at the same time revealing the back of her pants. They were completely transparent and revealed a different type of crack.

I quickly ended the Zoom call and decided now was a good a time as any for a strong black coffee.

❖

Large plastic shields were erected at reception to protect the staff from spittle.

Patients were not allowed into the building. They had to text the practice upon arrival and then sit and wait in their cars. When ready to be seen, a nurse would come to the front door in full PPE. This included a gown, FFP3 fighter-jet-style mask, plastic visor, scrub hat and goggles. The patient would then put on their own face covering and be rapidly escorted into the dentist's surgery.

Here, a large orange extractor funnel was ready to suck all aerosols from the room via an angled chute which was positioned by an open window. This was to minimise Covid transmission.

Ms Regina Connaught, a sixty-three-year-old female,

arrived for her emergency appointment at our Urgent Dental Care Hub (UDC). She was in agony. Indeed, had been for weeks. She hadn't slept in days and was desperate for some relief.

All of this had been recorded on the written referral received from another dentist. My nurse went to collect her and Regina – like everyone else – had to follow the same protocol as she was escorted in. If she wasn't nervous before, she sure as hell was when I gave her a muffled greeting from behind my PPE.

'Hello, Ms Connaught. Please, take a seat.' I indicated the dental chair. She looked at it and sat down. 'I understand you're having some trouble.'

'Sorry?' she frowned.

'You're having some trouble?' I repeated.

Regina looked at my nurse, who repeated the same question, but more loudly. Regina continued to look blank. It was then that I realised Regina was deaf and relied upon lip reading, which was impossible behind three layers of protective equipment.

'WHAT TROUBLE ARE YOU HAVING?' I yelled.

'Er, I'm here for an emergency appointment,' Regina ventured.

This was hopeless. I looked at my nurse. Carly shrugged.

'WHERE IS THE PAIN?' I shouted.

'My name? It's Regina Connaught.'

Oh, for fuck's sake.

'WHERE DOES IT HURT?' I bellowed.

'My skirt? I'm here about a toothache, not to discuss my clothing,' Regina snapped. 'Now can I tell you about the pain or not?' she said testily.

Hallelujah!

I gave her a thumbs up, whereupon she pointed to her upper left molar.

'It broke a month ago. I tried to fill it temporarily, but now I'm in agony. I can't sleep. It's constantly throbbing. I can't even have a cup of tea without it feeling like it's going to explode!'

Progress! I knew immediately that this was pulpitis

(the nerve of the tooth being inflamed and likely dying). I picked up an x-ray film and holder, showed them to her and mimed taking a picture.

'I'm not slow,' she said testily. 'Just say what you want to do!'

'X-RAY!' I hollered.

'Yes, yes, if you must,' she said fussily.

I wasn't sure if she'd understood, but somehow we muddled through and got a picture of her tooth. It showed decay right into the nerve, confirming what I'd suspected. Treatment was either root canal or extraction. I showed her the x-ray.

'The nerve in your tooth is dying,' I explained.

'I'm sorry, but I can't hear what you're saying. I didn't put my hearing aids in because my mask's ties pull them out.'

Okay*yyy*.

'NERVE,' I pointed. 'DYING,' I shouted.

'Oh,' she said. 'What can be done about it?'

My nurse found a pen and some paper, and I wrote out the treatment options. Regina was initially perplexed at my note, but no way was I going to attempt to explain the pros and cons of root canal at a million decibels.

'Yes,' she agreed, after reading the information. 'Let's take out the nerve today. I don't want to lose the tooth.'

'Great,' I said.

'What?'

Carly gave an imperceptible shake of the head as she handed me the anaesthetic. Luckily, the rest of the appointment didn't require too much talking.

When it was over, I tried explaining the tooth might be sore when the anaesthetic wore off but got the same blank expression. I resorted to typing up post-op instructions and printing them off.

The point of this story is to demonstrate how hard it was to communicate with patients, especially those with additional needs.

As the pandemic progressed, there were times when I completely gave up on the PPE, ripped off the mask and spoke face to face with the patient. There was only so much you could really do with all that clobber on.

❖

Temporomandibular joint dysfunction (TMD or TMJD - take your pick) was something that ran rife throughout the Covid period.

So, what is it? Well, it's a jaw-joint pain that is usually related to clenching and/or grinding. It is often muscle related (because the muscles are over-used) but it can also be multi-factoral and include skeletal problems (like arthritis), disc problems (the bit between the upper and lower jaws), occlusal issues (to do with your 'bite') and so on.

Often, a panicking patient squawks, 'Omigod! I HAVE TMJ!'

I refrain from answering that we all do! They are literally telling me that they have a jaw joint.

What they really mean is *TMJ pain* or *dysfunction*.

Anyway, dear reader, I've gone off topic. Back to the Covid years!

During this time, the incidence of pain related to clenching/grinding skyrocketed. I think many people were stressed out by the isolation that Covid brought. After all, human beings are social beings.

I remember one patient, Sally Wafflemire, who attended our UDC complaining of pain. She was a very prim-and-proper woman who, at forty-one, seemed far older than her years. She turned up wearing a formal skirt down to her ankles (as if to hide any flash of flesh). Her hair was pulled into the tightest bun with not one loose strand. Perched upon her nose were a distinctly old-fashioned pair of spectacles. I was instantly reminded of a Victorian schoolteacher.

She perched upon the dental chair side on, reminding me of a female horse rider sitting aside rather than astride.

'Right,' she declared. 'I have a toothache. It's in the upper right region. Fix it, please.'

Oh, wow, right into it, I privately thought.

163

'Of course. What sort of pain is it? Dull? Sharp? Shooting? And does anything make it better or worse?'

'It's a *toothache* pain,' she said. Her tone implied that I'd asked a stupid question.

'I understand, but need to know *what* does the pain feel like?'

She considered for a moment.

'A dull, aching pain.'

Hurrah!

'Does anything make it better or worse? Hot? Cold?'

'No. It's just *there*. All the time.'

'Is it worse at any particular time of the day?'

'Yes, in the morning, when I first get up. It then eases a little throughout the day. In fact, it often feels like it's moving to the back of my head.'

There was a huge clue in those last words – pain radiating away from the teeth and into the jaw/back of head, along with being worse first thing in the morning. In other words, after a night of gritting her teeth like a crocodile clamping its chops together.

'Okay, let me take a look. I'll also do an x-ray to check the teeth and work out what's happening.'

I did my due diligence. Checked the teeth. There was no breakdown. No fillings. Immaculate cleaning. Nothing was tender when tapped. No swelling. No raised lymph nodes. I took an x-ray to check there was no decay. There was none.

'Your teeth are in excellent condition,' I announced.

'But they can't be,' she said. 'After all, I have a toothache.'

'I understand. However, I don't think the problem is tooth-related. Rather, it's muscular.'

I was half-expecting Ms Wafflemire to sternly reprimand me and tell me I was wrong. However, she was silent.

'Let me demonstrate what I mean,' I said.

I slipped my gloved finger against her upper right molar, cheek-side. I then asked her to bite down hard (my finger was safely tucked to the side of the tooth). As she did so, I felt a hugely enlarged muscle press against my finger. Her response was immediate.

'O*www*!' she screeched.

'Is that the pain you've been experiencing?' I asked.

'Yes,' she said, massaging her cheek. 'That really hurt.'

'Have you recently been under any increased stress?'

'Who hasn't?' she quavered. 'Thanks to Covid, I've lost my job. I have no income. To top it all off I'm stuck in a small maisonette virtually twenty-four-seven.'

'I completely understand. This pain is very common. I suspect you're subconsciously clenching or grinding your teeth, which becomes worse at nighttime.'

'It can't be!' she protested. 'It must be a toothache.'

'Would you like me to test the muscles again?' I asked.

She considered for a moment, then shook her head.

'No. No, it's okay. I think you might be right.'

'I am,' I smiled gently. 'On the upside, there's a few things that can help.'

I then provided Ms Wafflemire with some physio exercises along with information on self-made night guards (unfortunately our labs were closed due to Covid). I also advised that she may need to return for a more heavy-duty solution when everywhere had reopened.

Ms Wafflemire stood up, her body tense. Misery was etched upon her face. Wrapping her skirt around her like a scarf, she then took herself off without so much as a thank you or goodbye.

'You're welcome,' said my nurse sarcastically, after Ms Wafflemire had departed.

'Now, now, Carly,' I murmured. 'Tea?'

'Always,' she replied.

❖

Throughout the pandemic, the Chief Dental Officer (CDO) was about as effectual as a chocolate teapot.

At such a time like this one, we needed strong leadership, direction and certainty. However, the CDO seemed to be missing in action.

Indeed, if you now read the press releases and interviews from this period, it sounds like CDO was a strong and pioneering figurehead. It wasn't like that. It was chaotic. A bun fight. No one knew anything. There was no certainty of being paid, or when we would reopen, or how to properly help patients. Every county had its own procedures and guidelines on how to get seen at these urgent hubs which fuelled the confusion and utter mess.

There talk of being paid a pittance and being redeployed into Covid hospitals as an auxiliary. There wasn't enough PPE for dental practices to stay open, so nobody quite understood the rhyme or reason behind the suggestion of sending dental staff into hospitals to treat Covid patients in a non-dental environment!

As I write this section, NHS dentistry is frequently making the headlines. A recent report by the Nuffield Trust claims that NHS dentistry is on the brink of collapse. Also, it will unlikely ever be saved due to the huge cost involved.

NHS dentistry has been completely underfunded by successive governments. It started with the design of the UDA system by Labour, then the successive reduction in investment by both Labour and the Conservatives.

However, I'm not about to wax lyrical about politics! You may vote, and if you choose to do so, then you must choose the better of two devils – but it's still a devil regardless.

During the pandemic, dentists were completely demoralised. We witnessed firsthand how little we were thought of in the NHS system, indeed initially working without pay.

This despair was compounded, at the time, by the country's chancellor who waggled a finger to camera and sternly told the self-employed to *pay their fair share of tax.*

Oh yeah? Well, we needed *paying* first, matey, in order to generate some money to give you your tax!

I went home. Resisted the urge to kick the door. Instead, I thought, *why the fuck am I in this profession?*

Indeed, when practices started to re-open, I knew it

was my time to go. I was working in a system that basically meant private dentistry subsidised NHS patients. You had to work at the speed of light or be financially penalised and earn less than the minimum wage per hour. Between the NHS and the Government, you were not regarded as a highly skilled medical professional, but rather a cheap commodity that could be squeezed and squeezed until there was nothing left.

This is why I eventually left the NHS and integrated into fully private dentistry. The pandemic shone a bright torch on NHS dentistry and revealed some dark corners. Indeed, if you look at the statistics around that time, you'll see that thousands of dentists quit their jobs and swathes of practices handed their NHS contracts back. Dental associates (in other words, workers like me) departed from the NHS all together.

❖

I **handed in my notice to Paul Slater in the January of 2021.** Before I handed my notice in, I had spoken to Paul. I had explained that I had discovered that the other dentists were actually on a higher pay than myself (despite being there less time than me). I asked if I could have my rate raised to be in line with them. I was told that now wasn't the time as there were still some Covid restrictions in place. I had invested several thousand pounds in an implant degree to provide this treatment at Paul's practice. I discussed the costs of the equipment and whether he'd look at investing in it (as it was nearly £7000). He declined. I then asked if I invested in it, could we change the split of costs until I had paid of this loan (e.g. any implants provided, I could take 60% of the profit instead of 50%). He declined.

I realised that there was no future at Paul's practice. I'd worked there for five years. Slaved away. Been taken advantage of along the way. There was no investment. No development opportunities. No furthering of experience. It was simply a drill-and-fill conveyor belt practice. He gave me a distinct vibe of *don't rock the boat*. Well, sorry. I wasn't going to rock the boat. I was going to completely capsize it.

It wasn't just Paul's apathy that led me to look for a new job. As I said, when the Government metaphorically put a middle finger up at NHS dentists during the pandemic, I'd already started thinking about leaving the NHS.

These two events eventually collided, culminating in me finally making the decision to go.

I approached several private practices with a revamped CV and portfolio of my dental work.

I received interest from a fully private practice. The principal's name was Frederick ~~Fartbox~~ Farbrow. He interviewed me, said he was impressed, and offered me a job between two of his clinics. We discussed terms. They seemed favourable. An email confirmed everything, and it was at this point I handed in my notice.

'What can I do to change your mind?' asked Paul.

'Nothing, unfortunately,' I said. 'I think this is a good opportunity to further develop. The job is closer to home. Also, there is mentorship available for implantology.'

I'm going to leave your place on good terms, I silently said. *I shall not tell you that your lack of investment was fundamental in driving me away.*

'I see. Are you sure? I could increase your rate.'

'No, unfortunately. I've made my decision. I think it's for the best in the long-term.'

'Okay,' Paul sighed. 'Well, this is all rather disappointing. After all, you've been here a considerable time. I'd ask that you stay until the end of the tax year, if you don't mind. Also, that you don't tell patients you're leaving.'

I agreed.

And so the three month notice period began.

A month later, I still hadn't received any contract from Freddy Fartbox, so chased him by both email and text.

He did finally send the contract some six weeks into my notice period. At this point I should mention that every contract is a *service user agreement* - not an employment contract (because we are self-employed). Therefore, such documents should be checked carefully.

The BDA (British Dental Association) offers such service, checking contracts. So, I sent mine off and they looked through it. It was returned a week later with the advice not to sign.

They had highlighted multiple issues hidden in wordiness which included:

...that if you take a day off, you are liable to pay the practice five hundred pounds for each day taken;

... that if you take more than a week off, then the practice can replace you without any notice;

... that if a patient refused to pay, you were *entirely* responsible for coughing up the shortfall (in addition to having done the work for free!).

I could go on. But won't.

Instead, I called Mr Farty to discuss the points the BDA had raised. I could hear the shrug in his voice.

'That's the contract,' he said. 'Take it or leave it.'

Oh fuck, was my initial reaction. *What the hell have I done?*

A million similar thoughts whooshed through my head in that moment. I'd got ahead of myself. I should have waited. I'd leapt from the frying pan to the fire. I shouldn't have been so impulsive about handing in my notice. Shouldn't have handed it in AT ALL!

But... but... I'd so wanted to get out of an unhappy situation.

'If there's no room for discussion or negotiation' – I sounded far braver than I felt – 'then I won't be able to proceed.'

'Your loss,' snapped Mr Blowoff.

The line went dead.

Terrific. Not.

This time, there was no panic. I'd chosen to leave Paul's. There was no going back. There was only looking forward.

I took a deep breath, sat down, booted up my laptop and got emailing. My CV and portfolio was sent off to six local private practices with a covering email. Twenty-four hours later, I had five interviews lined up. The following week, I received five offers. I was elated!

I got the best vibe from a principal by the name of Mr Thomas Green. His practice had become fully private in the last eighteen months. He'd previously had a small NHS contract but had handed it back when the Covid restrictions had destroyed patient care.

Thomas was a tall, slightly awkward chap. At interview, he offered me the job there and then. As an experienced implantologist, he offered mentorship and help with cases. The pay rate was slightly more aggressive and weighted in the practice's favour. Nonetheless, I had a positive vibe about Mr Green and his practice.

I didn't immediately accept the job. I explained that I'd received other offers and wanted to think carefully as it was an important decision.

Thomas understood. He asked if there was anything he could do to seal the deal. I reassured him that I was interested, but also wanted to discuss things with my partner before making any final decision.

I went home, told my partner all about it, weighed everything up, and decided to go for it. I then formally accepted the job at Thomas Green's practice and can say it was a great decision.

If you've read this far, dear reader, I'd like to say thank you. Covid was a bit of a heavy topic.

In my next section, you'll be pleased to instead read some entertaining stories about loony patients and the realities of private healthcare. So, stay tuned and let's continue the journey together.

7

Private Dentistry

In April 2021, I started working for Mr Thomas Green at the Marigold Dental Practice.

I don't know why, but I remember feeling very nervous. Maybe it was because there was a lot more pressure. Perhaps it was also because fully transitioning to private healthcare seemed such a big step.

In those first few months, I felt inadequate. It's hard to explain. Like... the work wasn't to the same standard as the other three dentists already there.

Also, I had big boots to fill. I was replacing a sixty-year-old dentist who'd previously owned the practice, whereas I was a fresh-faced dentist in my late twenties. It was a stark comparison.

So many patients asked if this was my first job... if I was a student... if I was on work experience... if I was the son of the retired dentist... if I knew what I was doing (oh, please, not again!). Such comments didn't exactly help my confidence.

Despite feeling this wobble of uncertainty, I never showed it. These were internal battles. Sometimes, inside my head, it'd be like the building was burning down and I'd be freaking out, but to the outside world I presented myself calmly, like an actor confidently taking the stage, performing without hesitation or any apparent worry.

I think a lot of dentists sometimes suffer from this. It's called *Imposter Syndrome*. This is exactly how I felt, probably for the first year of my career in private care. Worrying that at any moment, Thomas would say this wasn't working out and I should leave.

Luckily, that never happened. In fact, six months later, on a night out, he told me I was a great fit in the practice and that my name would soon be on the door.

True to his tipsy promise, my name went on the front door, alongside his two other dentists, also on the stationery and letterheads.

Thomas was a good boss and great mentor. He helped me out on the occasions shit happened. He was approachable and always reassuring.

I felt like I'd landed on my feet and my career really took off. My skills improved, as did my confidence and knowledge.

I wouldn't go so far as to say that I fell in love again with dentistry (because I still hated the litigious nature and stress of the job) but, workwise, this was the happiest I'd been in a *loooong* time.

So, having set this new scene, let me tell you some juicy stories!

❖

One patient who made me feel especially young, was the incredibly ancient Brenda Martinez (ooh, meow, that was a bit catty).

Brenda was in her late nineties. She had the weathered leathery skin of a serious sunworshipper. Her hair was the colour of baked straw. Her makeup was somewhere between that of an orange drink and Madge from Benidorm.

She was now visiting for her routine check-up. We were still having to wear face masks because of Covid, but things had eased.

Brenda entered my surgery with her mask firmly under her chin.

'Sorry,' she apologised. 'But I'm not wrecking my makeup for Covid or anything else.'

Fair. If Brenda had put the mask over her nose and mouth, she'd have seriously jeopardized several layers of foundation.

'Oh. You're not Harold.' Harold was the retired dentist I had replaced. All the patients had been informed of his pending retirement and that I was replacing him, so she definitely knew that Harold wasn't going to be here...

'Yes, Harold has retired now. I'm here in his stead, nice to meet you.' She sniffed and looked at me like I'd made a bad smell.

'How old are you? You don't look old enough to be a dentist.'

'That's quite a compliment.'

'It wasn't meant as a compliment.'

'Oh well, perhaps it's the contrast between Harold, who was at retirement age, and I'

'Oh. I'll be sure to tell him that. He's a close, personal friend of mine.' He really wasn't.

'No problem. Would you like to take a seat?'

Finally, Madge Mrs. Martinez sat in the dental chair. I was able to complete her check-up without too much further sass. At the end, I showed her the x-rays and explained everything looked fine. Foolishly, I asked if she had any questions.

'Yes,' she said, chin jutting again. 'How old are you?'

You're not letting this go, are you, you old bat!

'I'm nearly thirty.'

'So, in your twenties. A *baby*. Is this your first job?'

'No. I worked at another practice for five years before coming here. I've also lectured at a university too.'

She gave me a withering look.

'Let's see your face then.'

'Sorry, but no. There are regulations in place about always keeping masks on.'

With that, Brenda leant over and pulled off my mask. She then patted my bearded cheek and cackled.

'Good looking, kid.'

My mouth dropped open, as did Val's, my nurse. We were momentarily lost for words. I hastily pulled my mask up again.

'Right,' I said, trying to regain the upper hand. 'Your next check-up is due in six months.'

173

Brenda stuck her orange nose in the air and stalked off. For an old girl, she could certainly shift.

As the door shut behind her, Val gave a contemptuous snort (her name was actually Valentina, but she preferred the short version). She flicked her blonde ponytail off her shoulder and turned her cappuccino-brown eyes my way.

'What an old bag,' I said.

'Harald *hated* her,' Val confided.

'She indicated they were besties,' I said wryly.

'Ha! In her dreams. Everyone thought they were friends with Harold. It's because he lives locally. He wasn't personal friends with any of the patients here, trust me.'

Meanwhile, in reception, Brenda was causing a kerfuffle.

'I don't want to see that child again,' she ranted to Penny while waggling a gnarled finger. 'He might be a sexy young thing, but I want someone who knows what they're doing. That lad hasn't got a clue. He's basically a student doing a bit of work experience. I'm paying privately, so I want a *proper* dentist.'

'I can assure you that all our dentists are highly qualified,' Penny retorted.

'Don't try and pull the wool over my eyes. Sort it out.'

'Right,' Penny huffed. 'You can see Mr Green, the owner.'

'Good. And I want my examination done again at no cost. Understood?'

'Perfectly,' said Penny, trying not to fracture her crowns as she gnashed her teeth together.

During the lunch hour, everyone got together and chatted. Penny told me about what had happened in reception with Brenda. It transpired that Ms Martinez had a bit of a reputation for being an old harridan.

I was very relieved that this crusty old girl permanently switched to seeing Thomas. He, in turn, politely but firmly informed Brenda that he didn't employ children, and if she ever spoke to his staff disrespectfully again, she could go elsewhere.

Thomas had some balls taking on Brenda Martinez

because she wasn't a character for the fainthearted. Indeed, I said he deserved an award.

He gave me a deadpan look.

'An award, eh? Would that be... a little *plaque*?'

❖

I once had a patient called Graham Paul.

He was as wide as he was tall,

He complained all day,

I wish he'd just go away...

And that's my patient Graham Paul.

My nurse, Val, affectionately referred to Graham as *BFG*. No, not Big Friendly Giant. Rather, something ruder! In essence, Graham was a pain in the bum.

Before Thomas Green took over the Marigold Dental Practice, Graham was the practice's contracted cleaner with a small team of staff.

It transpired that during their cleaning hours, multiple boxes of stock including gloves, tissues, whitening gels and much more, had mysteriously vanished into thin air.

Naturally, Graham and his team hadn't been responsible. Regardless, when Thomas had taken over the business, he'd let Graham and his team go. Unsurprisingly, stock stopped disappearing after this...

Rather more surprisingly, Graham remained a patient of the practice and I inherited him. He had a standoffish manner and could be quite demanding.

As a more... *robust* gentleman, Graham snacked a lot. Biscuits. Sweets. Chocolate. All the things that are perfect for ~~fantastic~~ dreadful teeth. Every six months, Graham would have his check-up. Every six months, he'd leave with at least two fillings.

I'll never forget the first time I provided him with white fillings. First, let me backtrack and explain something.

Let me back-track a little... Dentists are taught to mimic nature. What I mean by this is, teeth are not flat, shapeless, white blobs. Teeth have ravines, hills, cusps, morphology, anatomy. We are taught (and are trained) to place fillings that closely resemble what the tooth may have originally looked like. This skill can feel quite rewarding when you finish a filling and you can't tell where tooth stops and filling starts.

For his latest filling, Graham wanted a white (composite) restoration on a back tooth.

I numbed him up, cleaned out the decay and put on a rubber dam. *What is a rubber dam*, I hear you ask. It's a sheet of thin material that goes over the tooth. White fillings don't like saliva. It causes poor bonding. It's important to stop a patient from touching it with their tongue. Therefore, the rubber dam isolates the tooth and avoids this issue.

Anyway, rubber dam on, my nurse and I got to work. I gave Graham a beautiful restoration. At the end, I paused to admire my work and thought *wow, it looks exactly like a pukka tooth.*

'Good job,' murmured Val approvingly.

'Thanks,' I grinned.

I removed the rubber dam to check Graham's 'bite'. But before I could go any further, Graham's humongous tongue began rubbing backwards and forwards over the tooth.

'I'm not happy with it,' he declared. 'It's all bumpy. It's not smooth.'

'It's not meant to be. I've mimicked the tooth's previous cusps.'

'No, you've mucked up. It's not meant to be bumpy.'

'Let me show you in the mirror so you can see what it looks like.'

'No,' said Graham, pushing the mirror away. 'I don't want to see it. You've done it wrong.'

'Graham,' I said firmly. 'Look at the tooth.' I offered him the mirror again. 'It's perfect. You can't even see the filling.'

'No,' he said, batting the mirror away. '*I* am the customer, and *I* am paying, so *I* will have what *I* want,' he ranted.

'No problem,' I said.

I tipped the chair back. Val looked on in disbelief as I proceeded to remove the entire filling. This time I didn't bother with the rubber dam. I recleaned the tooth with etch, rinse, dry and bond. Next, I thumbed a big blob of white composite into the cavity, and 'set' it with the light. The whole thing took less than three minutes.

Graham's probing tongue instantly began exploring the abysmal, totally flat restoration.

'Perfect,' he said.

'Glad you're happy,' I said.

Now get the fuck out of my chair!

❖

Along the way, there were some genuinely lovely patients who were so grateful, especially when my dentistry changed their life.

I don't say that lightly. I'm talking about patients whose quality of life has been badly affected due to having very few teeth, or even no teeth, and feeling unable to ever smile. These patients are basically considered to be a full mouth rehab.

My first true experience of this was with Mrs Jane Bird. Mrs Bird was in her mid-seventies and suffering from the early stages of Parkinson's disease She always attended with her husband, Mick. Together, they were a bit of a comedy duo. They reminded me of the Chuckle Brothers. With them, it was very much *to me, to you.*

Jane had severely worn and broken teeth. They were dark in colour, likely because the dentine (the soft-yellow part of a tooth) was on show. However, she was *stable.* In other words, there was no decay or severe gum disease. Harold (the retired dentist) had previously been looking after Jane's teeth for some twenty years.

'I don't like my teeth,' Jane confided. 'They're so jagged that my lips hurt if I smile.'

'We want you to fix them,' put in Mick.

'Harold told me they were fine,' said Jane. 'He didn't want to do anything to them.'

'Nice chap, Harold,' Mick interrupted. 'But I think he was old school. You know, *don't rock the boat.*'

'Okay,' I said. 'Let me make a suggestion. 'I'll have a look. Take some scans of the teeth. A few photos. Then we can put together a proper plan of action.'

And that's what we did.

With the collated information, I then conferred with my boss. Thomas helped me plan a restoration case. It was incredibly complex. Help was required from the lab. Jane had worn down her teeth so much they were meeting edge to edge. I needed a mockup of Jane's smile, which included opening up her 'bite'.

A week later, Jane and Mick returned. I ran through the plan with them thus far, explaining as I went.

'So,' I concluded. 'For a few months, your bite will feel rather odd – like you're only biting on your canines. You'll need a nightguard to protect the teeth, or you'll break the temporary crowns.'

'No,' Jane pouted. 'I don't want a nightguard.'

'Oh, yes you do,' said Mick.

'Oh, no I don't,' she retorted.

Children, children, I nearly said aloud.

Mick squared his shoulders.

'We're paying a lot of dosh for this treatment, so you'll wear it, and that's that.'

Jane made a harrumphing sound.

'So' – I ventured – 'is that a *yes* to the nightguard?'

'I guess so,' said Jane reluctantly.

Over the following weeks, everything was prepared. We went through the consent process. The risks. The benefits. And then the treatment began!

After a long, three-hour appointment, Jane's temporary crowns were fitted. The transformation was both immediate and striking.

'Give us a smile, love,' said Mick.

She was so used to not fully smiling, that when she obliged, it was without showing any teeth.

'Now with your teeth,' Mick encouraged.

Slowly, through her dribbling numbness, Jane beamed.

'Wow,' said Mick, his eyes widening.

I passed Jane the mirror so she could see for herself. As she stared at the reflection, a true smile lifted the corners of her mouth.

'Oh!' she gasped. 'Oh, my goodness.' She couldn't take her eyes from the reflection in the mirror. 'Thank you.' She continued to stare in wonder. 'Thank you, thank you, thank you!'

'These are only temporaries,' I reminded. 'You'll have them for the next few months, and I'll be reviewing you every four weeks. When you've adapted to your new bite, then I will replace them with porcelain crowns. They will feel much nicer to the tongue,' I added.

'They feel so much smoother than my old teeth,' Jane marvelled. 'I'm so happy!'

'I'm very pleased to hear that,' I said, returning her smile.

I basked in the glow of this hugely successful first experience of a complex case. I was also very grateful to Thomas who helped bring about that success and the learning that went with it. He was a fantastic mentor.

Before Jane left, I took some photos of the temporaries, and then rebooked to see her in four weeks' time. I then waved goodbye to an ecstatic Jane and delighted Mick.

❖

The next six months flew by. Jane returned to the surgery for the next stage. Making her definitive porcelain crowns. She came through the door, hanging on to Mick's arm and sporting a new pink cane.

'Hello,' she chirped. 'Like my stick?'

'Lovely,' I said. 'It goes with the coat.'

Jane was wearing an oversized pink fluffy jacket that made her look like a Care Bear.

She took the chair, keen to get started.

Today's appointment was fast and straightforward. I had scanned the prepared (drilled) teeth prior to fitting the temporaries. All I now had to do was scan the temporary teeth in her mouth. This would then show the lab Jane's bite.

'All done,' I said.

'Is that's it?' she said in surprise.

'Yup. See you in two weeks for the finished result.'

A fortnight later, after numbing up Jane, I removed the temporaries, and fitted the porcelain crowns. Once again, she looked in the mirror and this time was even more jubilant.

'They're amazing!' she exclaimed. 'Even better than the temporaries. Woohoo!'

And with that, we were done.

Jane went out into the world with a fully rehabilitated mouth.

* * *

Ten months later, Mick telephoned the practice. He left a voicemail asking if I could urgently return his call.

I immediately felt a knot of dread in the pit of my stomach. A wave of negative thoughts washed through my head:

Jane's crowns have fractured...

She hates the colour...

She can't tolerate the bite...

With a netful of butterflies flapping about under my ribcage, I picked up the phone.

'Hello?' said Mick.

'Hi, Mick,' I said. 'I'm returning your call.'

'Thank you.' He sounded very subdued. 'I have some bad news.'

Oh God, I thought. *Here it comes.*

'It's Jane.' Mick's voice cracked. 'She's dead.'

The words reverberated through my mind, and yet I couldn't take in what Mick had just said.

'I... I... *what?*' I stuttered.

'We were on a cruise,' he explained. 'Everything was fine and dandy. We were having a great time. Then, three days in, Jane said she wasn't feeling right. We were in Norway at this point. She didn't want to leave the boat to see the sites. No way was I going without her.' He paused. Cleared his throat. It was apparent he was starting to struggle with his emotions. 'So I stayed with her. In the cabin. She wanted to have a nap because she felt exhausted. I honestly didn't suspect anything was wrong. I mean, she wasn't in pain. Anyway' – he took a long shuddering breath – 'she didn't wake up.'

'Mick...' I said helplessly.

'Jane was taken to the ship's morgue. I visited her every day. She looked so beautiful you know. When she passed. And so peaceful.'

'Oh, Mick...'

So, I thought I ought to call and tell you what happened. And also, I cannot thank you enough for the confidence you gave her with your amazing dental treatment.'

The initial apprehension I'd felt upon first picking up the phone was now replaced with sorrow – sadness that Jane had only had a short time to enjoy her new smile.

'Mick,' I said quietly. 'I'm so sorry for your loss. Jane was a lovely woman, and it was my pleasure to treat her. I can't begin to imagine what you're going through.'

'Thank you,' he said, stifling a sob.

'If you ever need anything, don't hesitate to ask.'

Words. They couldn't bring back Jane, but they could hopefully comfort.

'Thanks.' At the other end of the line, came the sound of loud trumpeting into a handkerchief. 'I truly appreciate everything that you did for Jane. All the best.'

The call ended. For a moment or two I just stood there. Talk about a shock. I inhaled deeply, feeling a bit... weirded out. My patient had died. She'd died with the work that I'd given her. She would be buried with her new smile. How odd. And such a morbid thought, too.

I put out a hand to steady myself. I'd never been confronted with something like this, until now.

A local florist was sourced. A bouquet of flowers and a message of sympathy was delivered to Mick's house from me and the staff at Marigold Dental Practice, which Mick thanked everyone for. The whole episode was a stark reminder that none of us live forever.

Throughout my career, I've had a few patients unexpectedly pass away. It is always sad to receive such news. You get to know the characters that they are. You see them every six months, sometimes more. The relationship formed is unlike that of other medical professions. I can honestly say that I have raised a glass to several departed patients, and Jane was one of them.

❖

I've unintentionally offended many people over the years, and that includes patients.

Sometimes, the offence is due to the most trivial thing.

It can range from the mispronunciation of a surname (I once had a Mr Smythe who said, "If you ever call me Mr Smith again, I'll deck you.") to mistaking a cantankerous old man's wife for his daughter.

Enter Mrs Yvonne Schmellie, visiting for her routine check-up. It was her first examination since Harold had retired. Reception let me know my next patient was waiting. *Next patient.* No name. I checked my computer, then turned to my nurse.

'Val?'

'Yes?'

I tapped the computer screen.

'How do you pronounce this surname?'

Val scratched her head.

'No idea. I wasn't here when Harold was her dentist. Neither was Penny on reception.'

'Terrific,' I sighed. 'Well, bring her in. If we get her name wrong, we'll simply apologise and laugh it off.'

Val went to the waiting room, leaving the surgery door

open. Seconds later came the sound of a rumpus.

'How *dare* you!' screeched a female voice. 'HOW DARE YOU!'

Oh God.

'Do you think you're funny?' the voice demanded. 'I've been coming here for ten years. Ten *years*!' The voice had gone up an octave and was now quivering with indignation. 'And no one, *no one*, has ever called me Mrs *Smelly*.'

I stifled a giggle-snort while, at the same time, feeling mortified for Val. I could hear her apologising profusely and desperately trying to make amends.

'I'm so sorry.' Val's voice floated down the corridor. 'Can you tell me the correct pronunciation?'

'I'll give you a clue,' ranted the voice. 'It's not SMELLY!'

I nearly choked on another snort.

'I understand,' Val soothed. 'I am truly sorry. But, er, moving forward, how do I pronounce your name?'

'Work it out yourself,' scolded Mrs ~~Smelly~~ Schmellie.

'Well, I can't,' said Val in defeat. She'd clearly had enough of the patient's abuse. 'I've said I'm sorry. Either tell me the correct pronunciation, or I'll give up and instead call you by your first name.'

'It's *sh-mel-eye*, you silly girl!'

'Thank you,' said Val. 'If you'd like to accompany me, Mrs Shh... Mrs Smer... Mrs–'

It was too much. From the safety of my surgery, I silently convulsed.

'SCHMELLIE!' bellowed the outraged patient.

There came the sound of footsteps and, hastily wiping my eyes, I bolted over to my saddle stool and flopped down.

The ghastly Mrs Schmellie came through the door closely followed by a stressed-out Val. She shot me *the look* as the patient – feathers ruffled – sat down in the dental chair.

No way was I addressing this patient by her surname and risking any mispronunciation. Apart from anything else, I was terrified that saying her name might cause a violent outburst of giggles. The last thing I wanted was to collapse over the instrument tray in a state of hysteria.

'Nice to meet you, Yvonne,' I said, grinning manically.

'I *beg* your pardon,' she hissed.

My smile faded. Oh shit. Had I mispronounced her first name?

'Sorry?' I said.

'Do *I* know *you*?' she roared.

'Er, no. I don't think so. This is the first time we've met, so-'

'Young man!' she snapped. 'Are you not aware that it is RUDE to use someone's first name if you don't know them?'

What a witch. I gave her a benign smile.

'At the Marigold Dental Practice, staff like the personal approach to our patients' healthcare experience. This means I don't expect to be called by my doctor title and instead prefer the friendlier use of the first name. Likewise, I do the same for my patients. Well, *most* patients,' I added, letting her know she was now excluded. 'Does that make sense, Mrs *Smelly*?' I asked, deliberately saying her name wrong.

She turned a nasty shade of puce and looked all set to give me a verbal pasting.

'Shall we proceed with your dental exam?' I quickly cut in. 'Or would you prefer to rebook for another day?'

She wound her neck in and glared at me for a moment.

'Proceed,' she snapped.

I completed the exam which included taking an x-ray. I then showed her the picture and explained there was a small hole to an upper premolar.

'Are you *sure* there's a hole?' she questioned. 'Harold never mentioned a hole.'

'An x-ray reveals things between the teeth that can't necessarily be seen with a mirror. Do you see this black dot here' – I indicated the screen – 'between these two teeth?'

'Yes.'

'Well, that's a hole. If left, it will get bigger and eventually go into the nerve, which would be painful. It would be wise to treat it now, while it's small.'

'Very well,' she said imperiously. 'Draw me up a treatment plan.'

'Yes, of course,' I said, refraining from adding *Your Majesty.*

I turned to the computer and tapped away for a moment or two.

'Okay,' I said. 'That should now be ready at the desk for you.'

'Good,' she said frostily.

'Nice to meet you,' I said, trying to inject some sincerity into my voice. 'And have a good rest of the day.'

She stalked off, but then paused at the door. She gave a discreet cough. I glanced up from my notes.

'Was there anything else?'

'Nice to meet you too,' she said, taking me by surprise. 'And you may now call me *Yvonne.*'

'Thank you, Yvonne,' I said pleasantly.

She gave the ghost of a smile and then left.

I turned to Val who was giving the closed door some choice finger signs.

'*You may call me Yvonne,*' she mimicked in a silly voice. 'Stupid cow.'

'Not a fan, then?' I joked.

'No. She's a total bitch,' Val growled.

'On the upside, I don't think we'll ever forget how to pronounce her name,' I quipped.

And we didn't. Nor did we ever forget her. Every time Yvonne Schmellie's name appeared in the appointment book, we never mispronounced it because we instead called her something much ruder!

❖

Sometimes, I genuinely felt sorry for the people that walked into my surgery.

One such patient was Mrs Betty Valentine. She was eighty years old, polite and pleasant. She had quite severe arthritis and suffered Raynaud's syndrome (where the ends of your fingers go white due to poor circulation in the extremities).

Betty had, for many years, been Harold's patient. On her first check-up with me, she confided that she was concerned about a few of her old crowns. The gum had receded and there was an obvious colour mismatch between the tooth's dark root and its porcelain crown.

I checked the integrity of each crown. Took x-rays. Then assured Betty that – cosmetic appearance aside – the teeth were sound, and no dental work was needed. She was very relieved to hear this and left with a cheery farewell.

Three weeks later, her name was in my diary again for a 'Review'. No further information had been given. I asked Penny at reception if Betty had said anything over the phone.

'Oh, I think Mrs Valentine just wants to talk about her crowns,' she said.

'Strange,' I mused. 'We discussed them at her check-up.'

Betty arrived and my nurse led her into the surgery.

'This way, Mrs Valentine,' said Val.

'Thank you. What was your name again?' asked Betty.

'It's Valentina, but everyone calls me Val.'

'Valentina? That's nearly my name! Valentine... Valentina' – Betty did a seesaw motion with one hand – 'so similar!'

Betty took the chair.

'Hello,' I smiled. 'What can I do for you?'

'Well, I know we talked about the crowns last time, but I'm worried about this one in particular,' she said, pointing.

'That's okay. I can check it again to reassure you.'

'That would be great,' she beamed. 'Also, look at my fingers.'

She showed me her hands. The fingertips were very blanched due to her Raynaud's syndrome.

'Oh dear. Are you seeing your GP about that?'

'Yes, but the surgery doesn't care. No one cares about me.'

'Oh, don't say that,' I soothed. 'I'm sure they do. Do you

have children?'

'Yes. A daughter. But she never bothers to come round.'

'I'm sorry to hear that,' I said, feeling a pang of sadness for her.

'It's okay,' Betty shrugged.

'Meanwhile, let's have a look at this tooth.'

Once again, I checked the crown again, reassured Betty that all was well, and off she went. I didn't charge Betty for the appointment as I'd only seen her a few weeks ago and there'd been nothing to do.

Three weeks later, Betty Valentine was back. Val and I looked at each other in confusion.

'*Another* review?' I queried.

'I think she's lonely,' said Val.

Betty was called in. As she sat down, I had a feeling of déjà vu.

'Everything okay?' I asked her.

'Oh, it's so nice to see you and Val,' she said cheerfully. You're both the highlight of my day. You're both so kind and lovely to me.'

'I'm glad to hear that,' I said. 'Now then. I understand you're worried about a tooth?'

'Yes, this one here,' she pointed randomly. 'Also, my GP has now looked at my hands. He's referred me to a specialist so hopefully I'll get more answers. I was worried that my fingertips were going to fall off or go black because they were so cold.'

She waved one hand at Val, obviously seeking a comment of some sort.

'Gosh!' said Val politely.

'Well, I'm glad that's now in hand,' I chortled.

Ha! *In hand?* Geddit! I cleared my throat.

'So, tell me about this problem tooth?'

'I think there may be a hole in it,' said Betty. 'It feels so rough.'

I looked. Checked it with the probe. There was nothing wrong with the tooth.

'It all looks fine, but if it feels rough, would you like me to polish it?'

187

'Oooh, that would be fantastic!' she agreed.

So I gave it a buff with the ultra-fine soflex discs (a bit like the thinnest of sandpapers).

'That's so much better!' said Betty happily.

'Glad we could help,' I said.

And off Betty went. Again.

This time, I put a charge of forty-five pounds on the appointment. I felt bad, because she was a nice lady, but I didn't want to encourage an inappropriate relationship. Betty paid it without comment.

Three weeks later, Betty Valentine's name once again appeared in the diary.

'She can't have another problem,' Val said incredulously.

'She must be really, *really* lonely,' I said.

It was such a sad affair. Every three weeks or so, Betty Valentine would attend the surgery. The review fee didn't deter her, and she happily paid each time.

It was obvious she had come for some company and a chat. I felt genuinely sorry for her. Evidently, she lived on her own and rarely had visitors. And although Val and I were happy to chat to her, I had to make sure the conversation always returned to dentistry. After all, it was my job.

❖

You hear a lot of tosh as a dentist. I think I've already mentioned the myth of the knee on the chest for difficult extractions (which has never ever happened!)

Enter Agnes Reed, a seventy-nine-year-old female requiring extraction of an upper premolar. It had fractured and was causing pain.

Agnes walked with a stick. She had arthritis. She'd also had several spinal surgeries including cages in the vertebrae following removal of a mass.

Agnes was very nervous. She entered the surgery cowering like a dog on a visit to his vet.

'Hi, Agnes,' I greeted. 'Do you know today's plan?'

'Yes,' she wailed. 'You're going to rip out this tooth from my head!'

'Now, now. I can assure you that I've never 'ripped a tooth out' of anyone's head. However, I will remove your infected tooth.'

'When I was younger' – Agnes bleated – 'my dentist was a scrawny girl. She couldn't get my tooth out. So she had to get her mentor in. Both were holding the pliers between them. They had to put their knees on my chest to pull the retched thing out.' Suddenly the timid quailing Agnes turned into a ratty cantankerous woman. 'You'd better not do the same,' she snarled.

'I've never done that, and never will,' I reassured. 'If the tooth is obstinate, or breaks, sometimes I have to do a small surgical procedure. This requires a tiny bit of bone removal with water spray and feels something like having a filling.'

'Well I definitely don't want that, so make sure that doesn't happen, okay?'

'If it happens, it happens,' I said matter-of-factly. 'Your tooth is very broken down so there is a real chance that it might need minor surgery. Unfortunately, I cannot control such an outcome.'

Val and I did the look between us then swiftly moved on.

I ran through the consent process with Agnes. Told her the usual risks.

'You'll be a little sore afterwards. A bit of bleeding is normal. Some people get swelling or bruising. There's always a small risk of infection (dry socket). However, if you don't smoke that risk is about one in ten.'

Agnes said she understood and wanted to proceed. I numbed her up and started the extraction. This involves using a fine-tipped instrument called a luxator. This breaks down the ligament and starts loosening the tooth. Using an elevator, gentle pressure is then applied to get the tooth to move. The final step is with the forceps.

The tooth broke – which I had anticipated. It was so cavitated and decayed it was inevitable. I continued to apply pressure and wobbled the root. Finally, I felt the give and knew it was ready. I used some very fine tipped forceps and completed the extraction. From start to finish, Agnes had been in the chair approximately thirty minutes.

I dressed the socket, got her to bite on some gauze to stop the bleeding, then ran through the post-op instructions on how to look after the site. I then rechecked it, and let her go.

'She was feisty old bird,' said Val after Agnes had left.

'Not half,' I said. 'At least the extraction went well.'

'Small mercy,' Val sniffed. 'Hopefully we won't see her again for a while.'

Ha! Famous last words...

❖

Famous last words, indeed. Six weeks later, the spirited Agnes Reed tottered through my door leaning on her walking stick. She'd booked in under the guise of *review*.

Here we go, I thought, as she plonked herself down on the chair.

'What can I do for you, Mrs Reed?' I asked politely.

'Now, I'm not blaming you,' she began.

Okay, let's hear it, I mentally sighed.

'But you've basically destroyed my spine with your extraction technique.'

Huh? Well, I hadn't been expecting that!

'Sorry?' I frowned.

'You don't need to apologise.' She gestured with one hand. 'After all, you weren't to know.'

'Sorry, I... I wasn't saying sorry by way of apology. I said sorry as in pardon, because I'm confused.'

'Nothing to be confused about,' she snapped. 'You used too much force when you took out that tooth. You've damaged my spine. Since then, I've had numbness and balance issues, and it's all because of your extraction.'

'Respectfully, Agnes, do you not think that these issues are likely related to your previous surgeries and spinal cages?' I calmly suggested.

'No,' she said, pursing her lips. 'I've done my research. It's definitely related to your extraction technique.'

'Okay,' I said. 'Unfortunately, we will have to agree to disagree and–'

'Well, I don't agree,' she interjected. 'You're wrong.'

I ignored the interruption and continued speaking.

'But I recommend you see your GP to discuss referral for an MRI to check the spine for compressions – which is likely the culprit.'

'No,' she said, shaking her head. 'I've seen my osteopath and told him what you did. He said he sees it all the time. That dentists are far too forceful with extractions.'

We weren't getting anywhere here. How does a dentist gently extract a tooth? Perhaps I should've put on some romantic music. Dimmed the lights. Whispered sweet nothings to the wrecked tooth?

'Okay,' I said, my tone suggesting this conversation was over. 'I can only advise you of the medical facts. Sorry you feel it is related, but I do not agree. Is there anything else I can do for you today?'

Or was this review simply to rant about me breaking your spine? I silently seethed.

'No,' said Agnes, jaw jutting. 'That's all.'

'Right,' I said, trying not to gnash my teeth. 'I hope you have a good rest of day.'

Agnes harrumphed by way of response. I turned away and began typing up the notes while Val ushered aggy Agnes from the surgery.

'Want a brew?' said Val, upon her return. 'You look like you need a pick-me-up.'

'Yeah,' I agreed. 'A cup of positivitea!'

She came across sweet and innocent. But she was wolf in sheep's clothing. In other words, she was a complete *bitch*.

It was the middle of April. Outside, it was a balmy seventeen degrees with a slight breeze.

The temperature dropped when Edith entered my surgery. She was in her late nineties and was attending as a new patient, complaining of a broken front tooth.

In fact, this was the *only* tooth left in her head. She had fractured her upper left central incisor, which held her upper denture in place.

'Nice to meet you, Edith,' I said as she took the chair. 'So, please tell me how the tooth fractured.'

'Well, I was eating quiche at that cafe down the road. Have you tried it?'

'No, I don't think I have,' I said.

'Right, well, I have a good mind to sue them. That quiche had a *burnt* crust and that's why my tooth snapped in half.'

'I'm sorry to hear that.'

'Not as sorry as they'll be,' she said, flashing me a dark look.

The litigious nature of this lady immediately set alarm bells ringing. She was a walking red flag. Why has the world become so obsessed with playing the blame game for financial means?

The crust was burnt, so I'm going to sue you!

You hurt my feelings, so I'm going to sue you!

I didn't brush my teeth, so I'm going to sue you!

I am addicted to eating sugary shit, so I'm going to sue you!

This attitude ruins the world – not to mention other people's lives. Those who want to jump on the litigation wagon should perhaps start by letting the spotlight of attention fall upon themselves and take some responsibility!

'So, Edith,' I said, interrupting her diatribe. 'There are three options. First, I do nothing.'

'That's not an option,' she snapped.

'Second, I crown the tooth. This involves drilling and shaping it into a peg, then putting on a porcelain crown to give it some strength. In my opinion, this is the best option because it'll allow the denture to still fit snugly.'

Edith glared at me but didn't interrupt.

'Third,' I continued. 'I extract the tooth and instead add an additional tooth to your denture. This means you'll have *no* upper teeth so the denture will be quite loose.'

'What do you think I should do?' she said, pursing her lips.

'The decision is entirely yours.'

'Well, as it happens, I saw a Mr Tristan at the other dental practice down the road. He said something similar to you.'

Okayyy, I said to myself. *So, she is surgery surfing. That's never a good sign.*

'Can I ask, Edith,' I said mildly. 'Why didn't you let Mr Tristan do the treatment?'

'Because he was a *money grubber*,' she declared indignantly. 'He wanted my money, didn't he? He wasn't an honest man.'

Red flag alert! Abort mission! Get me out of here!

Everything in my brain was screaming.

'So, what do you want to do?' I asked tentatively.

She heaved a sigh.

'The crown, I guess.'

'Okay. I'll do a price estimate and send it to the desk. You'll need two appointments. This practice has a digital scanner. It will take several photos of your tooth and allow me to design a crown to go over it. I must then *mill* it from a porcelain block and glaze it in the furnace. This all takes time. You'll be here first thing in the morning with everything done mid-to-late afternoon. Is that okay?'

'Fine,' said Edith grumpily.

I then escorted Edith to the desk and palmed her off on Penny. I swiftly returned to my surgery but not before hearing Edith's bellow of rage about the price of her crown.

'HOW MUCH?!'

Edith returned a few weeks later, for her crown preparation appointment. As she stood at the desk, she made a waspish comment to Penny.

'That dentist. He better not keep me waiting.'

'Your dentist is running on time,' she said coolly.

'Pah!' Edith scoffed. 'He knows my money is about to walk through his door.'

She took herself off to the waiting room. A few moments later, Val escorted Edith into the surgery. I looked up and smiled pleasantly.

Edith pursed her mouth into the replica of a dog's arsehole. She threw me a dark look, then settled herself in the chair.

'Hello, Edith. How are you?'

'Annoyed. I'll bet you're on Cloud Nine stealing all my money, eh?'

Charmless old bat, I thought.

'If you're not happy about the treatment costings, you're welcome to find an NHS provider, or look at other options elsewhere,' I said smoothly.

I was aiming for diplomacy, but this old girl was already pissing me off.

'So, where do you get off charging me six-hundred-pounds for a crown, young man?'

'I don't set the prices,' I said. 'My boss does that. He's the owner of this practice. However, I think The Marigold Dental Practice is very competitive against other private practices in this area. Also, we provide everything in one sitting without the need for temporaries, or a two-week wait time. Then there's the small matter of using a state-of-the-art machine that cost sixty-thousand pounds. When you stop and think about all those factors, I'd say the price is a very fair one.'

'Well, you would say something like that, wouldn't you?'

'If you're unhappy, should we cancel today?'

'No, no.' More mouth pursing. More impressions of a dog's backside. 'Let's get on with it.'

'Are you sure, Edith?' I persisted. 'I don't want any trouble.'

There. I'd said it. My words hung in the air. She knew that I was on to her.

'Trouble?' Edith blew out her cheeks. 'From me? No, no. There won't be any trouble.' She was now quickly back-peddling. 'Let's get this done.'

I administered the local anaesthetic then prepared Edith's front tooth. This involved polishing one and a half millimetres off the tooth all around. Eventually, it resembled a cone which was scanned into the CEREC machine. This is a scanner that takes lots of photos and stitches all the pictures together to make a 3D digital model of the mouth.

'Okay,' I said. 'For now, you're done. Your next appointment is at three o'clock this afternoon. Go and have some lunch. You're fine to eat and drink but keep things cold or tepid. Don't have anything too hot otherwise it will irritate the tooth.'

'Hang on,' said Edith. 'I'm not happy about this. You're telling me that I must wait until three o'clock for you to make this crown?'

'Er, that was the appointment time that *you* booked,' I pointed out.'

'I'm in my nineties,' she protested. 'Do you honestly expect me to go away and then come back?'

'Would you like me to call a cab?'

'Absolutely not!' she exhorted. 'I'm not wasting money!'

'There's a Costa two minutes down the road.'

'At my age, a two-minute walk takes an hour.'

Fuck's sake!

'Right,' I said, throwing my hands up in the air. 'How about I forfeit my lunch break? I'll work through my lunch hour and have your crown ready in... what?... ninety minutes or so?'

'That's still a long time,' Edith moaned. 'And I'm totally parched.'

'Val will make you a cup of tea,' I cajoled. 'But remember. It won't be super-hot. I can't have you irritating the tooth.'

'I suppose,' said Edith, making it sound like she was doing me a massive favour.

'Take a seat in the waiting room. Val will be along with a cuppa shortly, and I'll get on with designing the crown.'

Edith stomped out of my surgery, banging her walking stick hard on the floor to convey her displeasure. Val stared after her, eyes narrowed and like flint.

'My God,' she breathed, before looking at me.

'I know, I know,' I said, tone pacifying. 'Let's just get through this. You don't mind working your lunch, do you?'

'No, of course not,' Val assured. 'Anything to get rid of that woman sooner rather than later.'

I cracked on and designed the crown, then left it to mill. It's fascinating to watch several drills in the space of half an hour carve up a solid block of porcelain until it resembles a tooth.

Afterwards, it would go into a furnace at a temperature of eight hundred degrees Celsius for another twenty-five minutes or so. This would strengthen and colour the crown.

Meanwhile, I went to check on Edith to see if she wanted another cup of tea. I was met with venom.

'That last cup was disgusting,' she complained. 'I want it good and strong with a dash of milk and two sugars.'

'Unfortunately, we don't have sugar,' I said. 'We have sweetener. Is that okay?'

'Actually, it isn't,' she said sourly. 'First, I'm given an undrinkable cup of tea. Second, I must sit on this uncomfortable chair. Third, you're telling me you don't have any sugar.'

'Well, we are a dental practice,' I said patiently. 'We don't routinely stock sugar for that reason.'

'I guess sweetener will have to do,' she said, giving me an eyeroll. 'But make it one. Do you hear? *One.*'

Coming right up, Your Majesty.

I went upstairs to the kitchen and made her a brew. Added one sweetener. Then I made sure I hadn't given her an inappropriate mug. There were a few on the draining board. The staff here had a sense of humour. My favourite was of a pissed-off unicorn supposedly singing:

With a f*ck f*ck here
And a f*ck f*ck there
Here a f*ck
There a f*ck
I don't give a f*ck f*ck!

Instead, I handed her a mug with the least offensive message.

If my mouth doesn't say it, then my face will.

I didn't smile as I handed her the cup. *That's it, Edith*, I thought. *Read and learn!*

She took a sip.

'It's not hot enough,' she grimaced.

'As I explained earlier, you can't have it too hot otherwise you'll irritate the nerve inside the tooth.'

'This isn't PG Tips,' she announced, banging the mug down on the magazine table.

'You're right. It's–'

'Cheap muck,' she interrupted. 'That's what it is.'

'Shall I take it away?'

'No!' she declared, snatching up the cup again.

'In which case I'll see you in a little while.'

And with that, I removed myself to wolf my lunch and glaze her crown.

❖

Exactly one hour later, I had the finished crown. Thanks to working my lunch hour while the practice was technically closed, it was the quickest restoration that I'd ever turned around. I'd bent over backwards for this miserable old bag.

Val brought Edith back into the surgery. She literally threw her walking stick into one corner to convey how put out she was with her treatment thus far.

'Hello, again,' I greeted. 'Do take a seat.'

Edith flung herself down so forcefully, the chair

momentarily protested. For an old girl, she had incredible energy.

'Don't you *hello again* me,' she exploded. 'You've kept me waiting for over an hour. Do you know how cold it is in that waiting room? I'm in my nineties. I could have *died* in there. *Died* from hypothermia.'

Our Edith was clearly a fan of hyperbole.

'In which case, thank goodness you only had to wait an hour thanks to me *working flat out for you.*'

She flashed me a look.

'I still could have died,' she growled.

'It's mid-April,' I pointed out. 'Outside it's eighteen degrees.'

'I'm one of the elderly,' she argued. 'Therefore, I'm vulnerable.'

You're anything but vulnerable, I thought unkindly.

'Shall we fit this crown and get you out of here?' I suggested, resisting the urge to fall to my knees and beg.

'Yes, but I want you to know that I'm not happy.'

Are you ever? I thought.

I reclined the chair, cleaned up the tooth, tried on the crown, made sure she approved of its appearance, then cemented it. I then checked her denture was a snug fit with it. It was. I then asked her to pop the denture in and out of her mouth to make sure there were no problems. She did so, and all was fine.

'Excellent,' I declared.

'No, it isn't,' she argued. 'The denture isn't fitting properly. It's too tight.'

'Okay. Let me loosen it.' I made an adjustment. 'Better?'

'It'll do,' she said begrudgingly. 'Anyway, I have something to say to you.'

'Oh?'

'I don't think I should have to pay for this treatment.'

'Excuse me?'

Inside, my brain was screaming something far less polite. *You fucking WHAT?*

'I don't think I should have to pay.' Her chin jutted forward. 'The waiting room was cold. Therefore, you should waive any charge.'

'Edith,' I said, sotto voce.

Anyone who knows me will understand this tone is not good. That they've wandered into dangerous territory. In other words, Edith was getting perilously close to pushing all my buttons.

I turned my chair to face my tormentor. Leant in.

'I have provided you with a high-quality restoration in an incredibly fast time, and sacrificed my lunch break to ensure you had the best experience. You will be paying.'

'I won't.'

'You will.'

'I won't.

'Yes, Edith. *You will!*' I asserted. 'I will now take you to the desk to settle up.'

I stood up, opened the door and waited for her to accompany me. Reluctantly, she retrieved her walking stick and followed me to reception where Penny was waiting.

'Edith would like to settle up,' I said. 'Goodbye, Edith.' *And good riddance.*

I turned on my heel and went back to my surgery where Val was waiting. She could tell I was quietly raging.

'You look like you'd like to be anywhere other than here,' said my nurse.

'Do you ever daydream about emigrating?' I said wistfully.

Val quirked her mouth.

'Fluorida?'

❖

Like me, you may have thought (and hoped and maybe even prayed) that the Edith Saga was over and done with. It wasn't. Just like a boomerang, she came back.

Two weeks after the crown fitting, Edith booked a review appointment. Over the phone, she told Penny that the crown had 'ruined' her denture.

She duly arrived at the practice, a little ray of sunshine

(obviously I am being sarcastic!).

'Let's get this over with,' I said to Val.

She went and collected Edith. There was no small talk between my nurse and patient. For different reasons, both women were frosty when they came into surgery. Val hadn't greeted Edith. And vice versa. A stony silence prevailed as Edith took the chair and Val stationed herself beside me.

'Hello,' I said coolly – possibly adding to the room's temperature dropping another degree. Edith would no doubt soon be complaining of hypothermia.

'I wish I'd never had this shoddy treatment done,' was my patient's opening gambit. 'Ever since you put this crown on, my denture has cut my tongue to ribbons. I'm so unhappy. It's dreadful. How could you do this to me?' Edith demanded.

'Woah, woah!' I said, as if addressing a runaway horse.

Edith looked momentarily taken aback but shut up.

'Please show me the denture,' I said.

She removed it. I then examined it and noted where it might have been rubbing. Smoothing it, I then handed it back to her. She popped it back in, then repeatedly ran her tongue over it, almost trying to find some fault or another.

'Better?' I asked.

'Yes,' she said grudgingly.

'Anything else I can do for you?'

'No. And by the way, I'm not paying for today's appointment.'

'Of course not,' I said. I gave her such a sugar-sweet smile it's a wonder her glucose levels didn't temporarily skyrocket. 'Your smile is payment enough,' I added.

She looked at me, eyes narrowed, unsure if I was being genuine or sarcastic (definitely the latter). Then she stuck her nose in the air and wordlessly took herself off.

Val and I exchanged *the look.*

I didn't see Edith again, but I have no doubt she's still alive and well. Still out there making some other dentist's working life as miserable as she possibly can with her complaints and accusations.

Patients like Edith wore their negativity like a fashion

statement, complete with matching eyebags and a frown so deep it could hold a week's worth of burnt quiche!

❖

I'd like to finish this section on a positive note. While working as a private dentist, although there were still a lot of complainers and whingers, I did have some uplifting moments.

At the other end of the whining patient spectrum were those who I were so thankful, so grateful, so appreciative, that it almost (I said *almost*!) made it worthwhile dealing with cantankerous old bats like Edith.

These lovely patients wrote thank you letters. Posted cards. Came into reception and asked Penny to pass on a gifted bottle of wine. These gestures meant *everything* to me. It didn't happen every day or even every month. Rather, every now and again. I cannot stress enough how it totally *made my day*. Why? Because it reminded me that my job *did* make a difference.

Jennifer Corringham, aged sixty-two, was one of my regular patients. She routinely visited every six months both the hygienist and myself and looked after her teeth very well.

When a child, she'd fallen in the playground and broken her front tooth. Over her lifetime, she'd had the tooth filled, crowned, root treated, re-crowned, and so on.

One day, Jennifer's tooth vertically fractured, leaving a semi-mobile root digging into her gum along with a loose tooth and much pain.

She attended clinic as an emergency where I delivered the bad news that the tooth could not be saved. After a discussion about options, Jennifer embarked on a six-month plan. This involved removing the broken tooth, having a temporary denture and then a replacement with a dental implant.

It culminated in a beautiful, perfectly matched, front tooth. Jennifer was shocked at how natural it looked. I was in the habit of asking patients how they'd found the whole process. After all, it was complex treatment.

Jennifer verbally responded positively, but when she additionally wrote a Google review, it really made my day:

If you are considering dental implant treatment, then I recommend a consultation at Marigold Dental Practice. I have just finished treatment for a single tooth implant. I'd been very nervous about the whole thing. However, my dentist carried out a thorough assessment and answered all my questions so thoroughly I felt confident to proceed. Throughout the surgery, my dentist made me feel completely relaxed and I was pain free. In fact, I felt no pain at all, just occasional pressure and pushing sensations. Afterwards, I was provided with excellent guidance – both verbal and written – on how to look after the area throughout the recovery period. I encountered no problems during the healing process. My treatment was finished today and I now have a brand new perfectly-matched implanted tooth. To say I am delighted is an understatement. You'd never know I'd any treatment done! I highly recommend my dentist at Marigold Dental Practice if you're considering a dental implant.

Words have power. *Immense* power. They can make you feel ten feet tall. Equally, an unkind word can crush you. In this case, Jennifer's words had such a positive impact I felt like I could have taken on all the Ediths of this world and still come out floating on air.

Even now, when writing this, I still feel that warm afterglow. That joy. That buzz that comes from making a positive impact on someone's life. Giving them back their smile. Simple but profound!

Not to be overly preachy, remember to *tell* people when they do good. All too often we moan when things aren't up to scratch, or too slow to say thanks for a job well done. I carry this thought with me every day. Be the good you want to see in the world.

So, dear reader, we reach the end of another section.

Private dentistry provided a lot of freedom, away from the conveyor belt of NHS dental care. It allowed me to develop – as a practitioner – without constraint. My first year in private care was a steep learning curve akin to university and foundation training all rolled into one.

I am so grateful that, during this time, I had such an understanding, intelligent and skilled mentor as Thomas Green. I truly felt that I'd landed on my feet at Marigold Dental Practice.

So, you might be thinking that there's surely nothing left to be said? But you'd be dead wrong. There are still a few more stories to tell. I invite you to turn the page to see what happens next!

8

The Good, the Bad and ~~the Ugly~~ Everything Else that I Probably Forgot…

There's a lot that happened related to dentistry or around my dental training, that may not really fit into the other sections. I felt like a chapter entitled *Miscellaneous* was a bit drab, so I renamed the section as above.

Here, I'd like to share my musings, ramblings, trials, tribulations, stories and experiences that were memorable but perhaps not directly related to my day-to-day practice.

Some of the stories are short, yet clearly notable to still so readily come to mind. Others are simply observations about the world around us.

Although I may not like to admit it, dentistry is a big part of who I am as a person. It is so different to any other job I've had (retail worker, recruiter, tutor, university lecturer). It is just *such a part of you*. I think that's why it seems to impact the world around me in such odd ways.

So, dear reader, without further ado, let's dive into the final part of my book. I hope you'll stick with me till the end. Oh, I've just seen what the next story is! Trust me, it's a good one!

❖

Breasts. Women have them. *Boobs.* So do some men. *Moobs!*

But what relevance do they have to dentistry? Well, none really, although they're relevant to this story.

If my nurse hadn't been in the room with me, I don't think anyone would've believed this happened.

It was three in the afternoon, and the last appointment of a Friday. A new patient had been booked in as an emergency and apparently in considerable pain.

Alina was a thirty-something-year-old Romanian lady. She attended wearing a black hoodie, the front of which had sequined cats stitched upon it.

Alina explained that she had a regular dentist in Romania who she routinely visited every six months. However, today she had a problem that couldn't wait.

'Doctor,' she said in a heavily accented husky voice. 'I have a swelling in my gum. It's been there for a while, but in the last few days it has spread throughout my top gums. It happened after I cleaned my teeth. A lump came up above my front tooth. I bought some antibiotics while in Romania and took them on and off. But then all these other lumps appeared and now it is really sore.'

'Sounds painful,' I said. 'Okay, let's have a look.'

I popped her back in the chair and noted what looked like an abscess (a swelling containing pus) on her upper left central incisor. The rest of her gums were full of small ulcers, and it all looked very sore. I initially thought it might be a reactivation of oral herpes. This is like a cold sore, but rather than appearing on the lip, it can break out across the gums.

I attempted taking an x-ray of the front tooth. However, Alina struggled with this, explaining she had a bad gag reflex. Consequently, I opted to do a panoramic x-ray. Basically, this is a machine that goes *around* the head, rather than a patient enduring an x-ray film in their mouth and potential gagging. I explained this to Alina.

'I think you will find this alternative more comfortable,' I assured.

'Thank you,' she replied.

'Would you mind removing your earrings?' I asked.

'No problem,' she said, pulling them from her earlobes. 'What about this?' she asked, pointing to some decorative metal studs at the neckline of the hoodie.

'Ideally, the x-ray should be done with no metal from the neck up. Perhaps it would be best if you remove the hoodie and then I'll take you to the x-ray room.'

'Okay,' Alina shrugged.

And with that she whipped the garment over her head.

I'd wrongly assumed that she'd had on a t-shirt underneath the hoodie. Instead, my nurse and I were treated to the sight of a very sheer lacy black bra. It left absolutely nothing to the imagination. Indeed, a pair of very pink nipples seemed to be waving hello to Val and me.

'O-Oh,' I spluttered, not knowing where to look. 'Um, Alina. Do you not have a vest, or something?'

'This is fine, no?' Her brows knitted together and she pointed to her bra. 'Or should I take this off too? There is a lot underwiring, no?'

'Nooo!' Val and I chorused.

'Er, the thing is' – I said carefully – 'the x-ray machine is next door. For now, perhaps you might like to put your hoodie back on.'

'Is fine,' she said, flapping a hand.

'Right,' I warbled.

In my peripheral vision, Val was doing her best not to wet herself with laughter.

So, I took Alina along the hall, ensuring my nurse came too. A chaperone is essential in crazy moments like this one.

I took the x-ray, then almost threw Alina's hoodie at her.

'Pop that back on,' I squeaked. I hastily cleared my throat. 'As quick as you can. You don't want to catch a chill.'

Val and I heaved a sigh of relief once those boobs were safely hidden behind Alina's sequined hoodie. I reviewed the x-ray, explained my findings, and Alina eventually left.

I later told Thomas about my stripping patient.

'What is it with your patients?' he hooted. 'You seem to

attract some right eccentrics. At least she didn't take her bra off, and you always had Val with you.'

'Indeed,' I mused. 'Otherwise, I'd have been at risk of a *booby*trap!'

❖

Banditry. Yes, it's a thing in dentistry. There are definitely *bandit dentists*, which is a 'catch all' term for any dentist that practices in a poor, unethical or downright dodgy way. That said, thankfully, they are few or far between, but every dentist will know of, or know someone, that is a bandit!

Let me tell you about Ron Trevor. At university, Ron was in the year below me. He didn't study much, partied like it was going out of fashion, failed a year at dental school and ended up re-sitting quite a few exams.

The problem was, Ron thought he was shit hot and all because he had a photographic memory! So, for exams, he'd just read the course notes the night before, then regurgitate everything in the exam itself.

Now, that's all well and good for passing *paper* exams, but it doesn't help when it comes to practical and patient exams – where you must *physically* do something or *explain to an examiner* the rationale of a treatment plan. That is where Ron fell apart. Nevertheless, he did eventually pass his exams and graduate from dental school.

A few years later, Ron ended up working at a practice I was at (I didn't stick around!). He believed himself God's gift to dentistry, despite his inability to complete simple extractions without fracturing each and every tooth.

Ron also had the ability to rub multiple staff members, patients and nurses up the wrong way. The Practice Manager not-so-secretively referred to him as *The Molar Mauler* and, when really pissed off, *The Whinging Wanker* (because he was always complaining about others not doing *their* job properly!).

The sad thing about Ron's banditry was that he didn't

realise that he was a bandit. He truly thought he was the bee's knees. I'll never forget him asking me for some advice on a case. A forty-year-old female patient had decay in the pulp (nerve) and needed either an extraction or root canal treatment. The patient opted to save the tooth, so Ron started a root canal treatment.

Mid-appointment, he decided it had gone so well that he would finish it there and then. Afterwards, he showed me the x-rays and invited me to comment.

The series of x-rays revealed that he'd perforated the tooth – in other words, drilled through the wrong part of the tooth, missed the nerves and created a hole that shouldn't be there. Even worse, he had decided to fill *through* the perforation. The final x-ray showed a load of *gutta percha* (a type of inert rubber filling material used in such treatments) shoved into the perforated area (the bone and ligament that holds the tooth in place) while *none of the nerve* had been removed or cleared at all.

'Erm, Ron,' I said tentatively. 'You've perforated the tooth.'

'Yeah, I did wonder.' He rubbed his chin thoughtfully. 'It wouldn't stop bleeding.'

'So why didn't you repair the perforation or extract the tooth?'

'Well' – he sucked on his teeth – 'I thought I'd angle the x-ray to hide the performation and then just see how it goes.'

I think Ron was faintly surprised at the look of horror on my face. Listen, we've all perforated a tooth during root canal treatment. It is a well-known risk that is consented for. But we do *not* shove a ton of filling material through that hole so it goes into the bone and soft tissues!

'I think you should call her back and extract that tooth ASAP,' I advised.

'Why?'

I stared at him.

I mean, like, where to even start?

'Because that tooth is *completely* fucked,' I said incredulously.'

'Oh. Oh. Right. So... you don't think it'll be okay?'

'No!'

Ron reviewed the patient a few days later, primarily because she was pain! He advised her that the treatment had failed and the tooth now needed extraction. He took out the tooth which healed without incident.

Not long after this, I left this practice. However, that shocking example of banditry left a real imprint on me. I don't think I'm God's gift to dentistry, of course I don't. But I am very competent. All these years later, that patient's x-rays still haunt me.

❖

Dentistry, believe it or not, involves a deep understanding of general medicine. I am aware that some people look upon us as glorified carpenters, but at university we studied all of medicine (alongside the future doctors in this world!) while *also* specialising in dental surgery. Almost everything affects the mouth. Let me give you just a few examples:

- *Diabetes* – a direct link to the periodontal (gum/bone) condition of the jaws.
- *Severe osteoporosis* - doctor has put patient on a bisphosphonate medicine that slows down bone turnover to strengthen bones - this affects *any* minor oral surgery a dentist does e.g. extractions.
- *Epilepsy* - anti-epileptics can cause a patient's gums to grow and swell in weird ways.
- *STDs* - these can present in the mouth. Oh, and yes, we can tell if you've had particularly vigorous oral sex from the bruising on your palate!
- *Anti-depressants* – at least one in ten people take anti-depressants. These often cause dry mouth and can increase decay.

Sadly, the list goes on.

I have often chuckled at patients' mispronunciation or misunderstanding of things when it comes to medicines, drugs, mouthwashes, teeth, and so on.

Here's some of the most common ones I've come across:

- *Corsodyl*: A mouthwash that contains chlorhexidine (an antibacterial) marketed towards gum health. Any dentist will confirm that nearly all their patients call this *Cordy-syl.*
- In the medical history questionnaire a patient fills in, there is the following question: *Have you ever had an adverse reaction to anaesthetics?* My favourite answer was: *Yes... to the heroin found in the anaesthetic* (there is no heroin in local anaesthetic!).
- *Ibuprofen* - there have been quite a few different pronunciations of this one! *Ib-you-pro-fen / eye-boop-rofen / ibi-you-profen / broo-fen.*
- *'I have TMJ'* – I think I've already mentioned this one but as it crops up almost every day of the week, it's worth touching on it again in case you happen to be panicking about it too! This is when a patient informs their dentist that they have pain relating to their jaw joint – the Temporo-Mandibular joint (abbreviated to TMJ). If you tell us you have 'TMJ' you're literally telling us you have a jaw joint. What you mean is: TMJD to TMD (temporo-mandibular dysfunction)!
- *'My teeth were fine until I got pregnant, and the baby sucked all the calcium out of my teeth!'* Again, I mentioned this earlier, but if I had a pound for every time I heard this, I could take early retirement. So, if your wife / girlfriend / aunty / cousin / the woman next door utters these words, tell them it really isn't true. It's a myth! And it comes about from pregnancy hormones increasing the body's inflammatory response to plaque. If the pregnant lady isn't cleaning effectively, her gums will swell and bleed. Also, cravings can kick in, which can lead to snacking on the wrong things, leading to decay. It is nothing to do with baby, per-se, and everything to do with sugar!

❖❖

My biggest fear? No, it's not spiders. Nor heights. Not even the Grim Reaper. Rather, it's bumping into one of my patients in public. The fear is so prevalent that, at one point, I used to work in a different county and travelled over sixty miles to get there.

In the end, I found the commute before a day's work beyond tiring – especially in rush hour. Eventually I *did* find a job a closer to home with only a twenty-five-minute commute time. I mentally kept my fingers crossed that this shorter distance would still ensure never bumping into a patient.

Unfortunately, I was wrong. Very wrong!

Sixty-year-old Thomas Jarvis was one of them. He was quite distinctive because of his height (extremely short), belly (shaped like a barrel), and his fashion-statement red spectacles which were at odds with his thinning grey hair. On his last visit to my surgery, I'd provided an implant in the location of his lower left molar.

Thomas's wife was also my patient. Both were very opinionated people and, as patients, overly demanding. In essence, they were both a pain in the bum. But such information isn't particularly relevant to what I'm now going to share!

Anyway, midway through his lengthy treatment plan, he casually dropped my worse fear into the conversation.

'I saw you at the gym the other weekend.'

My heart skipped a beat. This guy went to *my* gym?

'Oh?' I said cautiously.

His eyes bored into mine.

'Yeah,' he said softly. 'I think you were having a *leg* day.'

'Quite possibly,' I said, trying to remember when I'd last given my leg muscles a good workout.

'You looked good,' he said huskily.

I mentally took a breath. Was this married man hitting on me? This married *much older* man?

'Um, thank you,' I said awkwardly.

Thomas's eyes were still unblinking as he stared at me.

'Maybe you can help me with my workout, just like you're helping me now with my mouth.'

Okay, this guy was definitely hitting on me.

Val stifled a snort and gave me *the look*.

'I can definitely recommend a personal trainer,' I said diplomatically.

'I'd much rather have you putting me through my paces,' he said throatily.

'Ah, but it's teeth that are my remit. Not personal training,' I countered.

'Shame,' said Thomas lightly.

I managed to finish the appointment deflecting any further flirtation from Thomas Jarvis. After he'd left, I turned to Val.

'Blimey, that was fucking weird,' I said.

'Oooh, doctor,' she smouldered, morphing into a sex-starved character straight out of a *Carry On* film. 'What lovely legs you have. Can you help me with my butt lift, Doctor?' she whipped round and suggestively stuck out her backside.

'Fuck off!' I replied as Val convulsed.

Meanwhile, I fervently hoped and prayed that there would be no further funny business with Thomas Jarvis. But God wasn't listening.

As you know, this chapter is about bumping into patients in public. And yes. It happened at the gym. It was awkward as heck.

Thomas Jarvis approached me in the middle of a squat. I had my headphones on and, mentally, was miles away. He waved for my attention. Repeatedly. I snapped to, and my heart sank. But what could I do? It would have been rude to ignore him.

I stopped what I was doing. Put the barbell back in the rack. Took off my headphones.

'Ah, hello, Thomas,' I said politely.

'How *are* you?' he gushed.

'Very well, thanks. I was just midway through my workout.' *Get the hint, mate!*

'Yeah, yeah,' he nodded. 'And looking good,' he leered. And with that, he slapped my arse.

'Woah!' I said, taking a step away from him.

'Ha!' he grinned. 'Just a bit of friendly banter, eh?'

Matey, do you really think slapping my backside is banter?

I mean, I'd been hit on before by patients, but not married men, not at the gym, not in the middle of a workout when I'm in my short gym shorts.

'Right, well, I need to get back to my workout, Thomas. See you around, mate.'

'Trying to get rid of me?' he smirked, his eyes travelling up and down my body.

Yes!

'Um, I'm running short on time and would like to complete my workout.'

'Okay, okay.' He stuck his hands up in the air. 'I'll leave you to it, *big boy!*'

And with that, he pissed off.

I made a mental note of the time and day so I could take preventative measures to ensure that our paths *never ever* crossed again at the gym.

I briefly considered moving house, moving gym, and moving country, but then decided that might be a little extreme.

Anyway, the moral of the story is:

Do not stalk your dentist – you bloody weirdo!

❖

I've said it before and I'll say it again: Never treat your family or friends. This should be a cardinal rule of dentistry. They should teach this at university, and it should be at the front of every textbook in a size seventy font and in bright red capitals. If you disregard this advice, it will be the biggest mistake you will ever make.

And yes, I made this mistake. Repeatedly. And once you break this rule, you cannot unbreak it. Trust me, I tried.

My mother was and still is a menace to dental society. She has umpteen metal fillings dating back to the seventies. Of an anxious disposition, you will frequently find her with Doctor Google in one hand, and neuroticism in the other. She also has a deep distrust of any man in a white coat. In other words, she is every dentist's worst nightmare. Unfortunately for me, her regular dentist had retired, leaving me to take care of her mouth.

No matter where I worked – even when I was sixty miles away in another county – my mum would regularly turn up for her six-monthly check-up. She even managed to overcome her fear of motorway driving in order to make sure it was me who did her dental exam.

As a driver who never exceeded the speed limit (I'm not sure, even now, if her car has ever been driven faster than forty miles per hour), she would leave at the crack of dawn to ensure she arrived on time for her appointment. This often meant that she arrived early and then suffered a major attack of boredom in the waiting room. She'd then drive the receptionists nuts plumping sofa cushions and tidying the magazine rack.

When I was a locum, I thought she'd be too terrified to venture into the roughest areas imaginable. But no. She'd simply don a stab-proof vest and fight her way through the streets just to see me.

I will never forget when she fractured a molar.

'Darling,' she greeted. 'According to 'The Google', a broken tooth needs a dentist.'

(Yes, she is a bit dippy.)

I gritted my teeth and forced a smile.

'Okay. Well, let me assess it. We'll start with an x-ray.'

'You mean... RADIATION?' she shrieked. 'Oh no. No, no, no. I don't want any of that.'

'I can't help you without an x-ray.'

'But, according to 'The Google', radiation causes cancer and kills you.'

'The dose is very small. It's less than getting on a plane to Spain.'

'But I don't want an x-ray,' she protested.

'Mother,' I snapped. 'Enough.'

That's the difference between treating nutty patients and treating nutty family members. You can't snap at the general public, but you can at a family member.

'If you must,' she huffed.

'Yes, I must,' I said sternly.

Examination revealed a fractured cusp (prong of the tooth) but no caries (decay). I took the x-ray which showed quite a deep break, but thankfully not touching the nerve (a small mercy, as I couldn't face doing *another* root canal treatment for my mother).

I explained all this to my mother and said the tooth could be saved with a crown.

'That's what 'The Google' said,' she beamed. 'It's never wrong, you know.'

'Good to hear,' I sighed. 'Okay, let's get you numbed up.'

'I want the *heart patient* anaesthetic,' Mum declared. 'Because the usual one makes my heart go BOOM-BOOM-BOOM.'

'Sure,' I said, immediately dismissing her request.

I loaded up the syringe with the regular anaesthetic, then numbed her up. She immediately started to make a scene.

'I'm fainting,' she announced.

It was like watching a bit of melodrama at the theatre. Almost like Blanche Dubois (*Streetcar Named Desire*. If you've not read it, then do so, you uncouth heathen). In the play, Blanche sits on her chaise longue, puts her hand to her head, then pretends to swoon with shock.

I rolled my eyes and gave my mother a glass of water.

'Did you use the special anaesthetic?' she bleated.

'Of course,' I lied.

'Oooh. My heart is fluttering all over the place. I think I'm going to die!'

'Then could you do it quietly, please?'

'Don't say that!' she wailed.

'Then stop being so ridiculous,' I snapped.

Yes, more snapping. Definitely a family member in the surgery.

'I'm not numb,' Mum cried.

Oh God, I sighed. *Not this again.*

I took my probe and pushed it hard against her gum. Zero reaction.

'You're numb,' I announced. 'I just stabbed you with my probe.'

'Yes, I felt it,' she said disdainfully. 'I was just being a good patient and didn't complain about it.'

Give me strength.

'Okay,' I said. 'Let's get this done.'

Reluctantly, she agreed.

❖

In a normal patient (i.e. someone who isn't my mother), preparing a tooth for a crown would be a doddle. I'd numb them up, spend twenty minutes or so shaping the tooth, take an impression (mould) and send it off to the lab.

However, my mother was not a normal patient. Numb and dribbling copiously, she managed to swivel her head three hundred and sixty degrees to flash me a warning look.

'Before you start, I don't want *any* mercury in this crown. 'The Google' says that mercury causes dementia.'

Here we go. Nutcase alert. Alarm bells ringing. Woo-woo-woo. Red warning light.

'Mum, the metal in crowns is usually nickel-chromium. It's metal fillings – amalgam – that contain mercury. Also, there is no evidence of them causing dementia and they remain a safe and effective treatment.'

'Well, whatever. I still don't want it.'

'Fine. You can have an *eMax* crown. It is pure porcelain. Lithium disilicate. Would that be agreeable?'

'Let me just type that into 'The Google'.'

'No,' I snapped. (See? *More* snapping.) 'You can have either porcelain, porcelain bonded to metal, or metal. Now hurry up and choose.'

'Do the porcelain. Oh, and give me some more anaesthetic.'

'You don't need any more. You're dribbling all over the place.'

'More, more,' she whined.

'You've already had a full cartridge.'

'But it might still hurt.'

'It's not going to hurt,' I cried in exasperation. 'Now

PLEASE let me crack on.'

She made a harrumphing sound by way of response.

I started to prepare the tooth. Thankfully, she didn't flinch. I spotted some food debris packed into the fracture site.

'I need to clean this up. There will be a bit of vibration.'

I began running the slow handpiece to remove the debris.

'OUCH!' she screamed.

I rolled my eyes. Val and I exchanged *the look*. My nurse was bemused at my mother behaving like a total headcase.

'That did NOT hurt,' I said testily.

'It did,' said Mum, fighting her way out of the chair. 'I need more anaesthetic.'

'No, you don't. Now sit down and let me get on with my job because you're going to make me run late.'

Reluctantly, she sat back down, and the appointment continued with only the odd shout and bloodcurdling scream.

Everyone sighed with relief at the end of the preparation. The next thing to do was take moulds. You might remember that this involved a playdough-like material put in trays and pushed against the teeth. These impressions then go to the lab to create a replica of the patient's teeth and the required crown.

The gloop went into her mouth. Cue much arm-waving and panic. I couldn't be sure, but she might have been saying, "'The Google' never warned me of this!"

'That was HORRIBLE!' she cried after the trays were removed.

'Agreed,' I said, nodding my head. 'Every time I treat you, Mum, I think I age by ten years.'

You can always count on your family to rejuvenate and energise you. Not.

After she'd gone, Val and I had a much-needed cup of tea ~~and took 10mg of valium to soothe our frazzled minds.~~

❖

Dentistry isn't all about teeth. That statement may surprise you, dear reader, but it is the truth. Dentistry is so much more. It's part of your entire overall good health.

As I've said previously, the mouth affects the whole body. In my career, there were weird, wonderful, horrendous and truly harrowing events.

I saw cancers, neuralgias, cysts and weird conditions where not even a hospital was sure of the diagnosis. My job wasn't just to fix teeth, it was to screen for these diseases and ensure that anything dubious was picked up and then swiftly treated to minimise disability and suffering.

Take Lewis Goodman. He attended a routine check-up. Lewis had been seeing Harold, the retired dentist, for many years. He'd rarely needed any treatment. He also regularly saw the hygienist. In short, the ideal patient.

Lewis was in his mid-fifties and unremarkable. If I'd passed him in the street, I'd likely not have remembered him. But what I discovered at his routine exam changed all that. He was now someone I'd never forget.

As he took the chair, I asked the normal questions – how are you? Any problems? Brushing twice day? Flossing? You get the picture.

'I'm very well,' he said. 'And no, there haven't been any problems. Well, *not really*.'

'When you say *not really*, do you mean you haven't had any problems, or rather that something has been playing up?'

'I'm not sure if it's a dental problem.' He then pointed to the centre of his lower jaw. 'You see here?' He touched the area under the corner of his lip. 'It feels... *odd*. I don't really know how to describe it. It's a peculiar sensation. Sort of... woolly.'

'Like a cotton wool kind of feeling?'

'Yeah,' he nodded. 'That's a good description.'

'Okay,' I said. 'Let me have a look and then I'll take some x-rays too.'

I did the check-up. Felt along the jaw where Lewis had pointed. When palpating (touching), it definitely felt odd.

It was comparable to the shell of an egg or crepe paper.

I initially took a small x-ray inside the mouth to check the roots of the teeth and whether there was any infection. I was stunned at what came back. Blackness. The entire area under the teeth was completely dark, as if the jawbone was hollow.

Oh fuck, I thought.

'Something looks a little unusual on the x-ray,' I said to Lewis. 'I'd like to take a bigger picture to get in the entire jaw.'

'Yeah, fine, no worries.'

I took a panoramic x-ray which revealed half the jaw devoid of any bone – completely hollowed out and empty. The radiolucency (dark shadowy area on the x-ray) was pushing into the inferior dental nerve (the nerve that gives sensation to the lower half of the face). This was why he was getting such an odd sensation.

I was ninety-nine percent sure this was an odontogenic keratocyst - which is a type of benign tumour (but can recur as a malignant aggressive cancer).

'Lewis,' I said carefully. 'Let me show you the x-ray.'

I directed him to the computer screen and pointed at an area on the image.

'This dark shadow is a hollowing within the bone. It shouldn't be there. I think this is the cause of the woolly sensation you've been experiencing. I cannot diagnose it without a biopsy and, anyway, that's beyond my remit. However, if I were a betting man I'd say it's a keratocyst. It needs removing. Given the size of it, I'm going to organise a referral so that you'll be seen quickly.'

'O-Oh,' he stuttered, visibly shocked. 'Is it cancer?'

'I don't think so, but to be on the safe side I want you to see an expert.'

'Okay,' he gulped. 'I appreciate that.'

Lewis was seen within two weeks and keratocyst was confirmed with an urgent removal operation swiftly following.

Unfortunately for Lewis, where the keratocyst had got so big, it had damaged the nerve. He was left with partial numbness and a constant sensation of pins and needles.

However, he was just grateful that the thing had been removed, because he'd previously been at high risk of his jaw fracturing. It was a stark reminder to me to always thoroughly investigate and, if in doubt, refer.

❖

On the topic of dentistry being more than just teeth, I will never forget the nightmare I had flying home from a dental conference.

It was midsummer and I'd attended a weekend seminar in Portugal. My flight had been delayed by an hour. Then another hour. Then a further two hours. And finally, another hour.

The airport had directed all the passengers into the gated waiting area, where there were few seats and no air-conditioning. At around thirty-five degrees, it felt airless and stinking hot.

For those who hadn't secured a seat, they either stood or sat on the floor, slumped over their hand luggage. Everyone was fed up.

Eventually, the pilot came into the terminal to talk to the passengers.

'There's a major malfunction with the engine of the plane,' he announced.

It was one of those moments where total strangers shared anxious glances.

'Engineers are working on the problem. I'm going to give it another half an hour, by which time if they haven't resolved the problem then we won't be flying.'

God, I hope no one here is a nervous flyer, I silently thought as the pilot took himself off.

Five minutes later, there was a loud thud. Someone screamed and everyone turned to look. A portly looking gentleman had collapsed.

'IS THERE A DOCTOR HERE?' someone shouted.

I'm NOT a doctor, I told myself.

I waited. Counted to thirty. Hoped someone else would answer the call. No one did.

Ah fuck, I silently cussed. *I'm going to have to do this.*

I moved through the throng and looked at the gentleman on the floor. My brain did some quick calculations as I mentally skimmed through my medical knowledge.

The man was overweight. Shaking. Clammy. Sweaty. Pale.

I knelt alongside him.

'Hello there,' I said, making sure his head was cushioned and then raising his legs up onto his suitcase. 'Are you a diabetic?'

'Yes,' he confirmed, shakily.

Bingo. This was *hypoglycaemia.* In other words, a diabetic faint.

'When did you last eat?' I asked.

'About six hours ago,'

'I need sugar!' I shouted. 'Has anyone got sweets or biscuits?'

'I have!' said a woman.

She thrust a packet of biscuits at me. It would have to do.

'Sir, do you feel well enough to sit up and eat some of these? I think your blood sugar has dropped.'

Me and Biscuit Lady helped the man sit up and he began munching. As he did so, he regained some colour to his cheeks and the shaking stopped. Suddenly, a much older man had pushed through the crowd.

'Move out the way,' he said to me. 'I'm a retired GP.'

'Okay. I'm a dentist. I'm treating the patient for a hypoglycaemic attack.'

I was given a disdainful eyeroll. Mr Up-His-Own-Arse bent down and felt the diabetic man's pulse. The man batted him away.

'Mate, this guy has already helped me,' he said, pointing to me.

'He's a *dentist.*' He might as well have said *he's a dog turd.* 'He doesn't know what he's talking about. Now let me check your pulse in case you're having a heart attack.'

I raised one eyebrow but remained silent.

'Fuck off!' said Mr Diabetic to Mr Up-His-Own-Arse

221

(who was possibly about to become Mr Furious).

'Thanks for helping me, mate,' said Mr Diabetic gratefully. 'I really appreciate it.'

'You're welcome,' I smiled. 'I'm glad you're feeling better.'

He was completely coherent. There was no clamminess and the shakes were fully arrested.

At that moment, the pilot returned.

'Good news, everyone. The engines are working and boarding will commence in five minutes. Thank you for your patience.'

As everyone began getting to their feet, grumbling but glad to be on their way, I sent up a silent prayer that the flight would be less eventful than the pre-boarding experience. (And it was – apart from the cabin crew running out of gin and tonic!)

❖

There are dishonest people in all walks of life. It is an unfortunate fact, but a fact nonetheless.

There was once a serious theft at one of the more salubrious practices I'd worked at – which somehow made it more shocking.

It was a member of staff who committed the theft, but nobody ever found out for sure who the culprit was, although there was a suspicion of who it was.

I arrived at the practice at seven in the morning. I was the first there. I went in, turned off the alarm and made myself a black coffee.

It was a long commute to this place so, generally, I'd leave home as the sparrows were getting up to avoid the traffic. Once at the practice, I'd have breakfast and then chill out for a bit until the day got underway.

The rest of the staff – the nurses, receptionists and, of course, the principal – began turning up about forty-five minutes after me. So far, so good. A normal early morning.

About fifteen minutes later, everything kicked off. The

principal entered the staff room, where everyone was chatting over a cuppa. He shut the door so firmly that everyone stopped talking and looked his way. His face was thunderous.

'No one leaves this practice,' he barked. 'Everyone, cancel your first hour of patients.'

'What's happened?' asked one of the nurses.

'Money has gone missing,' he said, his eyes sweeping over each and every one of us. 'Over a thousand pounds,' he added. 'The police are on their way.'

Oh. My. God.

I couldn't believe it. We all looked at each other, suddenly wary. There was a thief among us. The principal left the room and chatter restarted. But now it was a hushed whisper as we all asked each other who it could possibly be.

'You arrived early today,' said one of the receptionists accusingly.

'I'm early every day,' I said defensively.

'Convenient story,' she said, folding her arms across her chest.

Wow, you fucking bitch, I thought. But I made no comment. The police were on their way. They could sort it out.

The boys in blue duly arrived. Bag searches were carried out. The alarm system records were retrieved, and the police started to interview staff.

But the money had gone. It was no longer on the premises. Everyone seemed to have an alibi. I'd never had a run-in with the coppers before. I felt unreasonably nervous as I got called into a side office to be interviewed by two policemen. The questioning was standard:
- What time did you arrive at work?
- Why were you here early?
- Were you aware that money had gone missing?
- Has anyone said anything to you about the money?

I answered honestly. I had no knowledge of where any cash was even kept, never mind if it went missing.

They let me go but, what with the bitchy receptionist's comment and then a police interview, I felt ridiculously shaken. Everyone was looking at each other. Everyone was talking behind their hands. Everyone was under scrutiny and suspicion. It was not a pleasant feeling.

By lunchtime, an event timeline had been established. The previous evening, reception had cashed up a large sum of money. It had been put in an envelope and then a sealed plastic moneybag. At this point, it was meant to be transferred to the office but was left on the practice manager's desk. The office had a lock-code on the door (but everybody in the practice knew it!). The following morning, a cash collection should have taken place with the money leaving the premises.

Instead, however, at four o'clock in the morning, someone entered the building, turned off the alarm, entered the manager's office, took the money, then switched the alarm back on and left.

The practice had no CCTV and no safe. Rather, it had worked on a *trust system*. Unfortunately, although the police and the principal had a suspicion that it was the receptionist (the lady that had accused me!), there was no evidence. The insurance covered the theft, and one member of staff was a thousand pounds better off.

After that, the practice became Fort Knox. CCTV was installed throughout the building. A new protocol for cash collection was introduced, including the installation a heavy-duty safe where codes were changed weekly, ditto the lock on the manager's door.

No stealing happened again, but it was horrible knowing there was a thief amongst us.

❖

You know what I hate? Patients who say they can't lay back in the chair. They are a total pain in the bum – and there's rather a lot of them!

One of my patients was a lady in her mid-seventies. Mrs Jean Appleby was adamant that she couldn't lay back in the chair. She said that not only did the dental chair give her back pain, but it also gave her vertigo. So, whenever Jean visited, she insisted on standing up which meant I buggered up my back treating her.

One day, she visited the practice with a broken tooth. A filling was required on her upper left back molar. Unless I hung upside down from the ceiling, no way was I going to be able to see what I was doing. Firm direction was required on this occasion.

'Right,' I said. 'Let's pop you back in the chair and I'll get this tooth fixed in a jiffy.'

'Not too far because I can't handle it.'

'Okay,' I said, pressing the *backwards* button. 'Tell me when to st–'

'STOP!' she shrieked.

'Jean,' I said. 'You're still upright. I cannot see the tooth.'

'Nooo,' she wailed. 'I'm getting vertigo.'

'I see.' I paused for a moment to think. 'Out of interest, how many pillows do you sleep on at night?'

It was a rather crafty question.

'Two,' she said, frowning. 'Why?'

'I've had an idea. Let me put the chair into the same position as two pillows.'

Success! Well, of sorts. The chair reclined forty-five degrees, so I was still hunched over her and did end up with backache. As Jean got up, she clutched her heart and complained of vertigo. I clutched my back and, together, the pair of us tottered over to the surgery door as we bid each other goodbye.

Funny story. A year later, I went skiing and another skier lost control and crashed into me. I was left with a broken rib and lots of bruising. Being self-employed, I still went to work and dosed myself up on painkillers. Enter Jean Appleby with another broken tooth.

'Remember,' she said, wagging a finger. 'I can't go back in the chair.'

'Sorry, Jean,' I apologised. 'I've broken a rib, so if you can't go back in the chair I won't be able to treat you.'

'How did you do that?' she gasped.

'Someone walloped into me when I was skiing.'

'Oh, you poor thing,' she said, looking stricken. 'Yes, just put the chair all the way back. I'll deal with it. I can't have you suffering with that injury.'

'Thank you,' I said.

The chair reclined with Jean in it, I completed the filling and she left with zero vertigo.

You bloody moo, I silently thought as she cheerfully waved me goodbye.

'How long you going to use that excuse?' asked Val, when Jean had left.

'For as long as I can get away with it!' I winked.

And I did. I used that excuse for over six months on uncooperative patients who either couldn't, or wouldn't, recline in the chair.

❖

Being self-employed has its pros and cons. Over the years, I've worked at several different practices – be that as a locum or an associate. The one constant about being self-employed is that if you don't work, you don't get paid. If a patient doesn't turn up, you don't get paid. If you want a holiday, you don't get paid. If you're sick, you don't get paid. So that's pretty shitty. But a self-employed person knows that that's how it goes.

In my profession, what makes being self-employed super shitty is when you come across an immoral practice owner. And there are quite a few of 'em out there!

As a dentist, when you go to work at a practice you're given a *contract.* It's not an employment contract. More, a service user agreement. The practice agrees to let you use the premises, provides you with materials and a nurse, and in return you hand over fifty-five percent of your earnings.

There is a standard fair template that the British Dental Association (the trade union of dentists) provides, but not all practices use this. Indeed, some practices issue contracts that are completely unfair and penalise the

226

associate for, well, dare I say *having a life*.

I have always paid to have my contracts checked, to ensure that I'm not entering a dodgy situation that is going to screw me over. This service is worth its weight in gold. I used it when Wayne Adams and his practice manager wife Sally tried to screw me over. I used it again when I had an encounter with the dastardly Dick Solowitz.

Dick had paid a visit to Turkey for a hair transplant and, while there, had also had his teeth done. They were so unnaturally bright, one needed to wear sunglasses if Dick smiled. And Dick did plenty of that when he was ripping off both his dentists and patients alike.

I put on my sunnies as he handed me my contract.

'Here you go. Sign it now.'

'Ah, thanks, but I need to have it checked.'

'Whatever for?' The megawatt smile was replaced with a frown.

'Well, because it's the terms I have to work by. So, I need to make sure it's fair and reasonable.'

'All my associates have this contract. If you're not happy with it, go elsewhere.'

'But you've not even given me the chance to read it, Dick.'

'Just sign it or piss off.'

So, I pissed off.

When I got home and read the document through, I gave a sigh of relief that I'd not been pressured into signing. It was written in a similar way to the unscrupulous Wayne Adams' contract. I wondered if the two of them were mates. They were certainly fellow dickheads.

I suppose with any job there are dickheads, but they seem to crop up far more when you're self-employed. There were terms in the contract like, if you took a day off, you'd be charged £500 for leaving the surgery empty. It was quite preposterous. Some days, it truly felt like everyone was out to get you…

❖

As an implant dentist, my patients are frequently apprehensive and nervous. I think I've already explained that an implant is a small titanium-based screw that is buried in the bone of the jaw and left to integrate with the body. Once integrated, a tooth is made that *locks* into that screw.

Patients often worry about this procedure being done under local anaesthetic. Many would prefer to be knocked out. Unfortunately, I personally don't do sedation. Why? To be brutally honest, dear reader, it attracts the nutters. And I already have enough of those!

Once I was established in my latest practice, I received referrals from some of my fellow dentists.

Louise Clarefield, a fifty-year-old lady, was referred to me by one of my colleagues. She had four crowns on her front teeth, all with root canal treatments, large posts and porcelain bonded to metal crowns. None of them matched. They were all different lengths. She'd also had repeated abscesses.

After assessing the situation, the best option was to extract all four teeth, scrape away all the muck in the bone from the abscesses, then place two implants with artificial bone.

The patient agreed, but said she was incredibly nervous. She wanted to be sedated. I said that I didn't offer this but could... perhaps... prescribe a valium (diazepam). This is a mild oral sedative/tranquilliser. I pointed out that she wouldn't be able to drive home from the appointment or operate machinery or sign any legal documents, and so on, for twenty-four to forty-eight hours after the procedure. Louise was very relieved and agreed.

At the consent appointment – where the dentist runs through the risks and benefits ahead of the surgery – Louise (who was *not* high on valium at this point) asked me some rather strange questions. Like:

Should she cancel her gym membership?

Should she apply for a credit card offering zero percent interest?

Did I think it wise for her to put her new driveway plans on hold?

My nurse was listening to this chit-chat with a raised eyebrow. Val caught my eye, and we briefly exchanged *the look.*

I wondered if Louise was possibly dropping hints about her financial situation. After all, implants are costly. I said that I couldn't give her any financial advice because I was a clinician.

Not even twenty-four hours later, I had an email from Louise asking me to write a letter to her gym stating she couldn't use the facilities because of her dental treatment. The reason was, she said, they wanted a three-month notice period and wouldn't waive it without a medical letter. I thought this reasonable enough, so obliged.

Louise's surgery day arrived. Her husband drove her to the practice. Val called her into the surgery. Louise settled into the chair, she had taken the Valium an hour ago, so it most certainly would've kicked in by now.

'How are you feeling, Louise?' I asked.

'I don't feel any different,' she slurred.

She was pretty stoned!

'Okay.' I winked at my nurse. 'Let's get you numbed up, Louise.'

I administered the LA, although Louise didn't seem to notice.

'When are you going to numb me up?' she asked.

'We've already done that,' said Val.

'Did you?' said Louise incredulously as saliva rolled down her chin.

The procedure got underway. It involved an incision running left to right, then pulling the gum back to reveal the bone. I gently extracted the teeth, trying to keep the bone intact. Two of the extracted teeth had been badly infected, so I scraped the bone, removing all the muck and leaving it beautifully clean.

Suddenly, Louise sat bolt upright.

'Floss!' she exclaimed. 'You said you'd give me some floss!'

Okayyy, I thought. *She's off her trolley..*

'You're doing great, Louise,' said Val, pushing Louise back down. 'Take a few nice deep breaths.'

She did as she was told, then started snoring.

'How much did you give her?' mouthed Val.

'Seven milligrams,' I mouthed back.

We continued.

I placed two implants along with some artificial bovine bone to support the deficient areas. I then stitched everything back together and was pleased how neat it all was.

'Louise?' I said.

'Hmmmm?' she said blearily, opening one eye.

'We're done.'

'Already?' she yawned. 'That was quick.'

'We're going to fit your temporary denture now,' I said.

'Okay. Can I have a cup of tea, too?'

'Not right now. You're very numb. No hot food or drink for twenty-four hours.'

'Oh, poo.'

I fitted the denture, then got Louise to take it in and out of her mouth. She did this with ease. I then invited her husband into the surgery as I wasn't sure Louise would remember any of the post-op instructions (even though I write them down for patients too). I ran through this with the two of them. They then left without shutting the surgery door behind them.

Louise's words floated along the corridor. I heard her chatting to the receptionist.

'You know, I've always wanted to be a receptionist. Should we swap? Oh, and you can have my implants!' she sniggered.

'Um, how do you want to pay?' asked Penny.

'Pay for what?' said Louise in confusion.

'By card,' said the husband smoothly.

'Oooh, a card! I want a card!' said Louise excitedly. 'Can I have one?'

'Yes, dear,' said the husband in a long-suffering voice. 'Let's get you home.'

And the moral of this story is that valium makes some patients even more bat-shit crazy than they were before.

230

Police were called many times when I was a **locum**. I have previously worked in some rough areas. Reception would often call the police if patients became aggressive and, sometimes, even violent.

But this story is a little different because, well, the *patient* called the police on a dentist!

Thankfully, that dentist was not me. It was one of my colleagues working in the locum practice at the time. So, let me tell you what happened!

A male patient in his mid-seventies – let's call him Colin Crankybiter – had come to the practice requiring extraction of an upper back tooth.

Colin was deaf and wore hearing aids. My colleague, Dr Singh, had numbed up Colin, run through the risks of extractions (soreness, bleeding, bruising, swelling, and infection).

As Colin was so nervous, he had decided to take out his hearing aids and keep his eyes tightly shut.

Dr Singh started the extraction. As I've explained previously, this involves applying pressure to the tooth to help loosen it up.

Midway into the procedure, Mr Crankybiter decided to bite Dr Singh. Perhaps because he was numb, Mr Crankybiter didn't realise this was hurting his dentist... quite a bloody lot.

'Colin, open, please!' said Dr Singh. 'OPEN! You're biting me!'

But Mr Crankybiter simply bit down harder.

'AHHHH!' screamed Dr Singh. 'OPEN! OPEN YOUR MOUTH!'

In desperation, Dr Singh began to tap on Colin's face.

Colin's eyes snapped open.

'You've assaulted me!' he declared.,

'You were biting me,' cried Dr Singh, practically in tears.

'YOU HIT ME IN THE FACE, YOU BASTARD!'

231

'Please calm down,' Dr Singh implored. 'Look what you've done to my finger!'

He showed Colin his finger, which was bleeding heavily.

'I'm calling the Old Bill, you fucking bastard!' said Colin.

He got up, mid-extraction and, with blood running out of his mouth, strode into reception and called 999.

'A dentist has fucking attacked me,' he screamed at the operator. 'I've been repeatedly punched in the face.'

He continued making a scene at reception, spraying red spittle over the desks.

Thankfully, the police arrived within ten minutes and ironed things out. They took statements from the irate Colin, the injured Dr Singh, his nurse and the reception staff.

'Right, mate,' said the bemused police officer to Colin. 'You've not been assaulted. Quite the opposite. If Dr Singh wants to pursue it, we could take *you* in for assault. You've potentially broken his finger and made him bleed, but *you* don't have a mark on you.'

'What are you talking about?' spluttered Colin. 'Look at the state of me. I'm covered in blood!'

'Yeah, because it's coming from your tooth, mate,' the policeman pointed out. 'The one that you were midway through having removed.'

'This is bollocking bullshit,' raged Colin.

'Okay, we're done here,' said a second policeman. 'Dr Singh, if you want to press charges, here's the crime reference number.'

The policemen left and Colin turned to Dr Singh.

'Right. Are you going to finish this extraction?'

'You must be kidding,' said Dr Singh.

'I'm serious,' said Colin.

It was one of those moments where silence is deafening.

'I think you should leave, Mr Crankybiter,' said one of the receptionists helpfully. 'And quickly.'

Colin looked at everyone in reception, and it was fair to say he looked flabbergasted. Then he snapped to, compressed his mouth into a thin (red) line, and stormed out.

He tried to slam the door after him to express his rage, but it was one of those soft-close ones, which made the scene awkwardly comical. Colin retaliated by kicking the door hard and then hopping around on one foot in pain.

Poor Dr Singh. But, to be honest, a small part of me was glad that I wasn't the only one who had loony patients!

❖

Let's finish with a heartwarming story, shall we? Yes, can you believe we are nearly at the end of this foray into the dental world. I want to share a nice story to finish with.

Thomas Nolan, aged sixty-six, attended the practice. He had severely broken-down teeth. He was a dreadful *bruxist* (someone that grinds their teeth) and had been left with jagged, rough, dark brown choppers.

He looked at me with real desperation in his eyes.

'I'm really fed up with them,' he confided. 'My daughter is getting married next year. I can't walk her down the aisle like this. And every morning, when I wake up, there's blood on my pillow and I have bleeding lips where, somehow, I've bitten down on them while asleep. Can you help me?' he implored.

'Thomas, I can help you,' I said. 'But it will be a process. I need to know you'll be motivated to look after the work I do.'

'I will do anything,' he assured. *'Anything.'*

'Okay,' I nodded. 'Let's do this.'

And so, we did.

I did photos of his teeth, scans of his mouth/bite, full mouth x-rays, digitally printed models and wax-ups.

In the planning stage, Thomas had already committed financially for us to *plan* the work, not even deliver it. I believed that he was going to be motivated to do whatever it took.

I ran through the plan, which was a full mouth rehab. It would involve a couple of root canal treatments on teeth he had nearly ground into the nerve, then opening the bite to mainly meet on his canines, allowing the back teeth to over-erupt (which they do when they're not meeting). He would have *temporaries* for six months and, when he'd got used to his new bite, then they would be replaced with ceramic crowns.

Part of the process would also involve wearing a hard splint. This is a special type of nightguard to inhibit grinding.

Thomas took it all in his stride. He was determined to see this through and he did everything I asked of him.

On the longest appointment, some two and a half hours, I prepared his front six teeth for crowns, and also fitted temporary crowns to open up his bite. At the end, I handed him a mirror. He took it, and broke down.

'Oh my God,' he wept, as he looked at his mouth. 'It's amazing. They're so smooth.'

He couldn't stop running his tongue over them.

'Remember,' I warned. 'These are temporaries. They're designed to *wear*. Consequently, they may chip or break. That's part of the process because I need to see where your bite is the heaviest. The treatment plan is based upon this.'

'Yes, I know,' he nodded. 'Even so, temporaries or not, I just can't believe how good they look! Thank you *so* much.'

The next six months flew by. During that period, he had several reviews and some minor adjustments. Eventually, the temporaries were removed and the porcelain definitive crowns (based on what his temporaries had been shaped to) were fitted.

This meant the bite was nearly perfect and only needed minimal adjustment. The new teeth weren't that hideous toilet-bowl-white that certain celebrities favour, rather a slightly off-white shade and looked so beautifully natural.

I was incredibly proud of the finished work. As I once again handed the mirror to Thomas, I smiled in anticipation of his reaction.

'Wow,' he breathed.

And then he was overcome with emotion which, in turn, made me well up. He reached for my hand. Gave it a squeeze. Then, composing himself, he shook my hand.

'Thank you,' he said. 'Thank you so much.'

Everything about this patient was a transformation. Not just his teeth, but also his confidence and overall demeanour.

A couple of months later, I received a card through the post. It was from Mr Nolan. Enclosed was a photo taken at his daughter's wedding. It was of him and the bride. In the picture, he was beaming away. The card read:

I am just writing to say thank you again.

Prior to seeing you, I'd visited a couple of other dentists. Each had said they could do nothing for me other than remove my teeth and give me dentures.

You've given me more than I could ever have imagined.

Thank you for making a father smile on his daughter's wedding day.

Best wishes

Thomas

I still have this card. Indeed, I have a special box in which I keep every card of thanks, every letter of gratitude, every note of joy from delighted patients. Sometimes, when I've had a bad day, when everything seems to have gone wrong, I go to this box. Then I sit down and reread everything within to remind myself that what I do *is* worthwhile and that I *do* change some people's lives for the better.

And to all those patients who have made me feel worthless, given me headaches and sleepless nights… thank you. Because I've written a book about it!

Epilogue

I started the prologue with the question: 'What made you choose to be a dentist?'

Having now written and rehashed the strangest, funniest, profound and (sometimes) most utterly ludicrous events experienced as a dentist... I can now answer that question and truly say: I haven't the foggiest idea why I decided to be a dentist!

Recounting these events has been therapeutic for me. It's been a stress buster. It has also reminded me of the good times, the amazing journey that I have been on, and to make light and laugh off some of the harder parts of my career.

At times, it has been challenging to put pen to paper and articulate the complexities of the dental field. I hope that I have made this both informative and entertaining. More importantly, I hope you have a deeper insight into the true warts-and-all world of dentistry!

At the time of writing this, I'm still practicing dentistry. However, I'm hoping (as one may hope to win the lottery) that, sooner rather than later, I can say goodbye to dentistry once and for all! Not because I hate being a dentist – because I don't. It is almost magical dealing with some patients... to fix what is broken, to give back confidence to people, to help those in pain fully recover... I think that's why I took this career path in the first place. BUT! I have also hated the flip side of the coin that this career brings... the stress, depression and deep anxiety over complaints, litigation, and the false assumption that all dentists are mansion owners with a Porsche parked on the gravel driveway while earning a living as pain-inflicting butchers! I mean, really? In which case, where's my Porsche and mansion?!

It's funny though (as in funny *peculiar*) because I feel that dentistry is part of my identity. My life is so intertwined with the field, that if someone asks me to describe myself, my first answer is, 'I'm a dentist.' But, actually, I'm so much more than that.

I'm a cat-father. A so-so skier. A gym-attendee. A lover of DIY. Dare I also say *writer?* Yes, I think I will! I'm also a landscape gardener (okay, it was just the one garden I designed – mine!). At home, you'll find me pushing a lawnmower, or a vacuum cleaner, or with my feet up on the furniture watching telly. Oh, and I'm more of an optimist than a pessimist.

And now I want to say thank you. Thank you, dear reader, for taking this journey with me. For seeing the tooth, the whole tooth and nothing but the tooth!

About the Author

Dr Bill is, at the time of writing, a twenty-one-year-old living in the body of a thirty-something-dentist. He was born in a rainy part of England and has worked several years in both NHS and private dental settings, as well as teaching in university settings. When not snapping pictures of his cats, he continues to practice dentistry, enjoys travelling, gardening and daydreaming about the time he can leave the industry, once and for all.

Printed in Great Britain
by Amazon

60090624R00139